THE HISTORY OF
FORT OCRACOKE
IN PAMLICO SOUND

ROBERT K. SMITH

EDITED BY
EARL O'NEAL JR.

THE
History
PRESS

Published by The History Press
Charleston, SC 29403
www.historypress.net

All images from the author's collection unless otherwise noted.

First published 2015

Manufactured in the United States

ISBN 978.1.62619.903.3

Library of Congress Control Number: 2014959942

Notice: The information in this book is true and complete to the best of our knowledge. It is offered without guarantee on the part of the author or The History Press. The author and The History Press disclaim all liability in connection with the use of this book.

Research and recovery accomplished by Surface Interval Diving Company:
Nonprofit Marine Archaeology and Exploration
"Preserving the Past, By Diving the Future"

SIDCO is a nonprofit organization dedicated to the proper archaeological
preservation of historic shipwrecks and submerged sites for the express purpose of
public education and display.

For Linda,
who gave me the support.

For Katie,
who gave me the inspiration.

For Mama,
who gave me the history.

For Daddy,
who shared the talent.

For Christ Jesus,
who gave me all.

CONTENTS

ACKNOWLEDGEMENTS

Those without whom this book would have been impossible:

Earl O'Neal Jr.
Ellen Marie Cloud
Paul Branch
Bobby Wayne Willis
Sam Newell
Jack Goodwin
Jessie Lee Dominique
Mike Austin
Rudy Austin
William J. Smith
Rita G. Smith
Mike Milton
Bruce Thome
Mel Covey
Ocracoke Preservation
    Society and Staff
Robin Payne
Walker Gillikin
Linda Lyons
David Moore

Richard Lawrence
Rob Reedy
Lindley Butler
Rick Allen
Edward L. Harding
Jamie Tunnel
David Pope
Eric Baptiste
North Carolina Maritime Museum
    and Staff
Graveyard of the Atlantic Museum
    and Staff
Teach's Hole Museum and Staff
Ocracoke Civic and Business
    Association
Janie Jacoby
Rob Covey
Jamie Gillikin
Greg Purdy
James Graham

ACKNOWLEDGEMENTS

Johnny O'Neal
Fowler O'Neal
Joe Schwartzer
Jack "Tony" Davis
"Bubby" Teeter
Tom Payne
Elizabeth Hathaway

Chapter 1

THE COLONIAL PERIOD

A FORT FOR BEACON ISLAND

Colonial Shipping and Trade

It can be argued that the area of Ocracoke Inlet was one of the most important ports in colonial America. There were probably more trade goods going in and out of that inlet than traverse some modern ports in America today.

Ocracoke Inlet is the only inlet that has remained open, to some degree, throughout the recorded history of the state of North Carolina, reaching back some four hundred years. As storms, hurricanes and nor'easters opened and closed other inlets, Ocracoke remained a fully functional deep-water passage with full shipping facilities until about 1840. The inlet was still used quite heavily by experienced captains until 1862. During the Civil War, Union forces sank two derelict schooners, part of the Stone Fleet, in the inlet proper to stop it from being used.[1] There were initial results in the way of shoaling, and over time the damage to shipping channels and passable waterways was significant. Ocracoke Inlet never recovered and today is open only to light vessels.

The facilities built at Portsmouth, Ocracoke, Shell Castle and Beacon Island made Ocracoke Inlet North Carolina's biggest and, at the time, most important port. By 1824, two-thirds of all commerce in the state was passing through the inlet. Traffic was highest in the years from 1822 through the 1840s, with some fifteen thousand vessels per year using the inlet and port facilities.

Though shifting shoals and moving channels prevented some of the larger ships from passing through, a well-established system of lighter ships would meet these ships and take on their heavy cargos. These "lighters" would then take the cargo through the shallow waters and on to Washington or New Bern. (Prior to the Civil War, the city of Newbern was spelled New Bern.) Other lighters would bring the outgoing goods to these large vessels for their return trip.

Through the years, starting in 1713, various taxes and fees were raised from the vessels using the inlet to pay for improvements to the port facilities in the areas of navigation (buoys, channel markers and lightships, beacons and pilots) and eventually even the construction of the first fort to protect the area's shipping.[2] The various attempts to fund upkeep of channel markers and clear waterways were marginal at best and did not finance the needed maintenance to the navigational aids, much less a fort. During years of war or poor relations between governments, the board of trade, based in Bath, would pass laws preventing ships en route from enemy interests from conducting trade at Ocracoke Inlet. In these times, smuggling was rampant, and this cost the port much money in missed fees.[3]

As things usually do, they *changed* here at Ocracoke Inlet. The channels moved and narrowed, the slews filled in and the shoals grew until the economics of keeping the port active far outweighed the cost of a new port at Morehead City, and the ships stopped coming.

SHELL CASTLE

In the late 1700s, a marvelous warehousing and lightering facility was constructed on an oyster rock near Ocracoke Inlet. This complex was constructed by John Gray Blount and John Wallace and was built on the edge of Wallace Channel. Meant to be a lightering station, the needs of the day caused the business to expand, even to include the state's second lighthouse. This light was fifty-five feet tall, pyramid shaped and wood framed and shingled.

The amenities on Shell Castle, which included a tavern and shipwrights, coopers and carpenters to make repairs, were invaluable to the merchant ships, which had braved high winds and heavy seas to deliver their needed goods.

A number of supporting shops were set up on Beacon Island itself, including a small factory for making barrel staves.[4]

The station on Shell Castle was unique because it was like a marine "strip mall" built right in the middle of the channel, on a bed of oyster and clamshells. It was something like a convenience store for colonial-era shipping. How Shell Castle ever stayed in one piece, sitting out there in the sound, open to every raindrop and every breeze that ever blew, is a bit of a miracle, to be sure.

The facility began to decline in the early 1800s due to shoaling of the channel by the shifting sands of Ocracoke Inlet, which cut off Shell Castle's access to the merchant shipping lanes via Wallace Channel. In 1818, the lighthouse was destroyed by fire after being struck by lightning. It has been suggested that the remaining bedrock base was later used during the Civil War to build up and improve the breakwater at Fort Ocracoke (see Chapters 3 and 5).

Ships and Shipwrecks

The story of any part of Ocracoke Island could not be told without mentioning shipwrecks and the treacherous shoals of Ocracoke Inlet. Any boat captain will tell you that it can be a dreadful experience to "cross Ocracoke bar" on a dark, stormy night, even with today's technologies of GPS, sonar and radar. The ever-changing shoals leave only a very narrow, curving and winding entrance to Pamlico Sound and the safety of Silver Lake on Ocracoke Island itself.

Many texts tell of the "first shipwreck in North Carolina" as being the *Tiger*, though records clearly show a number of earlier European shipwrecks along the Carolina coast.

Native Indian recorded folklore tells of a European shipwreck in or about 1560 on what is now Ocracoke Island, where a number of survivors made it to shore and began to make lives for themselves among the coastal Indian tribes. Soon they became homesick and, with the help of Indian carpenters, made a raft from parts of dugout canoes and other indigenous ship pieces. As soon as it was finished, they set sail for Europe, but several weeks later, Indian scouts found the torn remains of the raft on a nearby beach and the occupants were considered lost.[5]

There was another, much earlier, fully recorded casualty near Cape Fear in June 1526. A Spanish brigantine, under command of Lucas Vasquez de Ayllon, was lost while trying to reach the Spanish colony of Chicora, located at the time on the Cape Fear River.[6]

In about 1564, native records tell of finding a piece of shipwreck on the beach somewhere on the Outer Banks that was from a "Christian" ship. The iron fasteners holding the timbers together were removed and fashioned into hand tools.[7]

In 1584, explorations leading up to the appearance of English colonists and further shipwrecks continued with the travels of Philip Amadas and Arthur Barlowe. Sir Walter Raleigh sent these explorers to look for a suitable site for colonization, and their reports tell of thick flocks of white and blue herons, huge vines thick with grapes and great hammocks of cedar trees, some "the highest in the world."

Barlowe's reports were so favorable that Raleigh organized his colonial venture with sights on Roanoke Island, and his fleet set out for North Carolina's coast.[8]

Tiger itself was the flagship of this fleet of transatlantic travelers and commanded by Sir Richard Grenville. The fleet appeared on North Carolina's shores in June 1585, loaded with colonists headed by Raleigh himself and bound for Roanoke Island and a life in the New World. As the English colonial fleet approached Ocracoke Inlet, *Tiger* got aground on the shoals, just beyond the "bar" in the inlet.[9] Most historical texts stop right there and call it a shipwreck, but the little-known truth is that it was "lightered," which is the practice of throwing everything not absolutely needed overboard and lightening the ship's load so it will float on a lesser depth of water. *Tiger* was gotten off the shoal in about two hours, and once refloated, it was careened, or beached, for repairs to its bottom. The incident caused many of the supplies on board to be destroyed, and the blame fell on the pilot, Simon Fernandez. Governor Ralph Lane chronicles the affair in a letter to Sir Frances Walsingham, dated August 1585:

> *The other Ococon* [Wocowon] *in y Entry whereof all our Fleete strucke agrounde, and the Tyger lyinge beatynge vppon y shoalle for y space of* [2] *houres by the dyalle, we were all in extreme hasarde ov beying casteawaye.*[10]

North Carolina waters are deceivingly beautiful when a calm, sunny morning allows the ocean and the sky to haze together in the distance. No sound can be heard except the gentle lapping of the wake of the ship, until the weather turns into a desperate fight for one's life in waters so vicious that they emulate the furious actions of some giant washing machine. Even with today's electronics, high-power engines and hardened stainless steel fittings, that same washing machine can swallow a ship right out from under a person and leave him or her to the elements.

In colonial days, only eyewitness accounts and sworn documents could absolve a ship's crew from being responsible for its loss. Without the testimonies of the captain and crew, the ship's owner could hold them financially responsible for the loss of the ship and cargo. These records became public domain and were legally binding to protect those mentioned in the statements. The ill-fated crew would immediately seek out the nearest local courthouse and the registrar of deeds to document the events that led to the loss of their ship, its cargo and any of the crew. Here, several of the *Colonial Instruments of Protest* document a fraction of the losses associated with Beacon Island and Ocracoke Inlet:

1723 JULY 24

To all to whom this public Instrument of Protest shall come Hugh Drysdale Esq. his Majesty's Lt. Governor of the Colony and Dominion of Virginia and Vise Admiral of the same maketh known and manifest that on the 24th day of July in the 9th year of the Reign of our sovereign Lord George by the grace of God of Great Britain, France and Ireland, King Defender of Faith etc. Annoque Dominic 1723, personally come and appeared before me Thomas Fry, Master and Part Owner, Elias Audart, Mate, Samuel Rood, Mariner of the—Ship called the PARRE GALLEY, bound for the port of London in England from North Carolina in America.

At which time the Master made it appear to me that the ship was Plantation Built and belonging to His Majesty's Subjects and was of Burthen. sixty tons or thereabouts, loaded with 592 barrels of Tarr for the aforesaid port of London.

The said Thomas Fry, Elias Audart, Samuel Rood of the ship PARRE GALLEY did on Solemn Oath Declare;

That about 10 of the Clock in the morning on Saturday the 12th day of July they weighed anchor from Occocock Inlet in North Carolina in prosecution of their intended voyage to the aforesaid port of London. That on the Tuesday following, being the 15th day at 5 of the Clock in the morning the Ship sprung a Great leak and that having set both pumps and ply'd them to the utmost of the Power of all hands aboard the ship. Yet notwithstanding the water increased within the hold 9 to 10 inches an hour, inasmuch that the said Master and Crew were at length constrained to Quit the aforesaid Ship and betake themselves in order to preserve their lives, to their boat. That about an hour after quitting the said. Ship they Espyed a Ship who bore down upon them and took them up. The Ship so taking them up was called the CONTENT *from Liverpool, bound for Virginia, the Master named Fouler. The Master and Mariners by their nearest Computation reckoned themselves 15 or 16 Leagues East South East from Cape Henry at the time of their being obliged to Quit the said Ship. Thus Done and protested before me at Williamsburgh the day and year above mentioned.*

Hugh Drysdale[11]

Oct 30, 1749

By this Public Instrument of Protest be it made known… WILLIAM DOWWS, *Master,* PHILIP CALAWAY, *Carpenter, and* GEORGE MAY, *Mariner, lately belonging to the ship* Dolphin *being duly sworn…swear that on the 29ᵗʰ June last they sailed from Boston New England in the ship* Dolphin *bound for Ocracoke Inlet in the port of Bath in North Carolina, and from thence to London, that on the 3ʳᵈ day of August following they arrived at Ocracoke and moored and unrigged in Bacon* [Beacon] *Island Harbor, that on the 7ᵗʰ day of October following, them lying moored and unrigged in Bacon Island Harbor…there arose a storm of wind and rain from the NE by which the sloop called the* Endeavor of Boston, *Isaac Chikenders, Master, lying in sd harbor drove on the ship* Dolphin *bow, and forcing the sd ship to part her cables she had out to eastward and obliged her to ride by one cable and anchor. That on the 8ᵗʰ day of October at 4 o'clock in the morning the other anchor parted and the ship was drove on the shoal where she lay-beating till 9 o'clock, that the wind then shifting to the SW drove sd ship off the shoal. When the wind being extremely violet and seas boisterous, the master and crew cut away the ship's mast in order she might ride, and prevent her driving out of the harbor upon the shoal. Nevertheless the violence of the wind and seas kept sd ship from driving her anchor not holding, which obliged master and crew cut away the cable to prevent the, ship driving on the north breaker of Ocracoke Bar, a dangerous shoal, notwithstanding all their endeavors, the sd ship was drove on the north breaker of Ocracoke Bar, where she beat her rudder off, and part of her sheathing, that the sea being very high and boisterous popped them several times and tore in their dead lights, that the ship malting a great deal of water, obliged them to keep both pumps going. In this condition and—where they continued until one o'clock of 8ᵗʰ of October, when sd ship Dolphin was drove by the violence of the wind and sea on shore on Ocracoke Island, where sd ship had not long struck, until the sea have her laid broad side to the shore and made a free passage over her, so the crew could not stand to the pumps, and soon washed five feet water in hold, and the storm still continuing, the seas hove the sd ship on her broad side. The said deponents declare that on a survey made by several masters and a carpenter of ship* Dolphin, *then lying on shore on Ocracoke Island, they found her stranded and settled much in the sand, her rudder off, her stem part broke in two, and her planks—and her back broke, so that said ship could not be got and rendered unfit for service, for all which reason* WILLIAM DOWNS, *Master,* PHILEP GALAWAY, *Carpenter, and* GEORGE MAY, *Mariner, of the ship* Dolphin…*do Solemnly protest against storms, winds and seas for all damage suffered.*[12]

THE FIRST FORT FOR BEACON ISLAND: THE SPANISH INCURSIONS

The "oceans in the sea," or currents, made up a corridor of travel, so the shipping of the time had to follow the same route, like a highway in the ocean. A European ship headed to the New World left Europe heading south and then west to the Caribbean, then north to the Florida Coast, continuing north along the Gulf Steam, turning east at Hatteras where the frigid Labrador Current meets the warm waters of the south and continuing on past Bermuda straight to the southern European waters again. This route was used by every nationality, every type and every kind of deep-water, oceangoing vessel, because to deviate would mean months spent in contrary currents, dead-calm areas where the only way to move the ship was by oar and other delays. Every gold- and silver-laden treasure ship, every modest, dirty little cargo ship and every disease-ridden slave ship had to follow the same shipping routes. This, like so many other conveniences coveted by single-minded peoples, resulted in a recipe for war. Since the Spanish ships had to pass right by the English colonies on Core Banks, Ocracoke Island and Cape Hatteras, it was inevitable that someone was going to pick a fight.

In order to navigate the numerous channels and slews in Pamlico Sound and Ocracoke Inlet, a series of lighted beacons had been erected on some of the small landmasses in the inlet, including Shell Castle and, of course, Beacon Island. In other places in the inlet, lightships would tend a huge light suspended between their masts and showing the way. There was one thing on Beacon Island proper, and that was dry land. When it came time for a fort, one would think there would be no argument as to where it should go. However, the first fort for Beacon Island actually ended up on Core Banks, near Portsmouth.

Ocracoke Inlet would have been most effective, but it could be attacked by infantry forces and laid siege, making it a strategic gamble. An island installation, however, would require ships to oppose it—and very special shallow-draft vessels at that. Without some kind of boat, barge or landing craft, an island fort could not be attacked by infantry.

In the case of Beacon Island, the shallow waters surrounding the island proper made it impossible for any vessel other than small light-draft coastal shipping to even approach. All within an ever-growing field of artillery fire, long-range, oceangoing ships would have way too much draft to get close to any defenses there and would be aground before they could fire a shot. The island was closer to the inlet than Shell Castle and large enough to support a military base.

As if colonial life in coastal North Carolina wasn't hard enough, the average man and his family, not hurting anyone and just trying to make a living, sometimes fell prey to the politics of the day. The Spanish, who had colonies in Florida, often came up the coast, not as travelers, but in war parties made up of common thugs with nothing better to do than to harass these good people. Here we see quite a collection of war reports, some of which could almost have a hint of paranoia; either way, they illustrate the need for a fort.

PROTEST
1741 JULY 10

Be it known unto all men by this public Instrument of Protest, that on this tenth day of July in the fifteenth year of the r-reign of our sovereign Lord George, the second King of Great Britain, France and Ireland, and in the year 1741, personally appeared before me Gabriel Johnston, Esq. Capt.

General, Admiral and Commander of Chief in his Majesty's Province of North Carolina:

Benjamin Carkett, Commr. of the Sloop GUARNSEY of Edenton.

Andrew Frasher, Chief Mate of [illegible]

Francis Blakely, Seaman [illegible]

That they were bound on a voyage from Edenton, in the Province of North Carolina, from which she departed on the 7th day of June last, to Boston in New England, having on board the sloop; 600 barrels of pitch and tar, 50 bushels of corn, 400 pounds of dressed deer skins.

And then did take on board the sloop, in order to pilot and conduct her to Ocracoke Barr, one JAMES WAHAB, a man usually employed to pilot vessels through many channels lying between said town of Edenton and the Barr and Inlet of Ocracoke. Having proceeded with various winds, tides, currents, and weather till the 25th. At that time got as far as a shoal called the HORSE SHOE, distance from inlet 5 miles, at which time with a fresh gale of wind from the South, Southwest about 2 of the Clock in the afternoon, ran on a Shoal of land with vessel, which she struck with great violence, the tide running its last quarter Ebb.

The Deponents further say that they carried off an anchor and cable in order to hall the vessel- off the Shoal, but could not till about 8 of the Clock in the evening. The tide of the flood running very strong and the wind increasing, the Pilot ordered the Great Anchor to be let fall the Boltsprit into the water, in order to hold in case the other anchor and cable should fail, and to prevent the vessel from running any further onto the Shoal on which she did then lay almost afloat.

They further saith, that soon after, the Sloop did float and by the strength, of the tide, then steered over the Great Anchor so far that it came under her bottom, and pierced through the plank to cause her to leak great quantity of water so that both pumps could not keep her free. At 4 of the Clock the next morning, the 26th she was full of water and sunk to the bottom in 9 and ½ feet of water.

The deponents did. then proceed to unload the Cargo and put it on board a Sloop, one Capt. Draper, in order to put it on shore. The Pilot then left the vessel, and the deponents continued to labor in getting the stores, sails, and running rigging until the 2nd day of July, at which time they say a Sloop and Ship come off the bar and make a signal for a Pilot. None answering, they anchored without the Barr with the Sloop and Ship and fitted two Crafts with sails and oars, and about 60 people and proceeded over the Barr towards land. The deponents resolved, with their company of 13 in number to attack them at their landing, for which. intent they carried down their Jack and waved them to come on Shore, but the boats kept off, and went one on board Capt. Draper's Sloop and the other on board the Sloop GUARNSEY as she lay sunk, after which they landed on Ocracoke about 4 of the Clock, and approached the houses of OLIVER and KERSEY. They then fired a volley of small arms into the said Houses, and Capt. Carkeet, with others, heard old Mrs. OLIVER [illegible] in a most piteous manner.

The deponents then went to the boat of the Sloop GUARNSAY, which lay a distance from thence. and remained on the boat till next day when they went off in order to go on board their Sloop GUARNSEY, when they saw a large Sloop was got into the Harbour at about the distance of one quarter of a mile from their Sloop and they on board the sloop did send a boat full of men in pursuit of the Deponents, but their Boat happily got clear and further say that the next day they say a large Boat, and thinking it was Capt. Gales Pilot Boat, as they were at some distance from land, the Deponents then made towards her, but on approaching, they saw it was the boat that had chased them the day before. The deponents stood off from them and were chased for about 2 hours at a small distance by the said boat, but kept good their ground, whereupon the others distance from pursuing and stood back towards the Sloop in the Harbour, after which the deponents stood down also after them. In a short while saw several great smokes ascending, which the deponents do believe and imagine that the said people and crews of the Boats and Sloop had fired all the goods carried ashore by deponents, and carried off all the sails, cables and anchors, and further depose they believe they ENEMIES from seeing a SPANISH Pendant hoisted on the Sloop, and from their Manner and Action in all respects. Wherefore the said Benjamine Carkett, Andrew Frasher, Francis Blackley and James Fisher, do hereby solemnly protest against the Winds, Seas, Currants, Tides, and the depredations of the said Enemies for all damages, losses and expenses which have already accrued to, or shall hereafter be suffered and sustained by the owners, freighters and all and every other person or persons concerned in the said Sloop Guarnsey. In Testimony whereof they have hereunto set their hands and seals at Edenton, North Carolina, the day and year first before mentioned.

August 6, 1741
The Pennsylvania Gazette
Edenton July 10

"*The Spanish Privateers having the Boldness to advance a great Way within Occacock Bar, his Excellency our Governor has sent Orders to several Colonels of the Militia, to keep proper Detachments of their Men on Guard, in the Neighbourhood of the Sounds; and to have all their Men in Readiness to march on the first Notice: And in case the Privateers should land any of their Men to plunder the Inhabitants, or lay waste the Country, his Excellency has determin'd, if he has Timely Notice, to head the Militia in Person.*"

 A Spanish Privateer lately took a New-England Sloop in Pamtico River; and while they went aboard their own Vessel with some of the Loading of their Prize, they left two of the New-England Men on board their own vessel at Anchor: Mean Time, a fresh Gale happening to spring up, they cut their Cable, and run up the River; the Spaniards seeing this, sent a Launch after them, and pursued them almost to Bath Town; but finding it in vain, they thought proper to return and the Sloop got safe to Bath Town.

September 17, 1741
The Pennsylvania Gazette
CHARLES-TOWN, August 6

The Following is Part of a Letter from Captain Thomas Haday, to a Gentleman in this Town, dated Cape-Fear, July 7, 1741.

"*This comes to acquaint you of the Misfortune of having my Sloop taken last Sunday Morning, about nine of the Clock, about ten Leagues up the Sound within the Bar of Ocacock, by a Spanish Privateer's Long-Boat, in a Calm, being then on my Passage for the West-Indies: Upon which I immediately apply'd myself to the commanding Officer there, who sent an Express to this Place, which I chose to carry myself.*

 The Gentlemen here upon my Arrival have fitted out the letter of Marque Ship, Capt. Walker with 100 Hands; and a small scooner with 50 Hands. And I hope to have the Pleasure of serving the Spaniards brought in by them.

The Prizes that the Spanish Privateer has taken, are two Ships, three Sloops, and one Scooner: One of the Ships was Capt. Dupey, bound from Boston for Charles-Town. The Spaniards have built themselves Tents on Ocacock-Island; two of the Sloops lye in Teache's Hole, and the two Ships lye at an Anchor off the Bar. The Privateer is a high Stern black sloop with about 100 Men on board, and a very heavy Sailor. By the Accounts of several People who have escaped from them, they have burnt several Houses, and destroyed great Numbers of Cattle.

The Amount of our Cargo taken, being Provisions, the Sloop included, is upwards of Seven Hundred Pounds Sterling."

Extract of a private Letter from a Gentleman at Cape-Fear, dated Wilmington, July 21, 1741.

"We do not hear that our Privateer is yet sail'd, but rather a-Ground last Night, but expected to get off the Tide following."

About three Weeks ago Capt. Peacock, (who arrived here last Week) saw a fine clean Ship, with a Sloop on one side and a Scooner on the other, lying at Anchor off Ocacock Inlet, to which he gave Chase in order (supposing them to be Friends) to get some Provisions of them, which he was in great Want of; but by that Time he got within a Mile of them, they all weigh'd Anchor and bore away before the Wind, one of which he could discern to be a large black Sloop Spanish Privateer *as described in Captain Haday's Letter, and the Ship and Scooner he suppos'd to be her Prizes. Before the Spaniards weigh'd Anchor they were seen by Capt. Peacock, burning the Tents they had built on Ocacock-Island.*

A Scooner belonging to Capt. Thomas Henning, and a Sloop belonging to Capt. Jonathan Skrine, both of Winyaw, are supposed to be fallen into the Hands of the Spaniards, having both sail'd from North-Carolina about fifteen Weeks since.

Many other vessels bound for this Place, are suppos'd to have been taken by the Spanish Privateers which infest our Coast; particularly Capts. Skut and Wellon from Boston, and two Sloops from New-York.

June 16, 1748
The Pennsylvania Gazette
WILLIAMSBURG, *May 19*

Since our last, his Majesty's Ship Loo, of 40 Guns, Capt. Norbury Commander, arrived in Hampton Road, from Jamaica; and we hear is to stay to protect the Trade of this Coast, 'till the Return of the Fowey, or 'til he is reliev'd by some other Man of War.

Extract of a Letter from a Gentleman in Suffolk, dated May 13.
  I have just now received certain Advice of Three Vessels being taken out of Occacock Harbour, by a Spanish Privateer the 4th Instant, *viz*. Capt. Stephens, in a Brig. for London, Capt. Moor, in a Ship for Boston, and Capt. Williams, in a Sloop belonging to Bath. I dare say you may depend on it for Truth; and if you have Room to put it in your next Gazette, it may be a useful Hint to the Captain of the Man of War that is expected.
  There is a Harbour called Cape Look-out, a little to the Southward of Hatteras, where the Privateers rendezvous, and to which Places they carry their Prizes, 'til they are ready to carry them off the Coast to their respective Homes. It is as good and safe a Harbour as any in the World, secure from all Winds, and out of which you may get to Sea, even with the Wind that blows right upon the Land, in a Quarter of an Hour. The Privateers go there to wood, water and kill Beef; so that a Man of War might be almost sure of taking a Privateer or two, besides a good Number of Prizes, any Time between this and the last of October.
  The Pilot of North-Carolina was with me about 6 Weeks ago, in order to carry a Vessel consign'd to me round to Carolina, and told me, that for the Benefit of Trade in general, he would come to Virginia and carry a Man of War to that Place; and only expects the usual Allowance for Pilotage, 'tho it would be of great Prejudice to him, as he generally has as much Business in his Way as he can manage, besides he has One Hundred Pounds Sterl. from the Province.
  I dare say it would be of infinite Service to the Trade of this Country, if a Man of War would go there now and then; and the only Reason that they seem afraid to go near Hattaras, is, the Want of Knowledge of it: For by all Accounts a 20 Gun Ship might safely go over the Shoals; and as to Look-out Harbour, a 40 Gun Ship might go in Night or Day, without Danger.
I am, Sir, yours, &c.

June 23, 1748
The Pennsylvania Gazette
PHILADELPHIA, *June 23*

Sunday last came here one of the Hands of another Vessel bound hither from South Carolina, but was run ashore on Cape Hatteras in North Carolina, by a Spanish Privateer; by him we learn, that his Majesty's Ship Rye has taken and sent into Charles-Town, two of the Enemies Privateers; he also informs us, that as he came thro' Virginia, he heard that the Hector Man of War was to sail directly for our Capes.

July 6, 1748
By this Public Instrument of Protest…
SAMUEL WAKELY, *Mate,* JOHNSON HODGKINS *and* DAVID TROY, *Mariners, belonging to the Sloop* SARAH, *made oath…that on the 24ᵗʰᵉ day of May last, about nine of the clock in the morning, being at anchor in Lyn Haven bay, the sd sloop was taken by a Spanish privateer schooner, the commander whereof put eight Spaniards and a Linguistic on board of the said sloop, in order to have carried the sd vessel to the Havana or St. Augestine. And the sd Spaniards being unskillful navigators, obliged to entrust the deponents and with the crew and management of the sd sloop, who kept hovering about the coast between Cape Hatters and Cape Henry till the 15ᵗʰ of June following, at which time the parting of the mast, giving way, they prevailed on the sd Spaniards to suffer them to cut away the mast, to go to shore in a boat to get a spare, and the said David Tory together with two Spaniards and the Linguistic went on shore, where he met with* EZEKIAH FARROW *with two other men promised that night they would go off to the sloop to assist them but the weather would not then prevail, the next day this deponent cut away the mast and then desired leave to go ashore to grind their axes, David Tory, two Spaniards and the Linguistic where they met with* EZEKIAH FARROW, RICHARD BARBER *and* GEORGE SCARBOROUGH, JACOB FARROW, FRANCIS JAWSON (JACKSON), WILLIAM SCARBOROUGH, JAMES W. _____, . JASHUA WALL, *and* FRANCIS PUB,

Inhabitants of North Carolina, assembled together under a _____ assisted and helped these deponents to secure the Spaniards and the Linguistic, and then went on board the sd sloop, retook her and secured the Spaniards and sent them to Denton? (Kinston), and then the deponents were obliged to unload part of the loading, to wit; 427 bushels of wheat, 200 bushels of corn, 21 barrels of pork, one barrel of hogs fat, and about 5 ½ tons of iron, to raise a new mast. * The wind serving northerly, these deponents proceeded to Ocracoke and came into the said port on the day of the date hereof. And the aforesaid mate and mariners do further testify and declare that they did their utmost to protect the aforesaid vessel and damages for the benefit of the owners of sd sloop. Wherefor the said mate and mariners have desire to make Publication, that being taken by the said privateers at the time was the reason of the damages done to the said vessel and cargo on board the sloop. Therefore they do publicly and solemnly protest against all damages that hath happened by reason of the enemies privateers. I hereby set my hand and seal this sixth day of July 1748.

FORT GRANVILLE

In an attempt to stop these attacks, a fort was planned for Ocracoke Inlet—something that would protect the people from marauding Spanish ships. An attack of this sort, in which a crew of sailors attacks on dry land, like soldiers or infantry, is, by definition, an amphibious landing. The inlet itself was key to any attack from the sea. So the inlet is where the defenses had to be employed. Forts built on the oceanfront on either side of the inlet would be vulnerable to land attack and siege from behind. Two facilities could support each other in ideal conditions, but if one should fall, it could bring down both—certainly something to keep in mind when choosing the position on which to build a fort.

As it happened, the French and Indian War was also raging in the western part of the state, and North Carolina was receiving a fair share of refugees produced by this conflict. Be it Spanish or French to shoot at, a fort was needed against both.

At Old Topsail Inlet (modern-day Beaufort Inlet), a fort had been begun in 1756 but was never completed.

Near the newly formed town of Portsmouth, North Carolina, built on the northernmost point of land on northern Core Banks and on the southern side of Ocracoke Inlet, a new fort was planned. Rather than build on Beacon Island, the builders gambled on the possibility of siege, and construction began in 1755 on Fort Granville.

The Pennsylvania Gazette, May 29, 1755
NEWBERN, in North-Carolina, May 2

We hear from Portsmouth, that his Excellency our Governor is expected there the 7th Instant; at which Time the Commissioners for building the Fort at Occacock Inlet, are to meet his Excellency there, in order to consult on Measures for immediately carrying on the Fortifications there.

Named for Lord John Carteret, Earl of Granville, the installation consisted of a "fascine battery secured by piles" with two fascine fronts, one to secure the passage at two narrow parts of the main channel. The area behind the fascine fronts was to be protected by a strengthened barracks to house the garrison (this would also prevent a siege) and armed with eight eighteen-pounders and twelve twelve-pounders. A garrison of forty men, plus militia, was planned for manning the fort.[13] By October 1756, the fortifications were completed as planned and were ready for the garrison to move in.

In 1761, records show that at least a few guns of either six-pounders or twelve-pounders and as many as thirteen guns in total were here. In April 1762, a garrison of twenty-five men finally was issued to Fort Granville (for a period of six months). Later, this was reduced to five men, meant to maintain the fort and armament.[14]

Fort Granville was abandoned in late 1764 or early 1765. By April 1766, Governor Tryon wrote that Fort Granville was "never finished," and what had been done there was now in ruins, though earlier records clearly show that there had been guns en barbette and that a garrison had been assigned.[15]

BIRTH OF OUR NATION

For at least the first years of the Revolutionary War, Ocracoke was the child who was seen and "forgotten" by the British and allowed to bring in a goodly amount of needed war materials, supplies, arms, lead and a limited amount of powder. Their blockading abilities had been stretched to the limit on two battlefronts. Had it not been for Ocracoke's own organizational mistakes and logistical miscalculations, this inlet would have been a tremendous asset to the Continental army. As time went on and shortly thereafter, when money became worthless and only trade goods were of any value, tobacco, which was abundant at this port, became the new cash of the realm. The amount of smuggling was very heavy, but that's to be expected. There was trouble dealing with ports in the Caribbean, as English men-of-war patrolled heavily in those waters, looking for colonial ships and smugglers.

THE PRIVATEER COMETH

A great number of privateers (see accounts earlier in the chapter) were working from Ocracoke Inlet, and many more were on the way. These ships were a kind of "legal pirate," with letters given to them by the Continental Congress giving them permission to take English commercial ships by force and sell their cargo and vessel for a reward. A great many of these prizes were being transferred through Ocracoke Inlet on their way to market at New Bern. This brought attention to colonial operations at Ocracoke and placed the little port on the pages of a number of British intelligence reports. If British leaders intended to stop this port from delivering valuable war materials to the Continental army (they were probably not aware that the majority of goods coming into Ocracoke were nonmilitary, due to the poor management of the port at Ocracoke itself), they would have to extend their blockade to include the North Carolina Outer Banks. As the reader will see in this book, over and over, the coast of North Carolina is not, and never has been, a safe place for any kind of shipping, especially if you intend to anchor vessels (i.e. blockade) of any size outside the safety of the Outer Banks themselves.

The British had privateers, as well, and often loyalists were either employed on British vessels or willing to captain their own privateer ships for the British. On April 14, 1776, two warships, one British and one Tory, advanced toward Ocracoke to start trouble. The captain of the lead ship, John Goodrich, captured one ship, a schooner named *Polly*. The other ship, a British sloop named *Fincastle*, took prize of the sloop *Two Brothers*. *Fincastle* made off with *Two Brothers*, but *Polly* was too heavy draft to cross the bar in the falling tide. While Goodrich waited to get a tide high enough to make off with his prize, late at night, the pilots rallied and, with a force of twenty-three raiders under command of Benjamin Bonner, took both *Polly* and *Lilly* and delivered them to New Bern.[16]

The following is an extract from a letter from Halifax, North Carolina, dated April 22, 1776, and published in the May 8, 1776 *Pennsylvania Gazette*:

> *A few days past a ten gun sloop commanded by Capt. Wright (the same man who met with so warm a reception at Hampton, in Virginia) and a sloop of 6 guns, commanded by that infamous old piratical scoundrel John Goodrich, one of the parties of Lord Dunmore and Company, came over Ocracock bar, in this province, and took four vessels outward bound. The 10 gun sloop went immediately to sea with two of the prizes. The wind not being fair, Capt. Goodrich's sloop and the other two prizes remained within the bar. Twenty-three men, headed by a brave young man (Benjamin Bonner of Pamplico river) in four whale boats boarded the old pirate sloop of 6 guns, sword in hand, and possessed themselves of her, and the whole crew, with a tolerable cargoe of valuable articles. They also retook the two prizes. Seven of Goodrich's Negroes, a Captain, George Blair of the Queen's own royal regiment of Blacks, and a soldier of the 14th regiment, are among the prisoners. The sloop and two prizes are arrived safe at Newbern. Capt. Goodrich, Capt. Blair, the soldier and Negroes, are now within 15 miles of Halifax goal.*[17]

Eventually, more and more Continental privateers and even navy vessels used Ocracoke to deliver prizes and work out of, as the waters around the North Carolina coast have always been both an area conducive to piracy, legal and otherwise, and a protective environment for privateer vessels, allowing them to "leap" on their prey with efficiency and then return to protected waters.

As one could imagine, soon the British deduced the importance of Ocracoke and learned of the activities there from loyalists. Several appearances of British men-of-war led to the capture of a few American prizes.

At that point, there was much talk of how to defend Ocracoke, including militia, armed galleys and even larger vessels. There is some evidence that a battery was constructed but no confirmation of where.[18]

It was announced on July 12, 1776, that a company of about eighty men had been formed for the defense of Ocracoke; a paymaster had been hired to pay them; "guns" (it is not known if this means small arms or some kind of cannon), fife and drum and colors had been procured for the men; and powder and lead had been dispatched from the New Bern magazine.[19]

In July 1777, the Ocracoke Company assisted in the apprehension of William Brimmage, a Tory leader who had caused some trouble in Edenton.

Brimmage was a crafty one, though, and he later escaped and was recaptured and returned to Edenton.[20]

An officer and men were also sent to transfer three cannons from Cape Hatteras to South Quay, where several war galleys were being built and fitted out for their use.

WAR GALLEYS

During these years before the Civil War, often referred to as the Federal period, coastal communities depended on an ancient weapon to protect inlets, rivers and waterways: the rowing galley.

Cheap to build and easy to man, the rowing galley, or "gunboat" as they were often called, became a popular method of protecting the coastal waters of eastern North Carolina. Ideal for the small communities, they were often manned by raising a militia in a hurry, much like a volunteer fire department, or by armed troops, specially assembled to protect port facilities where forts were either not available or not financed. These vessels were from fifty feet long to over seventy-five feet long and carried a small number of large guns, accompanied by large swivel and rail guns and light arms. They were basically very large rowboats similar to those used in the Mediterranean Sea by Greek, Roman and Egyptian navies. These boats had multiple decks and magazines for gunpowder and cartridges and were partially powered by very long oars called "sweeps." The most basic version of these vessels was "sloop rigged," assisted by sweeps and normally supporting a gun deck somewhere around sixty feet in length. A larger gun—most wanted a long twenty-four-pounder—was mounted on the bow on a swivel carriage. Four more guns were mounted amidships in broadside, and a manageable number of swivel guns were mounted on the rails. The broadside guns were often long six-pounders or even twelve-pounder carronades.

These little gunboats had very shallow drafts, perfect for the sounds and shallow harbors of the North Carolina coastline, but this feature also made them very top-heavy. This was dangerous both in heavy coastal storms and on an open sea, and this kept the little fighters well inside the inlets and close to port. This restricted the boats to mainly defensive use only.[21]

Poor workmanship and inferior materials often handicapped the gunboats, and their best strategy was always to fight in groups or "packs."

The Continental navy galleys were built in a Virginia shipyard at navy expense and in the name of keeping Ocracoke open and mutually needed trade for both North Carolina and Virginia flowing. The first one, *Caswell*, was ready to launch in June 1778, under command of Captain Willis Wilson, followed by *Washington*. While both had been seriously impaired by supply problems throughout their construction and never actually served in battle, they proved somewhat effective in protecting the trade at Ocracoke. By 1780, *Caswell* had sunk at its mooring, eaten to a honeycomb by shipworms. Its crew and weapons were taken aboard *Washington*.

Ocracoke employed several of these galleys throughout the colonial and Federal periods. In June 1812, six of these vessels were deployed throughout the state coastal ports to defend these areas against British attackers. Gunboat numbers *7, 146, 147, 148, 150* and *167* were brought out of storage in Wilmington. One boat was stationed at Beaufort Inlet, two others were sent to Ocracoke and three gunboats were retained to defend the port at Wilmington.[22] Two years later, on August 27, 1814, one of these vessels, U.S. gunboat no. *146*, made history, of a sort.

At around 2:00 p.m., while preparing for a routine patrol, a sailor aboard was attempting to unload a musket by beating the barrel up and down against the deck when the rifle went off, igniting the powder magazine and blowing the boat to pieces. The crew of twenty-eight, some of whom were on shore at Shell Castle at the time of the accident, suffered eight killed and eight more wounded. The crew consisted of several free black men, at least one of whom was killed in the disaster. Commander Wolfendon, master of the vessel, was one of the men ashore at the time.[23] The vessel was lost, and its location is unknown. A month later, another source also mentions gunboat no. *140*, which also exploded and burned to the waterline on September 23, 1814, at Ocracoke Inlet. A beach wreck discovered on Bodie Island in 1939 was thought to have been the remains of this vessel.[24]

THREE ARMED BRIGS

Other earlier attempts to protect trade at Ocracoke came in the form of an armed brig named *General Washington*, which was purchased in January 1776, refitted at Wilmington and, by October, ready to begin the defense of the North Carolina coast, except for the completion of its crew.

Together with *King Taminy* and *Pennsylvania Farmer*, which were commissioned at the same time, the fleet made a formidable fighting force; however, the Provincial Defense Council, in command of the protection of the coast, decided to spread these vessels thin. *King Taminy* mounted some twelve guns and a number of smaller swivel guns; *Farmer* mounted twelve guns with swivels. Together, these warships were a threat to any British warships in the area, but alone, they would probably have to prove themselves.[25]

As it turned out, *General Washington* was reassigned to Wilmington a day later and never left that port. It spent its whole career here. *King Taminy* next started a life of escorting merchants and privateering. It eventually ended up back as a merchant vessel.

The closest any of them came to actually doing the job they were meant to was in September 1777, when *Pennsylvania Farmer* and an unnamed privateer managed to dissuade three British warships from entering Ocracoke and attacking New Bern.

By now, the British blockading efforts were improving, and there were more and more incursions by their warships all along the North Carolina coast, especially between Cape Lookout and Hatteras.

December 20, 1777
The Pennsylvania Gazette
NEWBURN, October 24

Since our last Capt. Ward, of the Independent company, stationed on Core Banks, has taken a prize schooner, called the Liverpool, *commanded by Capt. Mayes from Providence to New-York, loaded with fruit and turtle for Lord Howe. This vessel put into Cape Lookout Bay, under the sanction of a pretended friend; but Capt. Ward's vigilance soon discovered her to be an enemy, and in the night boarded her with some of his company, and took her.[26]*

THE YEARS BETWEEN THE WARS

Between the Revolutionary War and the War of 1812, continued harassment by Spanish marauders necessitated defensive installations be constructed to protect Ocracoke Inlet. To that end, in 1799, the U.S. government bought Beacon Island from John Wallace and John Gray Blont, who owned it (as part of the Shell Castle facility). This would be the first attempt to fortify Beacon

Island itself using federal funding. From 1794 to 1804, first system works were begun but not completed.[27] "First system works" tends to imply at least an L-shaped earthen parapet using driven pilings, sand and sod or perhaps barrels of earth or bales of some medium such as cotton or maybe even straw to stiffen up the center of the construction, or some combination thereof.

Another account, from an article in the *Newbern Gazette* dated May 1800, announced the government plans for parts of the fort and associated structures and even requested bidding contractors. According to the article, one detail that applied to all buildings is that they be one and a half stories tall. This is normal for structures built in coastal North Carolina, even today, and is done to provide extensive storage area well above any hurricane floodwaters. Houses in this area are also placed high on pillars and footings to keep the structures safe from floods. Some even have trapdoors in the living room floors to allow floodwater to enter the house, rather than float it off the "blocks" and cause its destruction.

Also described in the article are a barracks (sixty by sixteen feet); a "dwelling" house (thirty-eight by twenty-six feet), probably for the installation commander; and two other houses (twenty-six by twelve feet), use unknown. The buildings were to be built like castles, with six- by ten-inch corner posts and sills ten by twelve inches in size, which is five times bigger than the ones normally used today. The joists were to be nine by four inches and rafters six by four inches. Only the best possible materials were to be ordered, including sifted flaked lime, good quality oyster shells (concrete mix) and "pure heart lumber, free from sap."[28]

Though charts show some structure on Beacon Island, chances are very slim that any fort was started much past throwing up some sand bulwarks (see Chapter 2) and little other preliminary work. The real puzzle with this fortification is the timetable. After some ten years of work, from 1794 to 1804, the fort was "never completed." It sounds like a complete waste of time and money with nothing to show for it. Once again, the exact location could be anywhere on Beacon Island's original area, and though the fort was incomplete, somewhere nearby would be a collection of refuse accumulated by these workmen, which could be used to identify the location of this particular fort proper. Thus far, no such associated site has been found on Beacon Island or its perimeter, other than the period artifacts discovered by SIDCO divers on 0002OKI (official site number of Fort Ocracoke; see Chapter 4).

As a symptom of the lack of completion of this fort, we see another letter dated after the War of 1812, where actual guns were not only set aside and forgotten, but were so forgotten that they were awash at high tide:

Collector Office Ocracoke
April 19ᵗʰ, 1816
The Honorable
Wm H. Crawford, Esq.
Secretary of War
United States

Sir.

The cannon which were brought to this port during the war, for the purpose of completing the fort on Beacon Island, were thrown upon the edge of Shell Castle. They still remain there where every flood tide covers them, the carriages are rotting and the guns injuring. As an officer under the government I have thought it my duty to inform you of their situation presuming you were unacquainted with it.

Very Respectfully Sir
I Remain Your Abet. Servant
Thomas L. Singleton

INVASION OF OUR HOMELAND: WAR OF 1812

It has been said that "pride is a poor substitute for intelligence"; nevertheless, it has been the cause of more wars in human history than any other. Powerful leaders get offended by other powerful leaders, and the common man has to pay with his blood. Is this to say that all war is for nothing? The author supposes it depends not so much on who starts it, but why.

The War of 1812, in the author's opinion, is certainly one that comes close. England had received a "bloody nose" from a ragtag group of settlers, and the fact that those settlers now had a slowly growing navy was an insult to the pride of the country with the world's largest navy and the world's largest colonial interest.

In February 1813, British forces, including infantry and artillery units, were massing in Bermuda in preparation for a second attempt to bring the United States back under British rule. The artillery units were equipped with bombshells and even Congreve Rockets. The infantry units were formidable and included marines and even French prisoners of war, conscripted into fighting for the English.[29]

In the summer of 1813, a sizable amphibious force, under command of Sir George Cockburn, moved south against the U.S. coast from the Delaware River in an attempt to blockade and render useless the American ports. The blockade itself was somewhat inadequate and failed to make much of a dent, but the amphibious landings were more successful. They started in the area of the lower Chesapeake Bay. One of the primary goals for Cockburn's attack, especially on Norfolk, was the capture of USS *Constellation* and the destruction of the U.S. naval facilities there.[30]

American forces, made up mostly of militia, were caught completely unaware, and all along the coast, defensive positions, redoubts, batteries and small forts were "thrown up" in hopes of protecting the ports. Cockburn's force worked its way south, looting, pillaging and destroying harbors, towns and ports. They captured a number of small vessels and several privateers, as well.[31] Cockburn continued south, following the American privateer fleet and other support assets. In July, his armada anchored off Ocracoke Inlet. Because of the heavy draught of his oceangoing warships, he did not enter the inlet with his heavy vessels but rather sent a detachment of troops ashore in longboats to see what it could find. This force was supported by small vessels carrying rockets and light artillery:

> *Toward the middle of July Cockburn anchored off Ocracoke Inlet, and dispatched Lieutenant Westphall, with about eight hundred men in barges, to the waters of Pamlico Sound. They found within the bar the* Anaconda *of New York and* Atlas *of Philadelphia, both private armed vessels. They fell upon the* Anaconda, *whose thirteen men, after stout resistance, blew holes in her bottom with her own guns and escaped. The British plugged the holes and saved her. They then captured the* Atlas *and some smaller craft, but a revenue cutter escaped, and gave timely alarm at Newbern.*
>
> *Westphall proceeded to attack that place, but it was too well defended by the newly-rallied militia, to warrant an assault, so he proceeded to Portsmouth, not far off, took possession of the town, and for two or three days engaged in the pastime of plundering and desolating the surrounding country.*
>
> *The rapid gathering of the militia caused them to decamp in haste on the 16th, carrying with them cattle and other property, and many slaves to whom freedom was falsely promised. These Cockburn, it is said, sold for his own benefit in the West Indies.*

> *Leaving Pamlico Sound, the arch-marauder went down the coast, stopping at and plundering Dewee's and Caper's islands, and filling the whole region of the Lower Santee with terror.*[32]

Cockburn, several accounts mentioned, had this odd attitude toward deciding whether to loot a town or not. In what looks like an attempt to relieve himself of the guilt and responsibility of pillaging innocent townspeople and other noncombatants, he would order his men to take only what food he needed to sustain his force. Cockburn would even offer to pay a token, minimal fee for the stolen supplies. This was offered only if the townspeople did not put up a defense. If, however, his victims tried to defend themselves and their families, in any way, he would have his troops grab everything they could find and burn most of the rest.

Soon after entering Ocracoke Inlet, Lieutenant Westphall split his primary forces in two: one detail to take the two privateers and the other to raid Portsmouth. A number of small vessels and ships, including *Atlas* and *Anaconda*, were captured, but the American revenue cutter *Mercury* managed to get underway and carry the alarm to American forces at New Bern. Captain David Wallace, in command of *Mercury*, waited until all records could be gathered from the customhouse on Ocracoke and loaded aboard the cutter, thus saving them from falling into the hands of the British.[33]

Meanwhile, on Portsmouth Island, the second detail shot a villager named Richard Casey, who was trying to row his family to safety, and then began looting and committing minor vandalism. Eventually, Cockburn loaded a great deal of livestock and food aboard his fleet, cordially paid the town a fraction of what it was worth and departed the area to commit more mischief in South Carolina.[34]

In the same article mentioned earlier, we find the description of another abandoned fort used during the War of 1812 on Craney Island, near Hampton, Virginia. The author of that article, seen in the *Harper's New Monthly Magazine*, paints a vivid picture of a once-proud military installation left to waste after that war, as seen in 1853. The remains of the fort and the surrounding area were destroyed by fire in August 1861, as Confederate troops, under Magruder, moved through the nearby town:

> *It was the "ides of March" in 1853…On Craney Island were the remains of military works, constructed after the famous repulse of the British on the 22nd of June 1813.*

On the northern end of the island were the remains of a magazine, built of brick and earth. On the southern end, nearest to Norfolk, was a blockhouse in perfect order, within a large redoubt; and between it and the magazine, on the channel side of the island, were the mounds of the old connecting entrenchments. All this has been since changed by the fires of a terrible civil war.[35]

Back on Beacon Island, in 1853, a real lighthouse was finally built, regardless of what might have been there before; Beacon Island finally had a complete lighthouse. The building was a two-story keeper's quarters with the light mounted on the roof, elevating it to the height of thirty-eight feet. The original lamp was a fixed white light that was updated in 1855 with a sixth-order Fresnel lens. This is how it remained until it was destroyed with the fort in September 1861.

As we will see in the next chapter, there is always a bigger and better reason to fight, and each fight brings more need to protect one's own territory. The construction on Beacon Island will expand many times into an installation that, if tried, would have been found formidable indeed. Quite clearly, the decision to move the defensive facilities to Beacon Island was a strategically and tactically sound idea. In the end, of course, even that fort could not defend itself from time and the sea.

Chapter 2

A TIMELINE OF CHARTS

ANATOMY OF AN ISLAND

The Dynamics of an Island

It is said that we dislike change, yet everywhere we see man, we see him attempt to change everything to suit himself. In nature, change is automatic, almost mechanical, and whenever man and nature meet, man always tries to tame nature and control it. One of the most powerful forces in nature is water. In areas like rivers and streams, water will control the landscape and defeat our best efforts to control the surroundings.

Islands, inlets and rivers are always in a constant state of change, and it is very frustrating when we try to keep up with it, not to mention control it. Storms, extreme high or low tides and even wind direction effect change in a marine environment. Sand is moved around in a "washing machine" of forces, all acting to disrupt the terrain. What is covered by sand and sediment one day will be completely uncovered the next; sometimes the object will be uncovered for the first time in centuries, owing to certain conditions brought on by change.

One place where we see these changes happen on a daily basis is Ocracoke Inlet. Channels or "slews" will actually move from one season to the next, often complicating one's best efforts to navigate. Since its identification in 1998, Fort Ocracoke has transformed several times. So much so that the work season's first dives are often devoted to rediscovering the site. It often takes time to even find the channels leading to the site, leaving the team aground, wading along and man-hauling the company boats. Usually, it takes several expeditions to assess the entire site and document features that were not exposed the year before.

One of the best tools used in locating lost cultural sites is historic research involving charts and maps. Obviously, there is no sense in looking for two-hundred-year-old shipwrecks or sunken cities in an area that was an island for the last three hundred years and has only recently become a shoal or a new channel.

In the case of Fort Ocracoke, we are very fortunate that the area surrounding Ocracoke Inlet was heavily charted and recharted due to the natural changing of the terrain in contrast to the need to use the inlet as a port. The island on which the fort was located was named Beacon Island because at the height of the commercial use of Ocracoke Inlet, this island was used to build a large house with a light, or "beacon," on top. This was used for navigation by ships coming in and out of the maze of shoals, rocks and channels that make up the surrounding waterways. These charts show not only the existing terrain but also other means of navigation, including the Ocracoke lighthouse, lightships and channel markers, as well as the beacon itself.

The earliest chart we found was from 1795, and we were able to locate charts and mapping that ran the full gambit over the years leading to modern days. In this chapter, we will show the charts as they document the evolution of this island, as well as man's attempt to change the island to suit his purpose. There is evidence here of forts and military installations, as well as commercial use of the island and the surrounding waters, all chronicling the change that took place here over the years.

1795

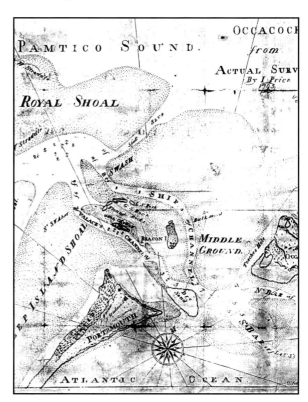

Top: Nautical chart of "Occacock," as surveyed by J. Price. Pamlico Sound is also called "Pamtico," and an emphasis is placed on Wallace's Channel, near the west shore of Beacon Island. Strangely, the four corner bombproofs and center magazine, along with what looks like the square building of the beacon, seem illustrated perfectly, but this chart was drawn seventy years too early, as the Civil War version of Fort Ocracoke was not constructed until August 1861.

Right: This close-up of the Beacon Island sketch better illustrates the uncanny detail displayed in this chart.

1806

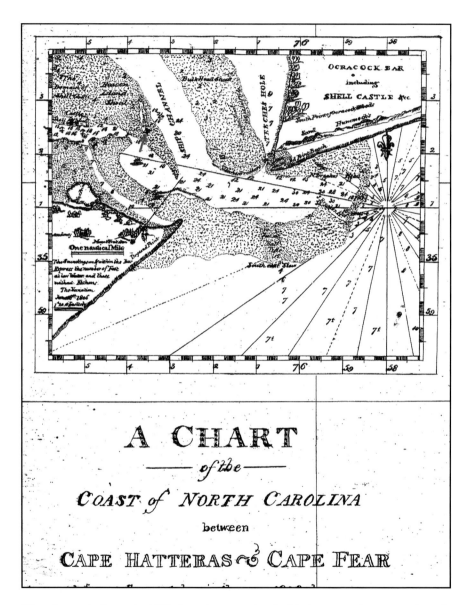

Though very similar to the 1795 chart shown previously, this document shows a number of differences in the movement of the navigable channels in the area of Beacon Island and the surrounding waters. The arrow shows the location of an icon almost exactly like the one in the earlier chart, once again suggesting some type of fortifications. *Chart supplied with the help of noted researcher Ellen Cloud, Atlantic, North Carolina.*

1808

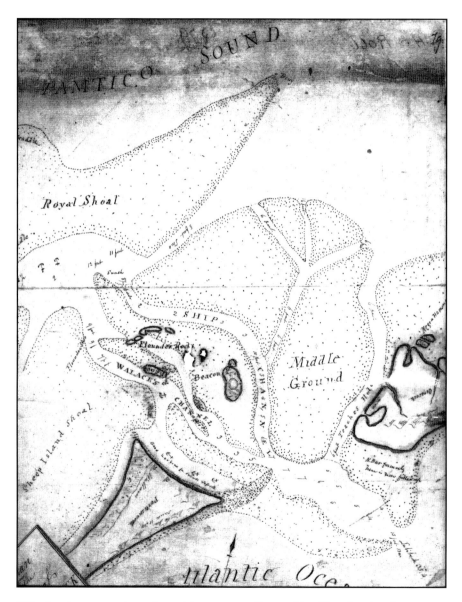

This plan shows not only a substantial structure on Beacon Island but also abundant anchorage areas and the channel to the north of Shell Castle. Notice that Beacon Island is shown here in two pieces of exposed land or marsh. *Courtesy of National Records and Archives Administration (NARA), from here on referred to as the National Archives.*

1820

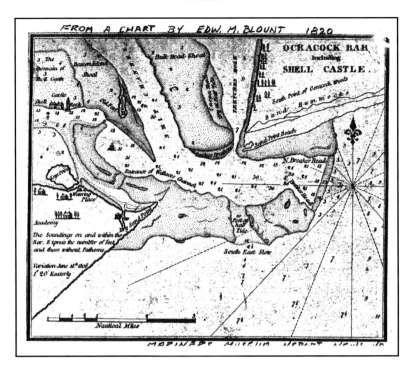

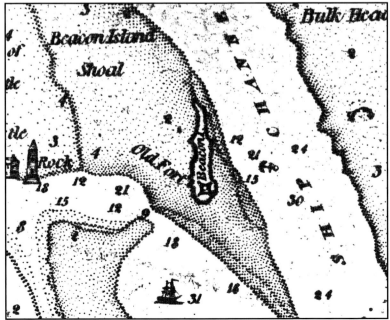

1821

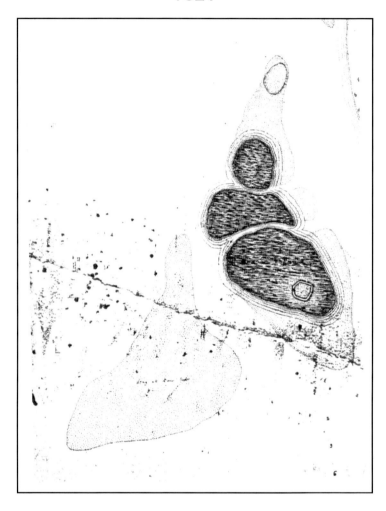

Above: This chart from 1821 shows a sizable earthen feature at the south end of Beacon Island, but little more is seen or described here regarding Fort Ocracoke. *Courtesy of the National Archives.*

Opposite, top: Nautical chart sketched by Edwin M. Blount, showing the channel leading to his Pamlico Sound port, Shell Castle. Notice again the diamond shape of the fort on Beacon Island, located just to the east.

Opposite, bottom: A close-up of the fort icon from the Blount Chart and the caption "Old Fort."

1827

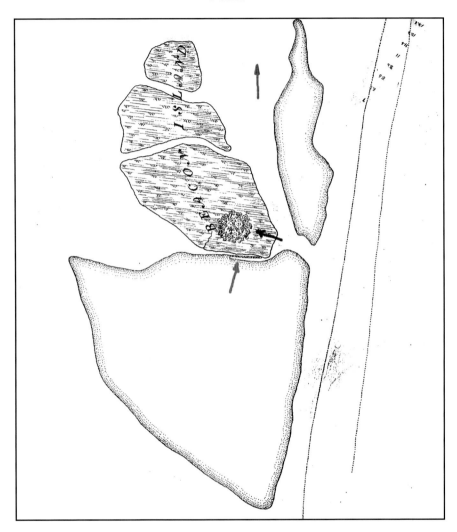

This chart shows a very detailed view of the topography of Beacon Island. The top arrow is the north pointer. The middle arrow points out an area of what appears to be heavy vegetation or perhaps even remnants of an earlier military installation. The bottom arrow directs attention to a small slew or channel that runs in the very same spot today, though the island was much bigger at the time of the 1827 survey. *Courtesy of the National Archives.*

1835

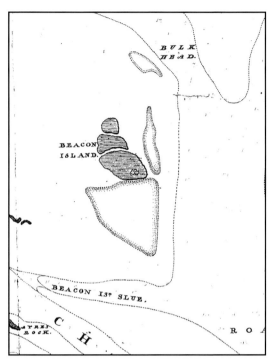

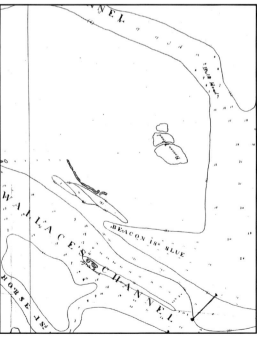

Top: This 1835 chart, by H. Dutton, is scaled "4 inches to One Mile" and is labeled "Map of Ocracock Inlet." The detail is excellent, and one major feature is the high terrain seen on the southern end of Beacon Island. The other interesting feature is the "Bulk Head" shown just north of the island proper. This is the first time we see a breakwater charted so close to the remains of the fort. Could this be the bulk of the ballast stone breakwater our divers found at the fort site?

Right: This chart also shows Beacon Island, but no mention of any type of military works is made. A feature that is once again seen is the mention of "Bulk Head," northeast of the island proper.

1852

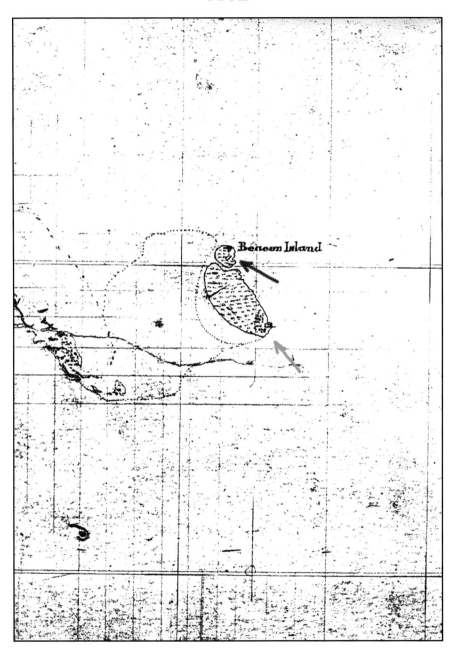

Another coastal survey started in 1851 and finished in 1852 shows little or no structure on or around Beacon Island.

1857–66

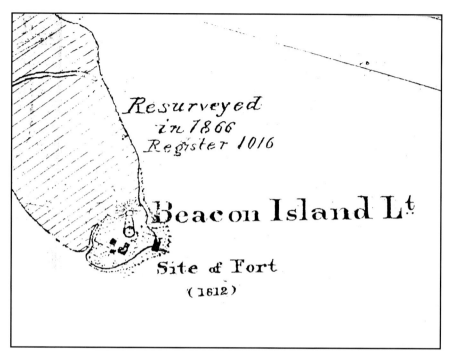

Above: This chart made in 1857 and then updated on the western half shows Beacon Island in great detail, including the Beacon Island light and structure labeled "Site of Fort" and dated 1812. It is unclear if this is referring to the Civil War Fort Ocracoke or remains of a fort from the War of 1812. This blowup shows an exaggerated drawing of the beacon, illustrating it more like a tall lighthouse, which may or may not have been an early version of the beacon light, as well as several block buildings of various sizes and an L-shaped building or feature. There is also a large rectangle where the breakwater is most probably built, which may be some kind of dock or wharf facility. This drawing may date back to pre–Civil War assets on the island proper and not show any part of Fort Ocracoke itself.

Right: A close scan of a charted light boat moored nearly due south of Beacon Island. Could this be the lightship that was "stolen" and later destroyed?

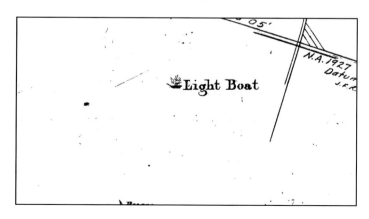

1866

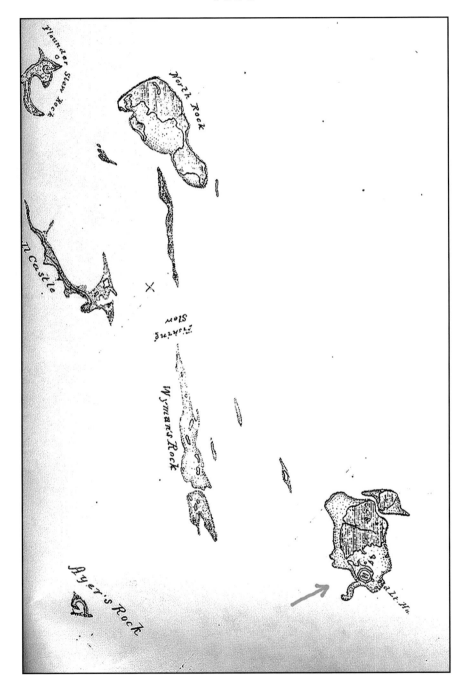

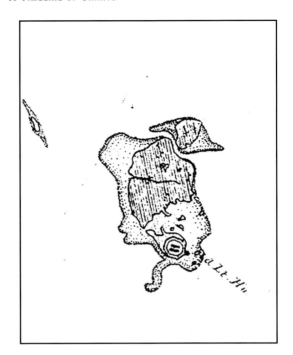

Right: A closer view of the structure(s) depicted in the chart opposite is seen here. The outer walls resemble the "eight-sided" fort design described by several eyewitness accounts.

Opposite: This chart also shows structures on Beacon Island. This version depicts a substantial remaining structure (see arrow) of what appears to be fortification walls and even a rectangular feature similar to the structure described as the magazine of Fort Ocracoke. These features are drawn representatively as awash and shoaling.

Sometime between the previously shown 1866 chart and the following 1945 chart, some act of nature caused the earthen walls and all the cultural features associated with the site to disappear beneath the surface of Pamlico Sound, and the site was forgotten by all but a few local fishermen and historians. There were several major hurricanes that hit the area between those dates—one in August 1899 (San Ciriaco), the Hurricane of 1913 and the storm of 1933, any of which could have caused the immense dynamic power needed to sink the entire southern section of Beacon Island.

1945

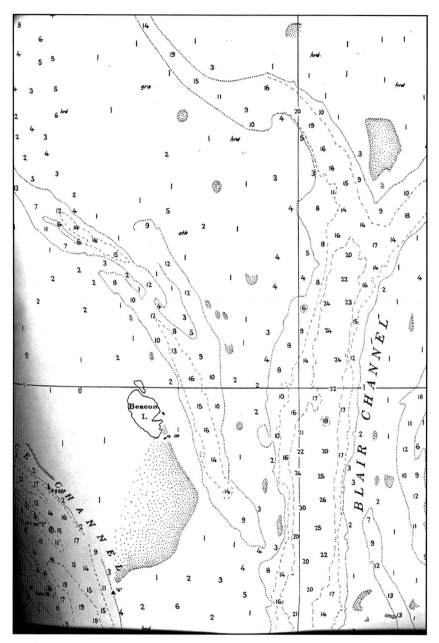

The survey/chart compiled in July 1945 shows an island similar to earlier descriptions, including the "slew" in the northern section of the landmass, but no evidence of any structures or elevated terrain.

2000

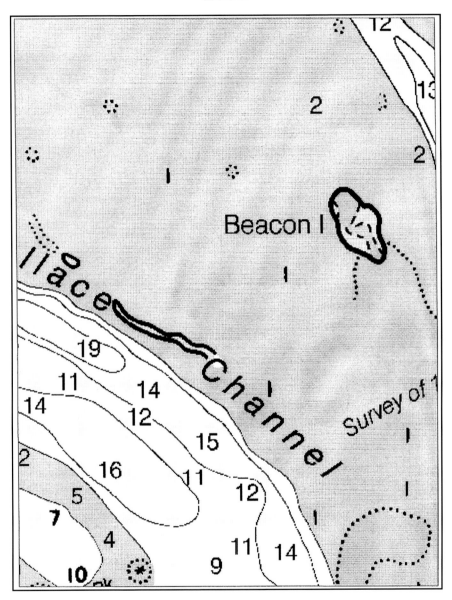

The modern-day depiction of Ocracoke Inlet, the NOAA chart no. 11550, shows a much smaller island, with much of the dry land becoming very shallow water surrounding what is usually described as a "grass lump." Since research is still ongoing, the exact location of Fort Ocracoke is not shown on this chart.

What Happened to the Fort?

How could such a huge piece of history be lost so completely? What "sank" Fort Ocracoke? What incredible force could wipe this site right off the charts? We now have that piece of the puzzle, given in the form of eyewitness accounts from those who were living at the time.[36]

Jessie Lee Dominic was the last child born in the town of Portsmouth in 1927 and the last to attend the Portsmouth School, which closed in 1943. She remembers playing on and around the remains of the fort while growing up on Portsmouth Island in the late 1920s along with Robert Fowler O'Neal, who lived on nearby Ocracoke Island.

They both describe the site as only a large mound of sand where the fort most likely stood and the remnants of the large house that supported the beacon. Almost directly below the beacon, a stone mound breakwater was exposed at low tide. This is the same breakwater that became the primary datum point of the entire site in 1998.

The force that turned a military installation, with earthen walls twenty-four feet thick, into a mound of sand is well known today to those who live on the coast: the hurricane. There are two hurricanes recorded in history with the destructive power and the proximity needed to make such changes: the infamous Storm of 1899 and the Hurricane of 1913.

The Storm of 1899

This hurricane, named San Ciriaco, struck the North Carolina coastline after making landfall in Puerto Rico, the Dominican Republic and Cuba. It slowly made its way north into the Gulf Stream, and on August 17, 1899, the San Ciriaco hurricane made its final landfall just shy of Cape Lookout. This was the storm that finally caused the abandonment of Diamond City on Shackleford Banks, for after this storm, the inhabitants had had enough. In Beaufort, light craft of every kind filled the streets along the waterfront. In Sea Level and Stacy, fourteen brave commercial fishermen were lost when the storm caught them off guard while working in Core Sound. On Ocracoke and Portsmouth Islands, many families were forced to "scuttle" the floors and chop holes in the flooring to allow water to come inside the house rather than wash it from its foundation. One eyewitness stated that no one, not even the older fishermen, could remember a hurricane so bad.

At the U.S. Weather Office in Hatteras, the anemometer registered sustained winds of 100 miles per hour, with gusts to 140, where it stopped reading when it was destroyed by the winds. Seven ships were wrecked on the shores of North Carolina, including the famous *Pricilla*. Six more ships, caught at sea, disappeared without a trace. In the aftermath of the killer storm, the sounds were littered with derelict light craft, dead animals, trees and bushes and the occasional human body. Those living in the remote parts of the coastal areas, above all, sorely needed fresh water, and food supplies were nonexistent. In the ruins of Diamond City, caskets and uncovered corpses lay drying in the sand, washed out of the graves by the tremendous tidal surge and overwash. The inhabitants of Diamond City who still had homes left began the task of floating their houses and belongings across the sound on barges to start over in Morehead City, Salter Path or Harkers Island.[37]

The Hurricane of 1913

On the very early morning of September 2, 1913, a tremendous hurricane struck the North Carolina coast and came ashore in the vicinity of Davis Shore in Carteret County. There was little or no warning to coastal residents, and many were lost. On Portsmouth Island, the water overran the island as high as 10 feet above ground level in some places. On Ocracoke, many houses were washed off their foundations, and a large steamer was washed into Ocracoke Village. The 319-foot, six-masted *George W. Wells* was piled up on the beach at Ocracoke, and as the storm passed, twenty-four people were rescued from the wreck. Pamlico Sound was reportedly "strewn with wreckage of small craft, trees and dead animals." On Ocracoke, Simon O'Neal reported finding a dead porpoise in the crotch of a tree. Inland, near New Bern, the bridge to Bridgeton was washed down and driven against the nearby railroad bridge. In other counties, at least seven major bridges completely disappeared, leaving only pieces of smashed driftwood. The hurricane also destroyed at least two concrete and iron railway bridges.[38]

The Hurricane of 1933

On September 15, 1933, another terrific hurricane devastated the coast of North Carolina. The path taken by the storm set off a chain of events that displaced the water in the northern sounds and forced it all into the already-flooded Core and southern Pamlico areas. This, along with the storm surge, decimated the coastal communities in Carteret and Hyde Counties as huge amounts of floodwaters completely overwashed Core Banks and Portsmouth, creating Old Drum Inlet in North Core, which is still there today. Twenty-one lives were lost in Down East Carteret County, and at Beaufort the wind speeds were estimated at 125 miles per hour. Once again, the Neuse River Bridge between New Bern and Bridgeton was destroyed, and the flooding moved inland. Many crops, ready for harvest, were completely lost in Craven and Beaufort Counties. The Down East community of Lukens was nearly wiped out, and the rivers and sounds were so full of dead animals that one report stated that disease was sure to strike if the animals could not be buried in a hurry. Many in the region lost everything they had, save the clothing on their backs.[39]

Conclusion

It is strongly suggested that one of these early hurricanes changed the fort into the mound of sand, and with the accounts given, it is most probable that the hurricane in September 1933 was the final blow to the fort, washing away even the sand mound that had been the walls, magazine and ruins of the beacon. None of the eyewitnesses remembers seeing anything above the water after this hurricane, with the exception of the small grass-lump island that exists today.

Both location and described landmarks verify the validity of the Fort Ocracoke site. Though this is circumstantial evidence, it is confirmed evidence that cannot be disproved. This, along with the other conclusive evidence seen in Chapter 6, goes to prove the identity of the site. In archaeology, 90 percent of all projects are identified using vast amounts of circumstantial evidence that, all collected and presented, prove the conclusions of the project.

Epilogue

In August 2005, Jessie Lee Dominique was killed in an automobile accident. Her contribution to historic preservation in both Carteret and Hyde Counties was tremendous, and she will be sorely missed.

Chapter 3

THE CIVIL WAR PERIOD

Beginning of Hostilities

During the early stages of the Civil War, as the North searched for an effective strategy against the South, it began its policy of a stranglehold blockade of southern ports. Southern commerce raiders struck Northern commercial targets off the North Carolina coast with great success. Small coastal steamers, normally used as passenger ships, were converted to lightly armed commerce raiders. These vessels were used because the Southern states had little money to purchase warships or vessels better suited for that purpose. Southern commerce raiding was so successful that Northern shipping tycoons loudly complained to the federal government and demanded that the Confederate privateers be stopped. One of the major passages used by these brave marauders was Ocracoke Inlet.

A naturally cut inlet in the Outer Banks between the villages of Ocracoke and Portsmouth, Ocracoke Inlet provided a protected corridor between the nearby shipping lanes and the safety of the shallows of Pamlico Sound. Rich commerce targets were sighted by lookouts in the Ocracoke lighthouse, and the privateers were signaled into action. Southern privateers captured Northern ships and their crews and either confiscated their cargoes or seized the entire vessel while operating from this inlet.

The waterways around Ocracoke, Portsmouth and Beacon Island were a center of maritime activity, even long before the 1860s. Various log entries from several sources describe the heavy shipping traffic in and out of Ocracoke Inlet and the adjoining waters as far back as the early 1700s.

Commerce Raiders like the CSS *Curlew*; the Confederate steamers *Winslow*, *Albemarle* and *Gordon*; the Confederate tug *Beaufort*; and the CSS *Ellis* are all mentioned quite frequently in period abstracts.[40] Well experienced and committed to the cause, their captains all knew a good location from which to conduct privateering operations. One eyewitness to this action, William Henry von Eberstein, had been a ship's captain before the war (it is unknown why he was not commissioned during his military career). He chronicles his involvement here:

> *Whilst there, we captured a schooner that came off the Bar from the West Indies. Colonel Martin put me on board, and gave me orders to get under way and proceed to New Bern, there to deliver her to the authorities there. This I did, with the crew detailed for that purpose from the sailors who had volunteered in the Washington Grays.*[41]

The support and aid given to the privateers ultimately led to the loss of Hatteras Inlet, Oregon Inlet and Ocracoke Inlet. The sheer number of privateer raids on Union commerce shipping was a financial hardship that the Northern insurance companies would neither bear nor forgive, and it was their complaints to the "right people" that initiated Butler's expedition to Hatteras. Funny how little things actually change over the years? Complaints from others might have been ignored by Union military officials, but not from the wealthy shipping magnates.

MAY 1861

In the South, men of vision and understanding knew that action had to be taken to protect the inlets to the sea, like Ocracoke Inlet—men like Warren Winslow, who was secretary of military affairs in North Carolina, and Henry S. Clark, the second governor of North Carolina during the Civil War. After realizing the great importance the Outer Banks held for the Confederacy, North Carolina's then adjutant general John F. Hoke ordered Colonel Ellwood Morris, an experienced engineer, to proceed to Ocracoke Inlet and begin building fortifications to protect that passage to the sea.[42]

Accompanying Colonel Morris was Major W. Beverhoot Thomson, who would eventually be the engineer in charge of building Forts Hatteras and Clark. In the following letter, Major Thomson reports on the conditions in Pamlico Sound and the need to begin shipping guns and other supplies to the coast:

Hatteras Inlet, May 23, 1861
J.A. Whitford Esq.

Sir,

I left Newbern on Sunday evening last, in company with Gen. Holms and Col. Morris to examine the sites and plans of the proposed redoubts at Beacon Island and at this point we got through with the examination the day before yesterday, and expected to have reached Newbern before this but have been detained here in consequence of a heavy blow from the NE, our boat being to [sic] light a structure to navigate the sound when very rough, as it is now. We splintered some of her timbers in the crossing the sound on our way here. We can not cross until the gale abates. The day Col. Morris & myself went ashore here we had an awful time in landing upon the beach from a life boat. On our return the boat made two attempts to reach the steamer and failed in both. A third however was successful with a through [sic] drenching by sea water. There is but one company of infantry from Edenton—No guns have arrived here from Norfolk as yet. I don't know whether the carriages will come with them. I understand that the adjutant general has countermanded the order to Richmond for the ironwork for the gun carriages ordered from Howard. The reason for this I understand is that the carriages are to be made in Norfolk.—I would simply remark that the carriages ordered from Howard are nearly complete. They will be required at Fort Macon, Newbern, Beacon Island and at this point, they will have to be paid for by the state, whether they are ironed or not they will I expect—all be needed and it seems to me there can be no necessity for going out of the state to have work done, when it can well be done here. I look at this on your own account not on mine, as it is no business of mine, further then my anxiety to get all of the guns in battery as hastily as possible—General Holmes told me the other day that he had waged upon the authorities at Raleigh that I be ordered to Wilmington in Whiting's place. Now I really (between orders) can see no necessity for this—they have at Caswell, Bowls and Radcliff, both

This period map from *Harper's Weekly* is the only source the author was able to locate that calls the fort "Ft Morgan." There are no primary source documents that use this name, and though it is used widely in many secondary books, the actual name of the fort was Fort Morris. There is no primary evidence of any other name.

*Engineers engaged in carrying out Whiting's duties. I am needed at Fort
Macon, as I am engaged in important works. Adding to the defense of
that important fortress it will take some time to finish—That work must
[illegible] I had when I get back to Newbern to hear from you—The
Morehead City work.*

Truly yours,
M. Bertrand Thomson[43]

Colonel Morris had made an earlier tour of both Ocracoke and Hatteras
Inlets and made strong cases for fortification of both in a report that
echoed the urgency of his assistant and opened many Confederate eyes. In
this report, he stated that "sand" forts should be erected at Ocracoke and
Hatteras Inlets and supplemented by a flotilla defense.

Due to the ever-increasing accuracy of "rifled" seacoast and navy cannons
of the day, ships' weapons were evolving from the smoothbore guns of the
War of 1812 and the Federal period. It was much easier to punch holes
in brick-and-mortar walls of forts with the new "hyper-accurate" weapons
(rifled and strengthened) being mounted on ships on both sides as fast as
they could be founded. Earthen forts, however, would have walls that simply
collapsed back into the damaged area, self-sealing the walls and stopping
any breach, even after continued strike by shell and shot. This was a critical
point, and ignoring it was the downfall of many masonry forts in the war,
including nearby Fort Macon.

Ellwood Morris was described as being "a scientific engineer of northern
birth and raising," but a southerner by adoption.[44] He must have impressed
his men because they bestowed on him the honor of naming one of the huge
eight-inch columbiads, mounted at Fort Ocracoke, after him, as stated in the
New Bern Daily Progress (see later in this chapter).

CONSTRUCTION OF THE FORT BEGINS

One month later, on May 28, 1861, work on Fort Ocracoke began in
earnest. The battery was also called Fort Morris, after its builder, and in
some texts it is called "Beacon Island Fort," but it has also been erroneously
recorded in some secondary sources as "Fort Morgan." In a letter of that
date, Colonel Morris stated that the *Fairfield* (at this time a supply vessel
carrying the aforementioned gun carriages; *Fairfield* later became CSS

Ellis) had not yet reached his post, although he expected it at any time.[45] He also stated that five gun positions had been made ready for guns, but only one gun platform was completed. Two other platforms were nearly complete. "In one day after debarking the cannon, I shall have five guns in battery," he promised.

DESIGN AND FEATURES OF THE FORT

The fort itself was built of barrels of sand covered with sand, earth and turf and was octagonal (several accounts say pentagonal) in shape.[46] The fort was described as having been built on Todleben's plan at Sebastopol (see maps of Sebastopol on the following pages).[47]

The following account was given in the personal diary of Mr. David Schenck, which describes some important aspects of the installation. The passage from his diary will be repeated in its entirety later in the chapter. This is done to ensure clarity and understanding of the text:

> We visited "Fort Morris" on Beacon Island this morning—The island lies in the mouth of the channel and completely commands the inlet.—The fort is a sand one, pentagonal and has already 8 barbette guns mounted with capacity for 50—Its magazine and horizontal redoubts are bomb proof—It is being erected under the supervision of Elwood Morris, a scientific engineer of northern birth and raising, but a southern adoption—It is built on Todlebins design at Sabastopol and though made only of earth it is so protected as not to be capable of washing away—over 200 free negroes are at work now on the fortification.

The walls were twenty-four feet thick.[48] These huge sand walls were said to have been protected so as not to be capable of washing away, which suggests some type of breakwater system, as seen during the archaeological surveys.[49] The fort was situated on the seaward side of Beacon Island, and eyewitness accounts suggest that an earthen mound may have still stood to some extent as late as the 1933 hurricane, which most probably finished washing all remnants of the walls into Pamlico Sound (see Chapter 2).[50]

Though it is very hard to tell, the chart here shows the basic concept for the fort at Sebastopol, as it relates to the description of Fort Ocracoke. The higher-scale chart also shows the general shape of that fort and how it could

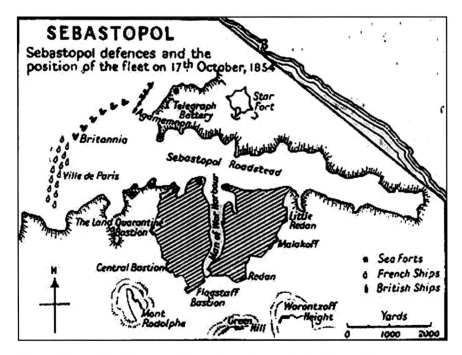

Chart of the battle for Sebastopol. Notice the star fort beside the Telegraph Battery.

be seen as "octagonal" or "pentagonal," as two of the accounts say. This description most closely fits two types of earthen fortification designs: the star fort and the field fort.

The star fort design, seen in the map of Sebastopol, is very much like a four-pointed star. This design uses pointed gun platforms and four corner bombproof shelters for the gun crews. This also allows room for the center magazine. The illustrations of star forts and field forts are graciously provided by the Civil War Field Fortification website.[51]

Here are D.H. Mahan's description and specifications for the "star fort":

Of Star Forts

Star forts are usually constructed either on a triangle ABC, of not less than 50, or more than 100 yards side: each side is divided into three equal parts, and on the central part an equilateral triangle DEF is described. The reason why the side of the triangle should not be less than 50 yards long has already been given in the latter part of [this text], *and they should not be more than 100 yards in length, because if it were necessary to occupy a*

62

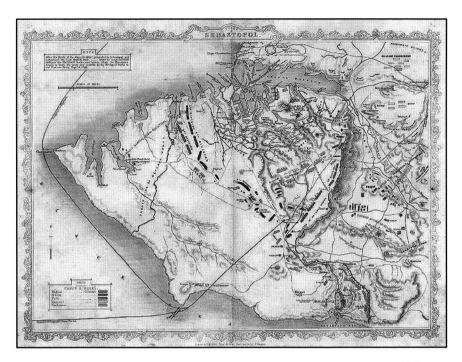

The Battle of Sebastopol in the Crimean War. Note the largest fort in the upper middle. *Courtesy of the Library of Congress.*

larger space than would be required for a star fort of those dimensions, a better outline might be adopted.

It is obvious that when building this type of fort it is extremely important to be sure the fort is not built too big for your manpower garrison. If the fort were too large to be completely manned by the troop complement, there would be sections of walls with too few men to defend them.

The field fort design is very similar to an inverted star fort. This type has many of the same features of the star shape but is much more complicated to lay out and takes a very large degree of accuracy in order for all sides to line up. This is most probably the design used on Beacon Island, as is suggested by contemporary charts, sketches and engravings and eyewitness accounts, although this is different from the design seen at Sebastopol.

The fort contained four shell rooms, each about twenty-five feet square, and a large bombproof about one hundred feet square. The magazine was contained in the center bombproof, which was framed in heavy pine timbers. There were twenty gun platforms, also built from pine, but the fort was said to be capable of mounting as many as fifty guns.[52]

Lieutenant James Y. Maxwell, first officer of the USS *Pawnee*, gives another firsthand account. This account is seen in its entirety later in this chapter, and this portion is repeated for clarity and a better understanding of the text:

> *It is called Fort Ocracoke, and is situated on the seaward face of Beacon Island; it was entirely deserted. It is octagonal in shape, contains four shell rooms about 25 Feet Square, and in the center a large bombproof of 100 feet square, with the magazine within it. Directly above the magazine on each side were four large tanks containing water.*
>
> *The fort has been constructed with great care of sand barrace, covered with earth and turf. The inner framing of the bombproof was built of heavy pine timbers. There were platforms for twenty guns which had been partially destroyed by fire. The gun carriages had been all burned.*
>
> *There were 18 guns in the fort, viz, 4 8-inch shell guns and 14 long 32-pounders.*[53]

EARTHWORKS

There are several important aspects of the fort seen here, not the least of which is the durability of earthworks at this point in history. In the War of 1812, brick-and-mortar forts were a highly accepted method of fortification and rightly so.

The weapons of that age were primitive smoothbore cannons, which had limited accuracy. Basically, if you hit a wall, you were doing pretty well. After the 1840s, cannons were drastically improved with the new method of rifling, in which the inside of the weapon's barrel was machined with an internal twisting pattern that caused the projectile to spin as it left the muzzle and flew toward its target. Now a ship could fire projectiles with such accuracy as to put its shells relatively close together and, in this manner, breach, or put a hole in, a brick fortification. To counter this threat, many fortifications were built using barrels of sand, sod, mud, clay or any combination of these kinds of earth. This way, the accurate combination of a series of projectiles hitting in the same area would simply move the earth and cause more sand and sod material to collapse down on top of the impression, sealing a breach that would otherwise mean disaster for the fort. As mentioned earlier in this text, this explains why the forts on the North Carolina Outer Banks were earthen and not brick and mortar. This also explains why this series of forts, if properly manned and supported, would have been so formidable.[54]

MAGAZINES AND BOMBPROOFS

The accounts say that there was a single large bombproof earthwork in the center of the fort that contained the magazine and other structures, but what is the magazine and how is it built? The magazine is simply the storage building for the fort's ammunition. It must be cool and dry and protect the contents from the elements. It must also be capable of protecting the contents from enemy projectiles, stray shell fragments, hot shot (cannonballs heated "red hot" and fired at an enemy to start fires in either a ship or fort) and other combat-related perils.

D.H. Mahan wrote a textbook for U.S. military cadets in 1849 and was an expert in the field of civil engineering.[55] His specifications were used to build works throughout the war. In *An Elementary Course of Civil Engineering*, he states:

> *Of Powder-Magazines*
> *Magazines are usually constructed either in the interior of traverses, or by the side of them. Sometimes casemates of timber are formed in the interior of large traverses to serve as barracks, but this would only be done in works of importance. These magazines and barracks may be formed in the same manor* [sic] *as the passages, with frames and sheeting.*
>
> *The best description of field powder magazines, is constructed of splinter-proof timbers of about 10 inches by 8, placing against a substantial and*

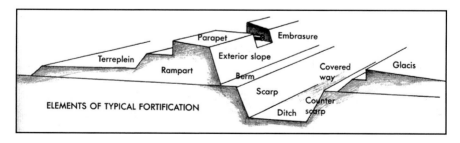

Elements and typical layout of Civil War–era fortifications. *From* Arms and Equipment of the Civil War *by Jack Coggins.*

well revetted [sic] traverse at an angle of from 45 degrees to 50 degrees, and strengthened externally with 2 feet of sod-work, or earth in sand-bags, the whole covered with tarpaulins; or the tarpaulin may be placed next to the splinter-proof timbers, or with an intervening row of sand-bags only; it is not then exposed to external injury; but if accidentally damaged, it cannot be readily repaired. If the site of the work be favourable to drainage, the floor of the magazine may be made with common gallery frames and sheeting, or in the same manner as covered passages.

Magazines are sometimes made with a double row of splinter-proof timbers meeting in a ridge; the bottom frame of the magazine should then be strongly connected at both ends, and at intervals of about 6 feet, by stout timbers framed into, or halved and bolted to the long sides of the rectangle; the ends of the splinter-proof timbers are then notched to fit into the bottom frame or sill. When timber cannot be procured for making magazines, casks or barrels may be buried in the traverse, reverse of the barbette, or parapet, to contain a small stock of ammunition.

There are two kinds of magazines: powder magazines and service magazines. Powder magazines are the main, long-term storage area for the entire fort. Often they would include several partitioned areas for storage of powder, storage of shot and shell and an area for the loading of shells and powder bags. There would be a gallery, or walkway, leading into the magazine but set at right angles to the actual entrance to the room. In this way, stray fragments of shell could not get direct, straight-shot access to the materials in the magazine. This was very important, as it can be imagined what chaos a hot shell fragment bouncing into the open entrance of a room containing ten thousand pounds of gunpowder would cause.

Service magazines were used to supply ammunition to the guns in use at the time of battle. As any weapon fires, it expends resources in powder and projectiles, which must be replenished very quickly. This remote magazine could supply the working guns until a lapse in the battle could allow resupply from the powder magazine.

Magazines were constructed of the same materials used to build the earthwork. Most people would think that this was a simple process and that it would not take a genius to design these types of structures, but nothing could be further from the truth. These features involved a wooden-framed inner building structure manufactured strongly enough to support the incredible amount of earth that it would take to insulate the contents and stand up to shellfire. There were several geometrical

A magazine structure at Fort Brady on the James River, most likely a service magazine. Notice it is sunken or built below the level of the ground. *Courtesy of the Library of Congress.*

configurations used to build the internal framing, but most were a square or rectangular house, covered with earth. Some used what they called "lean-to" or fascine designs based on triangular shapes and the use of kingposts and ridge posts.[56]

The structure and composition of the magazine had to be cared for and periodically inspected because earthwork materials would rot, erosion could occur in the rain or tide and rough use could even cause the feature to become weak and collapse or fail to withstand bombardment. There are documented instances in which magazines and bombproofs collapsed and killed their occupants, and the potential of shellfire getting close to a magazine and possibly exploding munitions inside caused several forts to

Bombproof earthworks at Fort McAllister, Georgia, with features very similar to those at Fort Ocracoke. *Courtesy of the Library of Congress.*

surrender, including nearby Fort Macon. Sometimes accidents could even cause catastrophic damage. After the fall of Fort Fisher in 1864, into Union hands, the victorious U.S. Army soldiers decided to hunt souvenirs. After several nice items were found in the fort's powder magazine, many soldiers ran in, trying to get the good stuff before it was gone. One of them had a lit torch. The resulting explosion killed hundreds of Union soldiers, and the carnage was so bad that no exact body count has ever been accomplished.[57]

More examples of bombproof works at Fort McAllister, Georgia. *Courtesy of the Library of Congress.*

Palisades

Part of a secondary arrangement of protecting walls used at the fort was a long fence made of sharpened pine poles, grouped very tightly together in a row, planted and set at a forty-five-degree angle. This is known as a palisade, and it is an effective obstacle used to slow advancing infantry. The feature, placed at the base of the forward wall, would slow the advance as men clumsily scrambled to scale the fence with its angle acting like the barb of a fishhook. This caused the enemy to "stack up," or place the men in a tight area where antipersonnel canister and grapeshot can be brought to bear, increasing its effectiveness tenfold. The only ways to breach a palisade would be to either go over, which would cause severe wounds from the sharpened ends and the height would make most difficult, or to dismantle the fence and

A heavily damaged palisade after the fall of Fort McAllister. Note how it is set at the base of the fort walls. *Courtesy of the Library of Congress.*

continue the advance by streaming men through the breaches, once again making a situation where grapeshot from the cannons was most effective.

It is unclear if the fence was placed in other areas of the installation or not, but the fence would have made a quite formidable battlefield obstacle.

Mahan described this feature as well:

> *Of Palisades and Fraises*
>
> *Palisades are made of large branches of trees, or young trees split or sawn in two or more pieces, according to their size. They are of a triangular form, each side of the triangle being 7 or 8 inches long. The palisade should be about 10 feet long. To plant it, a narrow trench is dug, from 3 to four feet deep, in which the palisades are placed upright, 4 inches apart. The earth is then filled into the trench, and well rammed to secure them below; and they are nailed to a band or riband 4 inches by 2½ inches, either within 1*

foot of the top of the palisade, or near the bottom of it. The riband must be placed on the inside of the palisade. It would be an advantage to have them also nailed to a riband, concealed in the ground, that the enemy might not be able to pull them up singly.

If the palisade be required to remain long in the ground, the ends should be charred or partly burnt; it will then be less injured by the moisture of the earth.

Oak palisades are the best. The upper part of each palisade is terminated in a point, to which an iron spike is often attached. The best position for a palisade is at the foot of the counterscarp, it is then sheltered from the direct fire of the enemy; but it may be received as a maxim, that a palisade is not of much use if exposed to the enemy's artillery, or unless, while destroying it, he is exposed to the fire of the work. Trunks of young trees 14 or 15 feet long have been used as a palisade with great effect. If more than 1 foot in diameter, they may be sawn down the middle to form two palisades.

Fraises are palisades placed horizontally, or but slightly inclined to the horizon. They are recommended by most authors to be placed along the crest of the escarp, in which case the work should have a glacis to cover the fraise from direct fire.

The stakes of the fraise should be 11 feet long, that they may be buried 4½ feet in the parapet, rest 1½ feet on the berm, and project 5 feet beyond the escarp. They are spiked to a riband laid on the berm, and on their upper end another riband is spiked, which being afterwards covered with the earth of the parapet, renders them firm and not easily to be displaced. The points should not be less than 7 feet above the level of the ditch.

The fraise might be more advantageously placed 2 or 3 feet below the crest of the counterscarp; there it would be concealed from view and not be liable to be damaged by direct fire; the enemy would also be exposed to the musketry fire of the parapet while destroying it.

Units and Personnel

Initially, the secession of North Carolina in May 1861 took the state officials in charge of defense and raising of troops completely off guard, and a bit of scrambling around ensued. The North Carolina Seventh Volunteers began a hasty organization. In the larger towns all over North Carolina, angry cries of patriotism caused men to pack a few things, say goodbye to their families

[Correspondence of the "Daily Progress."]
FORT OCRACOKE, BEACON ISLAND,
June 8th, 1861.

ED. PROGRESS: *Dear Sir:*—As we see your paper down here frequently, and, by means of it, discover what the world outside is doing, it seems but fair that that same world should know what we are doing in their behalf.— Briefly, then, the Fort is nearly completed; all our guns are landed safely and —— are mounted and in position. Magazines have been built and we have abundance of shot, shell and powder.

Two fine 8 inch Columbiads command the Inlet. The one first mounted of these has been named the "Nannie Daves" by an officer in the Fort, and the other has been justly called after the accomplished Engineer, who designed, and has nearly completed the work, the "Elwood Morris." With these two little implements, and some others that are now frowning over our parapet, besides those that will be in position in a few days, we are prepared to astonish old granny Lincoln's myrmidons, if they show their faces within range.

Over at Portsmouth, the "Morris Guards," under Capt. Henry A. Gilliam; the "Washington Greys," Capt. T. Sparrow; and the "Tar River Boys," Capt. Johnston, keeps watch and word, day and night, and, in case of a landing being attempted, will show the enemy that we are ready at any time to permit each one of them to "*hold, occupy, and possess*" six feet by two of North Carolina soil—*no more.*

For the rest—provisions are abundant, our spirits good, our aspirations high and holy, as of men engaged in a righteous cause, and we *fear not what man can do unto us!*

Truly yours, MUD FIDDLER.

and head into town to volunteer to fight. Far too many would never return. In homes, ladies' groups would gather to sew uniforms, bandages and flags. A celebratory atmosphere began to grow, as people finally had a chance to tell "Granny Abe" what they thought of him. As men gathered and began to muster, they held elections and voted on who their commanding officer would be and who would fill the other parts of a military formation.

Since so many eyewitness accounts are given, especially by ordinary individuals like Private William Parvin and others, it is very hard to keep up with the personnel and command structure of Fort Ocracoke and Portsmouth. Their descriptions of life at Fort Ocracoke often conflict with others and sometimes paint an incomplete picture for us today. Captain Thomas Sparrow was the senior commander of personnel at Beacon Island/Portsmouth and commanding officer of the Washington Grays. He was captured at Fort Hatteras and soon after was repatriated in a prisoner exchange. Before long, he was promoted to major. Colonel W.F. Martin, Sparrow's commander, was the commanding officer of the Seventh Regiment, North Carolina Volunteers, which was assigned to man the various forts from Ocracoke to Roanoke Island.

In order to clarify the companies at the fort, here is a list of them, including dates of arrival:

Washington Grays/Co. A (Heavy Artillery); Captain **Thomas Sparrow**; early May
Hertford Light Infantry/Co. D; **Thomas Sharp**; June 13
Hyde County Rifles/Co. B; Captain **James Leigh**; June 18
Morris Guards/Co. H; Captain **Henry Gilliam**; June 20
Tar River Boys/Co. C; Captain **George Johnston**; June 20
Confederate Guards/Co. K; **James Swindell**; early August[58]

It appeared that the work was continuing on the fort right up until the fall of Forts Hatteras and Clark since Colonel Morris and his assistant, Mr. Henry Brown, were still very much involved with the operations, including the recommendation that Von Eberstein be made ordnance officer.

Opposite: This article in the *New Bern Daily Progress*, dated June 11, 1861, gives great detail about the fort, including troop assignments and deployments. The status of the weapons is probably exaggerated for propaganda purposes. *Article courtesy of Ellen Cloud.*

JUNE 1861

According to local newspapers, Fort Ocracoke was nearly finished by June 8, the magazine had been built and filled with ammunition and several guns were mounted and "commanded the inlet."[59] We now know that this was highly unlikely and that, in fact, work was continuing on the installation right up until its abandonment in August. Meanwhile, a general request was compiled as to the eventual needs of the defense of coastal North Carolina. This letter was sent to Warren Winslow from Walter Gwynn in early June, and the supplies requested were approved:

To Walter Gwynn
Brigadier Gen. Commanding Northern Dept. Coast defenses
Requisition for Ordnance Stores for defense of Coast of North Carolina,
June 6, 1861

Percussion Caps
Friction Tubes
Paper Tubes for 8 in
   Columbiad Shells
Fuse Plugs for 8 in
   Columbiad Shells
Sabots for 8 in
   Columbiad Shells
Tin Stumps for 8 in
   Columbiad Shells
Flannel for Cartridges
Powder measures
Tangent Scales for 8 in
   guns
Quadrants Scales for 8
   in guns
Priming wires
Gunners Gimlets

Gunners Levels
Canister Shot (fixed
   if possible) for 32
   pounders
Grape " " " "
Signal Rockets " " "
Lead
Molds for musket balls
Powder
Portable Furnaces for heating
   Shot
Carpenters Levels
Cartridge Paper, 2 Reams
Twine for
   Cartridges—20 rolls
Thumb Stalls
Shot for
Roller Handspikes

Over

Requisitions Continued (page 2)

74

Hooks for Hot Shot
Saltpeter
Pitch Sights for 2- 10 inch
   Columbiads
Elevating Screws for " "
3 Sponges & rammers for
   8 inch guns
3 " " " 10 inch guns
20 " " " 24 pds guns
15 " " " 32 pds
   Columbiads
Rocket paper
Gunners Pouches
Worms & Saddles for
   24 pds
Saddles & Worms for

32 pds
2 Fuse Plug Reamers
8 pairs Port-fire Cutters
Port-fires
Quick and Slow Matches
Spherical Case not shafted
Bowman Fuses 100 doz.
Fuse Changers
Fire Balls
One six gun Barge Oars
   Awnings Cushions &
   complete
10 C. S. Flags
Water Tanks
Box Charts, books, Flags
   signals for Germantown

Walter Gwynn
Brigadier Gen. Comdr. North Dept. Coastal Defenses

Requisition for the Coast defenses of North Carolina, June 6th, 1861
Walter Gwynn
Brigadier Gen. Comdr. Northern Dept. Coast Defenses

60 8 in Guns with Barbette Carriages sponges Rammers Socks & Complete
4 XXXXII Cannonades
12 XXXII Guns 61 Cwt
6000 VIII in Shot
6000 VIII in Shell
1000 XXXXII Stand Grape x 500
1000 " Canister x 500
5500 XXXII Shot
2000 " Canister Grape
3000 XXIV Shot
3000 " Canister Grape

Approved

By order of the General
Warren Winslow W.W.

The list mentions the need for a six-gun barge, which would most likely be specific to the Beacon Island/Portsmouth installation. This explains the need to take the nearby lightship and begin converting it to a floating battery (see "The Floating Battery" later in this chapter). Also mentioned are supplies needed for three ten-inch columbiads. Since there were no ten-inch guns at Fort Ocracoke and the two columbiads that were there were eight-inch weapons, this list is most likely for the whole of the North Carolina coastline and not just associated with Fort Ocracoke. The requested equipment was most likely for ten-inch weapons at other installations.

As late as May 31, one account states that seventeen guns had arrived, but only five had been mounted in the fort.[60] Four more eight-inch guns lay on the beach at nearby Portsmouth Island, according to this account. One was mounted in a carriage, but the other three were still lying on the sand near the shore. One account states that these are only two seacoast howitzers (see letter from steamer *Albemarle Number 7* later in the chapter), and Maxwell describes other weapons here later in the chapter.

The operations at Ocracoke Inlet must have been a fury of attempted preparations, but even the basic equipment of an infantryman still had not arrived. The following report to Walter Gwynn from Captain Sparrow gives a picture of how unprepared for battle the Confederacy must have been:

To Walter Gwynn
Brig. Gen. Commanding
Northern Dept. Coastal Defense
Newbern

Report of Camp Equipment, Arms, Hospital Stores, etc. of the Forces at Ocracoke Inlet made by T. Sparrow, Senior Commanding, June 12th, 1861

WASHINGTON GREYS
10 Tents & fixtures
1 Capt. Marquee
3500 Rounds Ball Cartridges
1500 Caps
5 Camp Chests & furniture
99 Muskets Sharp. late patent "Springfield" 1850 with lock, bayonets attached
99 Canteens & Haversacks

The above except the muskets, were furnished by the Magistrates of Beaufort Co.

Articles needed
Body Belts
Cartridge Boxes
Knapsacks
Side Arms for officers
Bayonet scabbards
Cap Pouches
Bullet & Ball Moulds
Hospital Stores
Lead
Stationary
Powder
Camp Stools
Drum & Fife

Remarks

The tents are of very inferior material, too small for service, do not shed rain and will not stand the severe winds of the sea coast, they are now pitched at Fort Ocracoke, in double of one upon another, that they may shed rain. The camp chests are sufficient for the Co.

TAR RIVER BOYS
Capt. G.W. Johnston

13 tents
12 Camp Chest furnished
96 muskets
900 Ball Cartridges
2000 Caps for muskets
93 Canteens
100 Haversacks

Articles needed
Body Belts
Cartridge Boxes

Knapsacks
Bayonet Scabbards
Cap pouches
Drum & Fife
Side Arms for officers
Bullet or Ball Moulds
Hospital Stores
Ball Lead
Powder
Stationary

Report Continued

MORRIS GUARDS
Capt. Gilliam
Tents- have been ordered
85 Muskets
1000 Ball Cartridges
2300 Caps
12 Camp Chests & furniture
Drum & Fife

Articles needed
Body Belts
Cartridge Boxes
Knapsacks
Bayonet Scabbards
Cap Pouches
Side arms for Officers
Bullet & Ball moulds
Hospital Stores
Powder
Ball
Lead
Stationary
Canteens
Haversacks

HERTFORD L. INFANTRY
Capt. Sharp
No. of Men   *117*
Boys   *2*

                    119

Canteens, Haversacks, Blankets
Cooking Utensils

Articles needed

Arms
Ball moulds
Lead
Ball & Powder
Side arms for officers
Bayonet Scabbards
Cartridge boxes
Cap Pouches
Hospital stores
Knapsacks
Drum & Fife
Tents
Camp Chests

Respectfully,
T. Sparrow
Captain

JULY 1861

Several visitors came to see the fort during its construction, including Mr. David Schenck, who was a traveling companion to Commissary General Johnson (who may have been bringing supplies as the purpose of his visit). It is interesting to note that Schenck was "wrecked" and had to wade ashore on his return to Portsmouth from the fort:

Diary of David Schenck, June 27–July 1, 1861

I accompanied Col. Johnson on a tour of inspection to the coast today—Mrs. Johnson and daughter Jules went with us to enjoy salt water breezes and beaches—We left Raleigh at 8 O'ck. And arrived at Beaufort by 8 O'ck. in the evening enjoying the fine breeze and boat view from Morehead City to Beaufort…

We went to Newbern this morning in this way and took the steamer Post Boy, for Ocracoke Inlet at 12 Ock.—The ride down the Neuse was novel and exhilarating and our company being a pleasant one we greatly enjoyed our trip.—it is 84 miles, Capt. Osgood made the trip by 7 O'ck. to anchorage and we went over to the little ugly village of Portsmouth on the point in the pilot boat—We found a very inferior inn kept by old man Brady—There are four companies on Portsmouth Island under command of Capt. Sparrow—They received us with hospitality, glad to see any one from inland visitors to get news—

This place is forty miles from the coast and gets full benefit of sea breezes and is considerably visited to in the summer—But as rain water is the only available beverage it greatly lessened its blessings to one—

We visited "Fort Morris" on Beacon Island this morning—The island lies in the mouth of the channel and completely commands the inlet.—The fort is a sand one, pentagonal and has already 8 barbette guns mounted with capacity for 50—Its magazine and horizontal redoubts are bomb proof—It is being erected under the supervision of Elwood Morris, a scientific engineer of northern birth and raising, but a southern adoption—It is built on Todlebins design at Sabastopol and though made only of earth it is so protected as not to be capable of washing away—over 200 free negroes are at work now on the fortification.

On our return to Portsmouth three miles in a sail boat we came near being wrecked in a gale and escaped only by hard labor and with a thorough soaking among the breakers.

Another visitor to the fort was none other than Captain George Washington Curtis Lee, son of General Robert E. Lee and expert in the field of fortifications. Captain Lee toured all of the North Carolina forts just prior to the end of July in preparation of their coming under control of the Confederate government in the late summer of 1861. His findings were reported on July 24, 1861. The original records of this tour were destroyed in a fire, but a summary of the report states that Fort Ocracoke was "a well constructed fortification in a good position, but that [its] garrison of one eighty man company was too small." Lee believed that another garrison should be added when the fort was complete. His account of manpower differs from several others and could have been a misunderstanding of some kind. Lee goes on to mention the four other companies stationed at Portsmouth, and perhaps he felt that these were not assigned there to man the fort, whereas Von Eberstein tells us that the companies took turns garrisoning the fort proper.[61] He suggested that another battery be erected at Portsmouth to protect the approaches to the military installation there, and we know that one was under construction.

Armament of the Fort

Armament at Fort Ocracoke consisted of twenty guns total, though several eyewitnesses suggested it could have mounted as many as fifty. Nonetheless, it seems that at its strongest point, only a handful of guns were mounted and ready to fire in the fort proper.

Confederate battery of columbiads at Warrington, Florida, February 1861. *Courtesy of the National Archives.*

The actual number and type of guns at Ocracoke Inlet are a small mystery due to the vast differences in eyewitness accounts, not to mention secondhand stories. Twelve to fourteen of the guns were most probably thirty-two-pounder smoothbore cannons. It has been confirmed that there were the two eight-inch columbiads at the fort, and these would have been the most formidable weapons in battery there. Four more were said to be eight-inch navy guns, which were fairly large weapons firing a fifty-two-pound shell; however, with the combined weapons in the fort and at Portsmouth, it looks as though there were four eight-inch navy guns and four seacoast howitzers. It is still not clear which of the four were actually at which place. It is probable that at least three howitzers were at the fort.

Eight-Inch Columbiads

In the beginning of the Civil War, the Confederate armed forces were understandably short on arms, including sidearms, long rifles and, above all, heavy seacoast weapons. What was equally as important as the gun tube was the carriage. Seacoast cannons required specially built carriages, and most of the time, field carriages were completely inadequate. As much care was taken to construct and maintain the carriages as was taken for the gun tube itself.

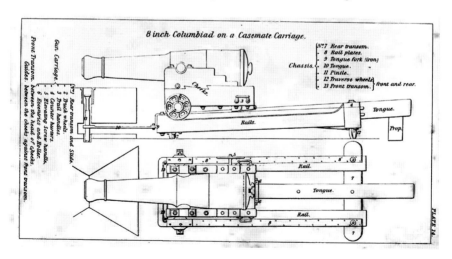

Overall view of eight-inch columbiad mounted on a "forward pintle" carriage in a masonry fort, for seacoast defense. Note the "front racer," allowing the gun to pivot on the front, as well as at rear of carriage. *Drawing courtesy of National Archives.*

In the first pages of *The Confederate Field Manual*, cannons and their classification are discussed:

> *Ordnance for the land service is made chiefly by private contractors, under the direction of officers of the Ordnance Bureau. The kind and calibers used are as follows:*
>
> *Guns/Seacoast/32-pounder-cast iron-1841*
>   *42-pounder- cast iron- 1841*
> *Columbiads/8-inch-cast iron-1844 & 1861*
>   *10-inch-cast iron-1844 & 1861*
> *Howitzers/ Seacoast/ 8-inch- cast iron- 1841*
>   *10-inch-cast iron-1841*
>
> *Note: Only the weapons associated with Fort Ocracoke are discussed in this table.*
>
> *There are in some of the forts guns of an older model than in the table. The 42-pounder gun and the 8 and 10 inch seacoast howitzers are suppressed by order of Feb. 9th, 1861. Some of the 8 and 10 inch columbiads have been rifled; the first to a caliber of 5.8 inch; the second, 6.4 inch. Their frequent bursting has caused this class of rifled guns to be discontinued. A few of the 8-inch siege howitzers were also rifled, for experiment, with a bore of 4.62 inch.*
> *Guns and howitzers take their denominations from the weights of their solid shot in round numbers, including the 42-pounder; large pieces, rifle guns and mortars, from the diameter of the bore.*[62]

The eight-inch columbiad fired a sixty-five-pound solid shot and a ten-pound powder charge. With a five-degree elevation, the gun's range was 1,800 yards. These guns were introduced in the United States in 1811 and were the primary seacoast weapons for many years during the 1800s. They were very versatile cannons in that they shared the features of the gun, as well as the howitzer and the mortar. The Confederate columbiads were primarily mounted on heavy seacoast carriages.[63]

The weapons called columbiads were called that after a famous period poem called *The Columbiad*, written in 1809 by Joel Barlow. Several authors have suggested that in the early Federal period, just before the Civil War (1809–41), nearly every weapon that did not fit in the other classifications (guns, howitzer or mortar) were called columbiads. This presents a classification problem for weapons made during this period. During the early part of this period, some guns as small as six- and eighteen-pounders were referred to as columbiads. Later weapons merely built in America were called by this term, further clouding the proper typifying of these cannons.[64]

There were only three sources for artillery for the Confederates: purchase from private or previously owned government mills, purchase from England

EIGHT-INCH SEACOAST COLUMBIAD ON BARBETTE CARRIAGE			
Powder (lbs)	Ball (lbs)	Elevation (deg)	Range (yds)
10	Shell (50)	1	681
"	"	2	1108
"	"	3	1400
"	"	4	1649
"	"	5	1733
"	"	6	1994
"	"	7	2061
"	"	8	2250
"	"	9	2454
"	"	10	2664
"	"	11	2718
"	"	12	2908
"	"	13	3060
"	"	14	3123
"	"	15	3138
"	"	20	3330
"	"	25	3474
"	"	30	3873
"	Shot	5	1697
"	"	15	3224

This information is taken from the *Confederate States Field Manual* and shows shot and shell sizes and powder loads for given distances.

Eight-inch columbiad mounted in a front-pintle carriage at Fort Delaware. *Courtesy of Wikimedia Commons.*

and other countries or seizure from captured U.S. Army forts and facilities, including Federal ships. Because of this, a great deal of mismatched guns were gathered for each new fort installation, based on what was available at the time. Then, of course, the carriages had to be built to suit the new use of the particular weapon.

THIRTY-TWO-POUNDER GUNS

According to *The Confederate Field Manual*, guns "technically, are heavy cannon, intended to throw solid shot with large charges of powder. It may be distinguished from other cannon by its great weight and length, and by the absence of a chamber."[65] The 32-pounder seacoast gun made up the bulk of the fort's weaponry. We believe that the fort's guns came from the Norfolk Naval Yards, and most of the guns would have been navy models as seen in the blueprint. Though antiquated by the new technology of the Civil War, they had served well during the War of 1812 and were in abundance at the time of the Confederacy's secession from the Union. Generally

Heavy seacoast thirty-two-pounder gun in front-pintal carriage. Note elevation screw under the breach. This gun is on display at Fort Macon, North Carolina. *Photo by the author.*

This is a heavy stand of eight-inch solid cannonballs, on display at Fort Macon State Park. These projectiles were fired from eight-inch weapons, such as the columbiad or howitzer, both of which were present at Fort Ocracoke. The solid shot used brute force to blast holes in wooden hulled ships. They were also heated in a special furnace and fired at the ships, red hot, to start fires in the ship's hull timbers. *Photo by Katie Smith, the author's daughter.*

THIRTY-TWO-POUNDER SEACOAST GUN ON BARBETTE CARRIAGE			
Powder (lbs)	Ball (lbs)	Elevation (deg)	Range (yds)
6	Shot	1.45	900
8	"	1	713
"	"	1.30	800
"	"	1.35	900
"	"	2	1100
"	"	3	1433
"	"	4	1684
"	"	5	1922

Diagram of thirty-two-pounder smoothbore in seacoast barbette. *From* Artillery and Ammunition of the Civil War *by Warren Ripley.*

mounted on wooden, front-pintle barbette carriages, they were capable of firing the full range of ammunition, including shot, shell, case, canister and grape. The gun tube was made of iron, had a 6.4-inch bore and measured 125 inches in length. The gun weighed 7,200 pounds. With a five-degree elevation and an 8-pound powder charge, the gun's range was 1,922 yards.[66] These guns were generally "smoothbore" and not rifled units ("rifling" was the method of lining the bore of the gun with grooves in a spiral fashion, causing the projectile to spin while it traveled to the target and increasing accuracy several fold), although 32-pounders were rifled later in the war, greatly adding to their accuracy and effectiveness. In the table provided, the ranges and elevation settings are shown. The range of these somewhat primitive weapons is very impressive.[67]

EIGHT-INCH NAVY SHELL GUN

Information for these guns has been hard to find. The guns themselves are at least as elusive as the text that describes them. These guns were the predecessors of the Dahlgren, Parrott and Brooks heavy cannons and were greatly antiquated at the outbreak of the Civil War in favor of the

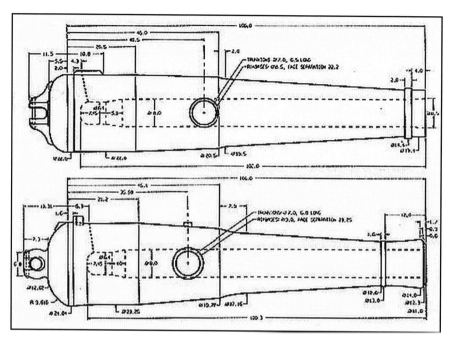

Diagram of eight-inch chambered shell guns. These are the drawings for the second set of foundered gun designs and the fourth set of designs for this weapon. *From* The Big Guns, *by Olmstead, Stark and Tucker. Provided by Paul Branch, Historian, Fort Macon State Park.*

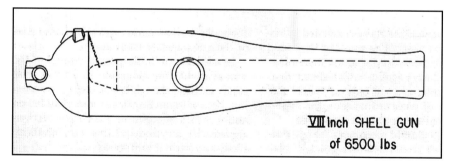

Sketch of the eight-inch shell gun by Eugene B. Canfield as it appears in *Civil War Naval Ordnance.*

newer, stronger weapons. The 4 eight-inch-shell guns left at Fort Ocracoke were described as "63 hundredweight" in one of the Union naval reports regarding Maxwell's actions there.[68] The eight-inch guns were founded in a variety of hundredweights, with the "63" being the focus here. They had been introduced in 1840, with 417 being produced between the years from 1841 to 1855. They were built for the navy in the Alger, Columbia, Fort Pitt and West Point foundries, and for a while they were required on the gun decks of first-class frigates and ships of the line. Regulations stated that 10 should be "carried and collected in one division of the gun-deck."[69] In 1846, the army accepted six guns, probably to compare with the 1844 eight-inch columbiad, which was by far a better piece.

Admiral Dahlgren described these guns:

> *They follow the form prescribed by Paixhans; they will be easily recognized by the straight muzzle common to the French canon-obusier of 22 centimeters; they have no sight masses; they are not turned on the exterior, consequently retain the outer crust, which gives them a rough appearance… In 1851* [others were] *cast, of the same bore length…but following the external form of other recent Navy cannon. They are turned, have sight masses, a bell muzzle, and a stouter knob.*

The guns were 101.3 inches long, with a bore of 8.5 inches, reducing to 8.0 inches in the chamber. The guns weighed in at around seven thousand pounds. The weapons fired primarily shells of around fifty-two pounds. With a nine-pound charge, the gun had an effective range of 1,770 yards with an elevation of five degrees.[70]

It is very possible that there was a combination of three eight-inch howitzers and one eight-inch navy shell gun at the fort and three or four eight-inch guns on Portsmouth, awaiting their mounting and fortification.

EIGHT-INCH HOWITZER

Because the Fort Ocracoke ordnance officer, William von Eberstein, ordered tangent sights specifically for three howitzers, it is believed that there were three of these weapons awaiting mounting inside the fort proper.

The Confederate Field Manual describes the eight-inch seacoast howitzer this way:

Howitzer—*The howitzer is a cannon employed to throw large hollow projectiles with comparatively small charges of powder. It is shorter, lighter and more cylindrical in shape than a gun of the same caliber, and it has a cylindrical chamber for the reception of powder. The chief advantage of a howitzer over a gun is that with less weight of piece it can produce at short ranges a greater effect.*[71]

The effective ranges for the eight-inch howitzer are listed on page 118 of *The Confederate Field Manual.* They include size of ball and size of powder charge.

According to *Artillery and Ammunition of the Civil War* by Warren Ripley, the eight-inch and ten-inch seacoast howitzers are the largest pieces in the howitzer family.[72] These weapons were introduced in 1838 and manufactured in 1841. The two sizes are virtually identical, with the exception of the projectile size. There is no evidence of any ten-inch howitzers at Fort Ocracoke, but three eight-inch guns were either at the fort on Beacon Island or at the battery being built on Portsmouth. The number and type of weapons destroyed by Lieutenant Eastman's marines on Portsmouth Island vary from two to four pieces and from eight-inch navy guns to thirty-two-pounders.

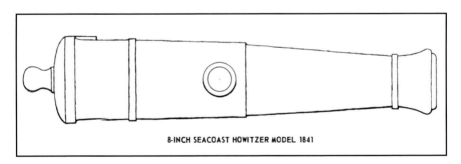

8-INCH SEACOAST HOWITZER MODEL 1841

Above: A diagram of an eight-inch howitzer. *From Harold L. Peterson Papers, 1963–1977, National Park Service History Collection RG 2, Location 11.2 lf., 1963–1977.*

Opposite, top: Shot and shell: a thirty-two-pounder solid shot with and without charge bag and sabot. The sabot allowed the round ball to be fired from a rifled gun. The sabot would guide the ball down the barrel and then be separated from the shot by the blast of the gun and fall away. A twelve-pounder is just visible to the right.

Opposite, bottom: A round shell with the fuse hole visible (far left) and a Whitworth "bolt" (second from left). The slots would fit inside the rifling of the weapon's barrel and spin when fired. An "Absterdam" shot (third from left) and a "flanged" shell (fourth from left) are also seen. *As seen at the beautiful exhibit at Fort Fisher, North Carolina; photo by author.*

EIGHT-INCH SEACOAST HOWITZER ON BARBETTE CARRIAGE			
Powder (lbs)	Ball (lbs)	Elevation (deg)	Range (yds)
4	45-lb Shell	1	405
4	"	2	652
4	"	3	875
4	"	4	1110
4	"	5	1300
6	"	1	572
6	"	2	828
6	"	3	947
6	"	4	1168
6	"	5	1463
8	"	1	646
8	"	2	909
8	"	3	1190
8	"	4	1532
8	"	5	1800

The information from this table was used to formulate shot or shell sizes and powder loads for given firing range adjustments. This table is taken from the *Confederate States Field Manual*.

"NOTHING MUCH TO DO EXCEPT DRILL AND STAND GUARD"[73]

The "Washington Grays" under Captain Thomas Sparrow are mentioned more than the other companies in research.[74] The Grays were formed in Washington, North Carolina, in very early May 1861 as Company A of the Seventh North Carolina. Two of the enlistees were William Henry von Eberstein and William Augustus Parvin, both of whom wrote memoirs after the war. The men came from all around to join the volunteer companies. William von Eberstein, who was originally from Chocowinity, enlisted on April 15, 1861. For volunteer troops, officers and noncommissioned officers were "elected" by the whole of the enlisted men. Von Eberstein was elected fourth sergeant.

Soon after enlistment, Von Eberstein, along with a detail of ten men and with ensign Benjamin Cowell in charge, was sent to take possession of

Fourth New York Artillery in defense of Washington with a seacoast howitzer. Note grapeshot and canister munitions at the sergeant's feet. *Courtesy of the Library of Congress.*

the U.S. Marine Hospital at Portsmouth.[75] This structure had been used as quarantine during port business but became the barracks on Portsmouth Island and was later called Camp Washington. Before leaving, the detail formed up in front of the home of Mr. Samuel R. Fowle on Main Street in Washington. After much ceremony, including the presentation of a bouquet and a speech by Miss Martha Fowle, the detail departed on the schooner *Petral*, owned by Mr. Fowle and captained by Adam Warner:

> *We left Washington N.C. in the early part of May 1861 with instructions from Thos Sparrow Capt of the company afterwards known as Co "A 7th N.C. Volunteers" to proceed to Portsmouth by river and on our arrival there*

to seize the U.S. Marine Hospital and hold it to be used as quarantine for the company which was to follow within a few days. The detail consisted of W.B. Cowell Ensign, Wm H von Eberstein Sergt, Harrison Hall Corpl, W.W. Cordon Corp, Thos O. Wroton private, E.B. Shaw Private, Chas K. Gallagher Private, others I do not recall their names but ten in all constituted the detail.

On the day of our departure our Detail was assembled and formed in front of the Dwelling on Main Street of Samuel R. Fowle where we were presented with a beautiful boquet accompanied by a very appropriate speech from Miss Martha M. Fowle. After which headed by the old Colored Fifer Dennis to the air or tune Who'll be King but Charley we moved off by the flank to the foot of Respess Street and embarked on board the schooner Petral *Adam Warner Capt and owned by Saml R Fowle.*

We proceeded down Pamplico River and across the sound a distance of eighty miles and performed the duty assigned to us which was very arduous duty. We arrived at night. We seized the U.S. Hospital and commenced unboarding the Petral *and land our stores on wood which we had to do by wading through the water over the shoals waist deep. this occupied all night and nearly the whole of next day. I tell you we felt very military for as soon as we left the wharf at Washington I placed a centry aft and one forward in the bow of the vessel over the stores and as soon as we got on shore at Portmouth and seized the Hospital I placed centries at every gate and one at the door of the House to keep the men from going out without permission. We commenced to have Military discipline.*[76]

William Augustus Parvin, a private in the Washington Grays, gives this account of the departure of the rest of the company from Washington on May 20, 1861:

I shall never forget that day, I think all of the people in Washington turned out that day dressed in their best and the ladies especially with flags a-flying. Drums a-beating and fife playing. Much later a man presented the company a beautiful flag and made a fine speech to the company and we had a fine company. 112 men rank and file a fine uniform of gray cashmere trimed in black. We also were well armed with improved Springfield Rifles. We went aboard the steamer and arrived at Portsmouth all right and landed and marched up to the United States Marine hospital and took charge of it and wed it for our quarters as long as we stayed there and there it was where I commenced to see what a soldiers life was.[77]

A soldier's life indeed—with adversaries like boredom, mosquitoes, disease, weather and the lack of the "glories" of war, it seems that one had quite a battle without the Yankees. Still, they seemed to get along well:

> *We drilled twice a day, target practice once a day, also guard duty to do. But we had a fine time. Plenty of good fishing and plenty of fish and plenty of game birds such as cerlew and willet, sea plover and yellow shanks and fine salt water bathing and surf bathing. We could catch all the oysters and clams that we wanted and we got so much rations and the people of Washington sent us so much provisions that we traded off some for watermelon and peaches and figs.*[78]

William von Eberstein's description was somewhat more military and lacked the simple man's view of their new duty station:

> *After some time, a few weeks, several companies came down and joined us at Portsmouth. Two were from the north counties, and one from Greenville,*

The U.S. Marine Hospital at Portsmouth, North Carolina, built in 1847. The structure was meant to be an "Old Sailor's Home" of sorts and was built using a collected fee paid by U.S. Merchant Marines of that period. It ended up being used as a quarantine facility for travelers using the port to enter or exit the country during its more active period throughout the 1840s and '50s. Notice the two main stories with large open porches on both levels and the tall brick and mortar pillar and footings under the building to keep it above Outer Banks storm- and floodwaters. *Referenced from* North Carolina Medical Journal; *courtesy of Earl O'Neal Jr. Re-penciled by the author.*

in Pitt County. We then organized in the 7ᵗʰ North Carolina Volunteers, with Colonel Martin commanding.

We did patrol duty on Portsmouth Island. Our men took turn and turn with the other companies to garrison Beacon Island, where Fort Ocracoke, as the Yankees call it, was situated. I was detailed to drill the different companies in Artillery Drill.

Whilst at Portsmouth, we had a pleasant time fishing, crabbing, clamming, and oystering. Nothing much to do except drill and stand guard.[79]

Not all the soldiers of the Confederacy faired as well. One commander in Virginia states that drinking water was very much a problem. He goes on to say that there is very little source of it occurring naturally on the barrier islands and that the streams are all salt water. We see this same situation at Fort Ocracoke and on Portsmouth. As written in the diary of David Schenck (June 27–July 1, 1861), "But as rain water is the only available beverage it greatly lessened its blessings to one."

The majority of water supplied for drinking on the Outer Banks at this time in history was rainwater caught and stored in large brick-and-mortar tanks called cisterns. Several accounts say that there were four large cisterns in the interior of the fort, and many of these kinds of tanks survive today in and around Portsmouth and Ocracoke Village.[80] We also know from Maxwell's account, and others, that water was brought from Washington and New Bern in barrels and stored inside the fort. On Portsmouth Island there were only the cisterns (see image on page 1891). Sergeant John Wheeler of the Hertford Light Infantry described the drinking water there as "oh, such stuff" (see Chapter 6).

Sickness, disease and sanitation were also severe problems for most of the coastal commanders, Confederate and Union alike. This letter from General J.B. Magruder paints a dark picture of the state of conditions on the Virginia Peninsula, only one hundred miles north of Ocracoke Inlet:

George Deas, Adjutant-General C.S. Army
August 1861

The sickness among the troops in the Peninsula is grave, both in extent and character, all diseases taking more or less a typhoid character, and many deaths occurring—at Yorktown about two a day…the Fifth North Carolina Regiment, composed of twelve companies and over 1,000 strong, is now less than 400 for duty…I have called out a large force of Negroes, at considerable expense to the Government, to complete the fortifications upon which our troops have been so laboriously working. The troops can no longer do this work, and I respectfully request that the Quartermaster-General be directed to furnish to the assistant quartermaster-general of this department, Captain Bloomfield, the funds necessary for the payment of the laborers without delay, as a great many of them are free Negroes who have families, who must starve if they are not paid, and to all I promised prompt payment. There are, perhaps, 1,000 now at work on the Peninsula.

It is hardly necessary for me to say that I wish the sanitary condition of the troops to be as little known as possible, for obvious reasons.

J. Bankhead Magruder
Brigadier-General Commanding

General Magruder tried to imply that disease and medical conditions were improving, but one wonders how such severe losses could be stopped.

THE FLAGS OF FORT OCRACOKE

Private Parvin mentions a flag, beautifully made and presented to the company by the ladies of Washington, and later Von Eberstein tells us what happens to the same base banner (see "War Comes to Carolina" later in this chapter). But just what flag flew over the walls of the fort? It is believed that it could only be one of two flags of nationality: either the First National Confederate or the First North Carolina Secession flag.

As states began to secede from the Union in mid-1860 and the Provisional Congress of the Confederate States of America assembled, one of the first items of business was the creation of a national flag. There were several designs proposed, but the flag known as the Stars and Bars was adopted as the very first national Confederate flag, though it was never "officially" designated so by the later official Confederate Congress.

Initially, this flag had only seven stars, representing the first seven states to leave the Union: Texas, Louisiana, Alabama, Mississippi, Georgia, Florida and South Carolina. Later, as more states left the Union, stars were added until the flag bore thirteen stars, with anticipation of Missouri and Kentucky becoming members of the Confederacy as well; however,

Left: First National Confederate Flag, seven-star variant. The flag consisted of a red and white stripe with a blue star-studded field in the upper left corner. *Photo by Katie Smith, the author's daughter.*

Below: First North Carolina State Flag, also called the North Carolina Republic Flag, was a dark red or burgundy, left-hand field with a blue upper and white lower adjoining stripe. A single star and the dates May 20, 1775, and May 20, 1861, are printed in the burgundy field in white lettering. The 1861 date was the day North Carolina seceded from the Union. North Carolina was the last state to join the southern Confederacy. *Photo by the author.*

of course, history tells us that the latter two states never left the original Union. This flag ran into trouble at the Battle of First Manassas in July 1861, where its similarity with the Stars and Stripes of the Union caused great confusion.

The Provisional Congress laid down specific rules and specifications governing the designs of the flags of the Confederacy, and the official Confederate Congress followed suit. The designs and specifications for the unofficial Confederate flag, the Stars and Bars, were:

> *The Flag of the Confederate States of America shall consist of a red field with a white space extending horizontally through the center, and equal in width to one-third the width of the flag. The red spaces above and below to be of the same width as the white. The union blue extending down through the white space and stopping at the lower red space. In the center of the union a circle of white stars, corresponding in number with the States in the Confederacy.*[81]

The North Carolina Secession state flag is very similar to the First National Confederate in that the "bars" concept is also used in a rectangular pattern of different color order.

North Carolina's flag uses only three fields, while the former uses four fields and the red and blue are reversed. The red used on this flag is much darker, almost a burgundy. With the Seventh North Carolina Volunteers being state troops, it is very possible that the flag over the fort would have been the North Carolina flag. In fact, Captain Sparrow mentions being in a lighter "duty"-type stance, awaiting orders from the Confederate army, when the news of the Union attack on Forts Hatteras and Clark arrived (see "War Comes to Carolina" later in this chapter), and he and his men are forced into combat much earlier than expected. With this, it can be reasoned that the First National Confederate flew on the flagpole of Fort Ocracoke or that both flew from the pole. We may never know for sure.

AUGUST 1861

On August 19, 1861, Richard C. Gatlin was notified that he had been appointed "Brigadier-General in the Provisional Army and assigned to the command of the Department of North Carolina and coast defenses of that State."[82] He would be taking over for Brigadier General Walter Gwynn, who was the current commander of the northern department of coastal defenses.

The Union navy was also now becoming aware of Fort Ocracoke and its strong position. In a letter from Daniel A. Campbell, master of the brig *Lydia Francis*, which was wrecked at "Hatteras Cove" on May 6, they learned much about the installation. His vessel, being en route from Cuba to New York, was considered enemy commerce to the Confederate privateers. Captain Campbell was detained at Fort Hatteras (while it was still in Confederate hands), and while going through the process of prisoner transfer, Mr. Campbell was moved several times—from Hatteras to New Bern, then to Raleigh, then to Ocracoke and Hatteras and *then* back to New Bern, finally being released through Oregon Inlet and boarding USS *Quaker State* for Hampton Roads.[83]

While traveling, he got a good look at some of the Confederate installations of eastern North Carolina, and he described Fort Ocracoke as such:

> Ocracoke Inlet,—*Captain Campbell states that on Beacon Island, about 4 miles from the bar, at the mouth of the inlet, the rebels have erected an octagon-shaped fortification; and at that place, and in barracks at Portsmouth, on the beach, on the south side of the inlet, there were reported to be about 500 troops. He was not allowed to land there.*
> Daniel A. Campbell
> *New York, August 12, 1861*[84]

Even in August, gun carriages were continuing to arrive. On August 9, at 10:00 a.m., the schooner *Isabella Ellis* finished landing gun carriages at the fort before continuing on to Oregon Inlet.[85]

In early August, Miss Martha Matilda Fowle, along with her father, sailed to the fort aboard his schooner *Minot*, which had transported many of the troops to Beacon Island from Washington just a few months earlier. There had been a number of young ladies from surrounding counties who had traveled to Portsmouth and Beacon Island, escorted by parents or family members. Miss Fowle writes:

> *We stopped at Portsmouth on our return and were joined by Mary, Magg, Anna Marsh and Mattie Telfair. Helen and Laura Shaw came down also. Clara Hoyt, Kate Carraway and Sallie Howard, and there were many*

other ladies in the house. Here we spent two weeks very pleasantly and formed some agreeable acquaintances, of whom I would mention Lieuts. Perry and Moore of the Hertford Light Infantry. Lieut. Perry fell in love with Mary at first sight and there commenced his attentions to her.[86]

The following letter, dated August 12, is a list of ordnance supplies needed at Fort Ocracoke. It is compiled by Sergeant von Eberstein and gives us a more comprehensive accounting of the number and type of guns at the fort. As Von Eberstein was the ordnance officer, it is doubtful that anyone would know more about the guns mounted there than him. (See "Armament of the Fort" earlier in this chapter.)

GEN. J. WHITFORD
Ocracoke Inlet
Ordnance Officer
August 12th, 1861
Newbern NC

Dear Sir,
Enclosed is a memorandum of ordnance stores & other articles absolutely needed at Fort Ocracoke. The guns & gun carriages especially should be painted at once. Please send all that can be proceeded as speedily as possible.

Very respectfully,
T. Sparrow, Capt.
Commander Forces at Ocracoke Inlet.

(ATTACHMENT 1)

Fort Ocracoke
August 11th, 1861
CAPT. SPARROW
Commanding the troops at Ocracoke
Sir,
According to orders from Brig. General Gwinn, I am notifying you of the different articles needed at Fort Ocracoke.

8 Gallons Lacker to black the guns
3 Kegs white lead to paint gun carriages

1 Keg Black lead for same
8 gallons Linseed Boiled oil
2 Gallons Spirits Turpentine
4 large paint brushes
2 small paint brushes
2 8 inch scrapers for columbiads
2 scrapers for 32 Pounders
1 good spy glass for use of Fort
3 sets of Tangent Sights for 8 inch Howitzers
1 No. 44 gwt 63 gro 3 lbs 10
1 " 40 " 64 " 2 " 10
1 " 25 " 66 " 3 " 10
10 sets Tangent Sights for 32 Pounders
1 No. 64 cwt 58 gro 1 lbs 16
1 " 27 " 47 " 0 " 11
1 " 157 " 57 " 2 " 27
1 " 18 " 47 " 2 " 20
1 " 30 " 47 " 1 " 21
1 " 19 " 47 " 1 " 25
1 " 14 " 43 " 3 " 14
1 " 15 " 48 " 0 " 15
1 " 29 " 47 " 1 " 00
1 " 17 " 46 " 32 " 06
2 Sets of Sights for 8 inch columbiads
1 No. 2 weight
1 No. 1
1 BBl of common oil
4 Elevating Screws for 4 Barbette Carriages
10 Barbette Carriages
1 Large sized Monkey wrench
2 Sledge hammers
1 doz. Handspikes
1 doz. Steel Priming wires
also fuses for the shells
10,000 lbs. Powder
600 22 lbs shot
100 8 inch ball
Grape & Canisters
Yours Respectfully

Sergeant William von Eberstein
Ordnance officer
Ordnance Dept.
New Bern, August 13th 1861

Recd. this 13th day of August, 1861 of [illegible] *left out on board schooner Minot for Capt. T. Sparrow, Ocracoke with the following ord & ord stores:*
50 Kegs Cannon
3 Kegs White Lead
1 Keg black lead
I Keg oil
1 Keg Spirits Turpentine
1 bundle of (6) paint brushes
1 monkey wrench

signed P.J. Marly
in behalf of [illegible]
New Bern, August 12th 1861

Part of the [illegible] *for making cartridges*[87]

From the list of items needed, we can deduce that at least three of the "8-inch navy guns" that Maxwell reported were, in fact, howitzers, bringing the armament tally for Fort Ocracoke to twelve thirty-two-pounders, one eight-inch navy gun, three eight-inch howitzers and two eight-inch columbiads being on loan from Fort Macon. These are also the guns retrieved by the CSS *Albemarle* on the day before Maxwell arrived at the fort. It is unclear why more weapons were not recovered on the same day they recovered the two columbiads in early September (see "The Destruction of the Fort Is Complete," later in this chapter).

By mid-August, after the visit from Captain Lee and as the fort neared some form of completion, Colonel Bradford, the state's chief of ordnance, made his tour of the installation. He said that Fort Ocracoke was capable of resisting any bombardment directed against it, with twenty-four-foot-thick walls, an earth bombproof mound covering the eighteen-thousand-gallon capacity cisterns and two spacious galleries for the storage of ammunition. The magazines, under the traverses, were shellproof. The work had continued to settle, making it necessary to raise the walls of the parapet from time to time until the settlement ceased.[88] This may explain why work had continued through this date and that "200 free Negroes" had been reported working through June 30, as seen in David Schenck's diary entry.[89] Colonel Bradford went on to say that the two eight-inch columbiads were mounted and ready along with seven thirty-two-pounder smoothbores and that they had been mounted on the "channel fronts."

MUTINY AT PORTSMOUTH

Not long after news of the Confederate victory at First Manassas (Bull Run), excitement and envy of the "glorious" life of a combat soldier ran amuck through the ranks of the Portsmouth garrison.[90] Many of them longed for action and disliked the life of inactivity. They began to speak their minds and murmur among themselves. Some of the company commanders were more diplomatic than others. When many of the men grumbled and complained, Captain Thomas Sparrow of the Washington Grays came up with an interesting way to solve the problem. He staged a vote or election to decide if the company wanted to stay at Portsmouth, as members of the North Carolina State Troops with a twelve-month enlistment, or join the Confederate States Army and be transferred to the front lines in Virginia. Out of 112 men under Sparrow's command, 100 voted to go to fight in Virginia. Captain Sparrow arranged to trade the 12 remaining men with Captain Gillian for 12 of his who wanted to leave Portsmouth as well.

Captain Johnson, on the other hand, was not so open-minded, and when his men wanted to hold an election he would not have it. The men ignored his orders against the election and held an unofficial vote. Some of the men even wanted to vote Captain Johnson out of command. They selected a soldier named Howard Muswall for their new leader.

Tempers flared, and Johnson's company was to be placed under guard by some of Sparrow's men. As tension mounted, some of the men barricaded themselves in the house that served as their quarters on Portsmouth. Outside, one of the Confederate gunboats anchored nearby (Captain Cook commanding) was ordered to train its guns on the structure.[91] At the fort, Ordnance Sergeant William Henry von Eberstein received the same orders, and he aimed the two columbiads at the house as well. Colonel Martin asked for volunteers to form up and go arrest the men, and the Washington Grays marched to the front door of the building and called for the "mutineers" to come out and surrender:[92]

> *This the mutineers did quite meekly, and that was the end of the difficulty. The ringleaders were court-marshalled some time afterwards, but through the influence of their commanders and their many friends, they were turned loose with a reprimand from the Commanding Officer.*[93]

Just prior to this incident, Sergeant von Eberstein was promoted to ordnance sergeant of Fort Ocracoke. His duties were to take charge of the ordnance and to train the men in artillery drill. He describes the unfortunate event that gave him his promotion:

> *As the Ordinance Officer on Beacon Island, a Lieutenant Brantly, having been removed from his office for drunkeness and bad conduct at the instigation of Colonel Morris, the Chief Engineer of the battery, Colonel Martin ordered Captain Sparrow to send me to take and occupy Lieutenant Brantly's Place.*
>
> *I then proceeded to take charge of the heavy guns of the battery and all Ordnance. I was also to instruct Leith's and Swindell's companies in Artillery service. This was in the month of August, 1861.*[94]

WAR COMES TO CAROLINA

On August 29, 1861, a combined force of Union vessels and troop transports, U.S. Army and Marines led by Major General Benjamin F. Butler, attacked Forts Hatteras and Clark, with amphibious landings near Fort Clark. After a gallant effort on behalf of both sides of the battle, the two forts fell to the Union invaders.

On the morning of August 27, 1861, the post was preparing a court-martial for the mutineers from Captain Johnson's company when the steamer *Gordon* appeared in Ocracoke Inlet. Captain Sparrow gives this account of the news:

> Portsmouth N.C., 27 August, Tuesday. *The privateer steamer Gordon ran into the inlet sometime in the afternoon and put David Ireland and two others of the crew in the shore. They reported in camp,*

the appearance of a fleet of United States steamers, seen off Hatteras, after they left that inlet. This news corresponded with a letter previously received by Captain W.T. Muse of the Navy, giving news of the expedition. Captains Lamb and Clements were at Portsmouth from Hatteras attending a court-martial. These gentlemen expressed their desire to return to their commands at Hatteras that night. I detailed Privates Wm. H. Hanks and Woodley to take the steamer M.E. Downing *to carry them. They left in the steamer about 10 o'clock.*[95]

With this news, two of the presiding officers, Captain Lamb and Captain Clements, wished to postpone the court-martial and return to their units at the besieged forts. They were most anxious to return, so Captain Sparrow sent Private Hanks and Woodley, both from his company, to take the officers back on the steamer *M.E. Downing*. This was the end of any court-martial proceedings for the mutineers. Once this business was ended, life at Fort Ocracoke returned to "normal," but there must have been some tension in the air. That afternoon, the fort was inspected by Lieutenant Colonel G.W. Johnson and Major H.A. Gillam; Von Eberstein was their guide, and drilling of the men continued as always:

During the afternoon I went to Fort Ocracoke with Lieutenant-Colonel G.W. Johnston, Major H.A. Gilliam, Captains Luke, Company D; John C. Lamb, Company A, and Clements and took with me Sergeant William H. Von Eberstein to assist in the defense of the fort, and to act as Ordnance Officer. He went immediately to work preparing cartridges and putting things in order.

On August 28, at 1:10 a.m., a report from a gun from the fort was heard, as reported by nearby ships, indicating that something other than target practice was happening. The shot may have been a signal to all Confederate units that the attack had begun on Forts Hatteras and Clark.[96]

That morning, Captain Sparrow had planned on a leisurely day at the fort, as he had been "released from service in the Seventeenth Regiment, and was expecting orders to…Virginia" and, evidently, the war. He did not expect to be needed. Soon a dispatch arrived from Colonel Martin ordering all forces to go to Fort Hatteras to support the defending Confederate installations there. Martin also requested Sparrow by name to lead his men to the imminent battle. Captain Sparrow describes the morning of August 28:

August 28, Wednesday. *I rose and dressed at reveille and went on drill with the company on the parade ground, near the church. Drilled two hours.*

On return from the drill, Major Gilliam called me to the front fence and stated that Colonel Martin had sent a dispatch ordering all the forces at Ocracoke to Hatteras and requesting me to go. (I had been released from service in the Seventeenth Regiment, and was expecting orders to join Colonel Tew's Regiment in Virginia.) I at once gave orders for the men to get breakfast, prepare two days' provisions, pack their knapsacks, take tent flys (for they had no tents) and prepare to embark.

Captain Sparrow issued special orders to the soldiers left on Portsmouth Island for one reason or another. These orders would be useless in the hours to come:

I appointed T. Hardenburgh, a lance Sergeant, and left him in charge of the camp, giving him written orders. Among these was one, that he should request Mr. B.J. Hanks to take certain of my command expected from Washington, on the steamer Col. Hill, *to Hatteras in the afternoon. Another was on approach of an enemy to take all the valuable baggage and the remaining men in camp to Fort Ocracoke, and if defeated in an attempt to do this, then to make the best of his way up the sound to Washington.*

The Washington Grays, forty-nine in number, exclusive of commissioned officers, were in line, uniformed and equipped at 10 o'clock. I marched to the wharf, and embarked them for Hatteras, on the schooner Pantheon. *The Morris Guards, Tar River Boys and the Hertford Light Infantry, embarked in other vessels.*

The Morris Guards took a vessel at Beacon Island, and so had several hours advantage. The others were towed by the steamer Ellis. *Captain Muse embarked on her. So they had an advantage.*[97]

From 8:00 a.m. to 8:00 p.m., troops boarded ships and departed for Fort Hatteras in hope of supporting that installation while it was under attack. The steamer CSS *Ellis* left for Hatteras at 11:15 a.m. with Captain Sharp's company:[98]

Wind and tide being against us, we took a longer route round Royal Shoals, and so were the last to arrive at Hatteras. The Ellis, *with her tow, was only a half mile or so ahead of us when we arrived.*

When within ten or twelve miles from the inlet, we began to see the fleet off the fort, first from the rigging, then from the deck. As we drew nearer we began to count them—one, two, four, ten, thirteen! There is a large fellow—there three others—there the small ones! Occasionally a gun was heard, then another—then three or four in quick succession.[99]

The *Ellis* landed troops at Fort Hatteras from 8:00 a.m. to 12:00 p.m. and stood by, under direct fire, while the battle raged.

THE FALL OF FORTS HATTERAS AND CLARK

The CSS *Winslow* delivered Commodore Barron to Fort Hatteras in the early evening of August 28. A short time before his arrival, the battery at Fort Clark had expended its ammunition and been abandoned. Not long after, Union troops had landed and taken control of Fort Clark and were now fortifying the battery and installing several field pieces that would be used to shell Fort Hatteras the next morning. Barron found both Colonel Martin and Major Andrews exhausted and eagerly in need of relief of command:

The Winslow, *Confederate States steamer, arrived after dark, bringing Commodore Barron, Lieutenants Murdaugh and Wise, of the navy. Major W.S.G. Andrews, Captain Muse and several of his midshipmen and sailors also came into the fort. Colonel Martin and Major Andrews voluntarily surrendered the command to Commodore Barron, who thereupon, assumed it.*[100]

The Confederate soldiers and sailors spent a long night preparing to defend the larger fort (Hatteras) in the morning. They unloaded ammunition, food and supplies from the supporting schooners and privateer vessels anchored on the sound side of Hatteras Island. They attempted to repair and adjust the damaged parts of the fort and refortify and repair the parapet. They even tried to disembark a ten-inch columbiad and move it into the fort proper, but they were unable to find suitable block and tackle gear. Scouts were sent out to ascertain the strength of the Union troops occupying Fort Clark, but after a heart-stopping moment of misidentification, they returned to Fort Hatteras just before dawn. They arrived back too late to tell Commodore Barron that only a small, token Union force was holding Fort Clark and there was little to stop the Confederates from retaking the smaller fort. At that point, it was too late to mount a counterattack against Fort Clark, as the second day of bombardment was about to start.

Unfortunately, most of the Confederate reinforcements waiting on board the anchored vessels in Pamlico Sound, and the supplies being unloaded during the night, had the arrived too late to change the outcome of the battle. Once Fort Clark ran out of ammunition and fell into Union hands, the battle was tactically decided. The reinforcements that landed after the supplies made no difference in the battle and were captured with the two forts. The Confederate "guardians" of Hatteras Inlet had simply been outgunned by the Union fleet, and Hatteras and the majority of Fort Ocracoke's combatants were now in Union hands. The Union navy detail and marines now had a beachhead in North Carolina, and most of the Confederate fighting force that *would* have been used to throw them back was captured in the process.

When one thinks of "articles of capitulation" or "unconditional surrender," the graveness and utter sense of loss this phrase implies often escapes attention. The *Articles of Capitulation* for the Battle of Hatteras reminds us just how serious this contract is:

> *U.S. Flagship Minnesota,*
> *Off Hatteras Inlet, August 29, A.D. 1861*
> *It is stipulated and agreed between the contracting parties that the forces under command of the said Barron, Martin, and Andrews, and all munitions of war, arms, men, and property under the command of said Barron, Martin, and Andrews, be unconditionally surrendered to the Government of the United States in terms of full capitulation.*
>
> *And it is stipulated and agreed upon by the contracting parties on the part of the U.S. Government that the officers and men shall receive the treatment due to prisoners of war.*
>
> *In witness whereof we, the said Stringham and Butler, on behalf of the United States, and said Barron, Martin, and Andrews, representing the forces at Hatteras Inlet, hereunto interchangeably set our hands this 29th day of August, A.D. 1861, and of the Independence of the United States the eighty-fifth year.*
> *S.H. Stringham,*
> *Flag-Officer, Atlantic Blockading Squadron.*
> *Benj. F. Butler,*

Major-General, U.S. Army, Commanding.
S. Barron
Flag-Officer, C.D. Navy, Comdg. Naval Defenses Va. & N.C.
Wm. F. Martin,
Colonel Seventh Regiment Infantry, N Carolina Volunteers
W.S.G. Andrews,
Major, Commanding Forts Hatteras and Clark.[101]

After the Union fleet acknowledged the Confederate flag of truce and the fighting was considered over, an incident took place that angered many of the surrendering Confederate men. Captain Thomas Sparrow describes what he calls an outrage:

> *General Butler, in the steamer* Fanny, *carrying two rifle guns, ran into the inlet and fired a gun at the* Winslow. *This was an outrage, as it was taking undue advantage of a flag of truce. Had the negotiation failed he never would have got out again.*[102]

Flag Officer S.H. Stringham's report of the matter coldly gives the basic facts and offers no apology for the illegal action:

> *At 11:30 Major-General Butler in the tug* Fanny *went into the inlet to the rear of the forts to take possession. Three steamers and several schooners with troops on board were in the sound watching the engagement. They all left as the* Fanny *approached. She fired at them with her rifled piece.*[103]

With shoals all around them and very little room to maneuver, the fleet of Confederate vessels supporting Fort Hatteras could not evade enemy fire and certainly could not return fire with the enemy well outside the range of their own weapons. The shot from *Fanny* must have caused little or no damage, and we have no record of what damage occurred to any ship during the entire affair, if any. It is important to note that the fleet of Confederate ships would not have been affected by the surrender agreement with Fort Hatteras, which explains the anger expressed in the records.

Sparrow goes on to describe the exodus of the supporting ships anchored on the sound side of Hatteras Island as the surrender continues:

> *During the morning the Colonel Hill had come down from Portsmouth before the firing began, but not in time, I suppose, to land more of my men,*

who were no doubt on board. After the surrender she with the Winslow *and all the other steamers and vessels made the best of their way up the sound. They were spectators of the whole bombardment, and a very grand spectacle it must have been to them.*[104]

The loss of Forts Hatteras and Clark was great indeed. Not only had a solid foothold been established by Union forces in a valuable strategic area of eastern North Carolina, but a huge amount of military hardware and nearly an entire regiment of Confederate soldiers were also destroyed or captured.

As for the men, these units were originally elements of the Seventeenth Regiment of North Carolina Volunteers. After their capture, they were taken to New York as prisoners of war.[105] Flag Officer Samuel Barron made his report to Confederate secretary of the navy Mallory from a Union prison ship:

The amount of loss on their side is not exactly known; 5 are ascertained to have been buried, and 11 wounded are on board this vessel. Many were carried away, Lieutenant Murdaugh, late of the U.S. Navy, among the number, with the loss of an arm.[106]

As for the military stores, one account listed the following:

By the surrender we came in possession of one thousand stand of arms, thirty-five heavy guns, ammunition for the same, a large amount of hospital and other stores, two schooners—one loaded with tobacco, and the other with provisions; one brig loaded with cotton, two lightboats, two surfboats, etc.[107]

This newspaper went on to say the following, which shows both an excellent understanding of the tactical situation in eastern North Carolina and a bit of foreshadowing of things to come:

If this operation (Butler Expedition) is followed up by the capture of the forts at Ocracoke Inlet, all but one of the ports of North Carolina, as well as those of Virginia, will be hermetically sealed; and by stationing sufficient forces at the two inlets all this stretch of coast may be effectively blockaded without the employment of any vessels.[108]

REACTION TO DEFEAT

The Confederate soldiers remaining at Portsmouth and Fort Ocracoke were informed of the defeat by the *Ellis*, which had returned to Portsmouth and received several families, before departing for Washington, North Carolina. At 7:00 a.m., the *Ellis* hailed and conversed with the sloop *Pine*, which was in route to report to Captain Leech (Leith) at Fort Ocracoke:

Raleigh, N.C., August 29, 1861
L.P. Walker, Secretary of War:
A fleet of steamers, with boats with men, left Fort Monroe on Monday evening, going south. Tuesday evening they appeared off Hatteras. On Wednesday, about 9 o'clock a. m., they attacked the fort. The firing from the fort ceased after some hours, and the result is only known from rumor, which says the fort was captured. The fort was scarce of ammunition, which contributed to its fall. It is a most important point during the blockade.

Henry T. Clark[100]
Goldsborough, August 30, 1861

General S. Cooper, Adjutant-General:
The steamer Winslow, *just arrived here from Hatteras, Captain Sinclair, reports the forts there captured by the enemy at 11:30 a.m. Commodore Barron, Colonel Bradford, and the garrison, numbering about 580 men, including the field officers of Seventh Regiment of volunteers, surrendered. I will make such arrangements as I can for present defense against further disaster. Please order General Huger to send four regiments and a light battery to the eastern counties, and a number of heavy guns with an engineer to fortify such points as may be necessary. I have only the Seventh Regiment of State troops at my disposal.*

R.C. Gatlin,
Brigadier-General, C.S. Army[110]

After hearing of the loss at Hatteras, Captains Leith and Swindell called a conference of their officers to be held in a large house on Beacon Island, which was used as officers' quarters (possibly the beacon itself, which was a sizable building with the beacon light on top). The conference included their two companies, a handful of officers, several civilians (including black workmen) and Mr. Henry Brown, who was the fort's assistant engineer. Along with Sergeant von Eberstein, these were all the Confederate forces that remained at Ocracoke Inlet. Sergeant von Eberstein tells what happened next in stark and vivid detail:

> *When Captains Leith and Swindell heard of this, they called a conference of their officers to be held in the big house which was on the island, and which they used as officer's quarters. I was invited by Captains Leith and Swindell and the other officers to take part in the deliberations. This invitation was as the Fort Ordnance officer, and me being in charge of Artillery. Mr. Henry Brown, the Engineer of the works was also invited. We accepted.*
>
> *After we had all got into the room, the consultation commenced. Captains Leith and Swindell proposed that we should evacuate the Fort in the morning, the reason was that we would all be captured some time or other. I recommended against such proceeding as evacuation of such a position when the enemy was nowhere near. I told them we could fight anything the enemy could send against us, as they must attack us with small boats, and that we could be reinforced and reattack from New Bern. I was seconded by Mr. Henry Brown and Lieutenants Fredrick and Henry Harding of Swindell's company. We were overruled by Captain Swindell and the balance of the officers.*
>
> *Captain Swindell went to Portsmouth at once, and seized two small schooners and brought them to the fort. We then commenced the most cowardly evacuation ever known. It was a complete disorderly thing. Captain Leith's company went in one schooner and Captain Swindell's in the other. One of the schooners went to Washington and one to New Bern.*[111]

The logs of the *Ellis* later mention contact at 9:00 p.m. on the thirty-first with the steamer *Governor Morehead*, which was headed to Fort Ocracoke after the troops that were evacuating. At 11:00 p.m., the *Governor Morehead* was returning from the fort with the schooner *Sarah* in tow with troops on board.

Von Eberstein continues with anger and shame as he describes the manner of the evacuation:

> *Mr. Henry Brown and four Negro men who were at work on the fort remained with me, for we would not join them. When they started,*

Captain Swindell took his company flag, which had been presented to him by the Ladies, and stuck it down in the southeast corner of the bomb-proof, and told us to leave it in that place when we left the fort, so the enemy might think the fort was still occupied. Thus, he abandoned the flag that had been presented to him to defend, and which he had promised to do with the best of his ability—even with his life's blood. A more cowardly act I never knew.

Knowing we could not defend the Fort against the enemy without reinforcements, we proceeded to dismantle it. I piled the guns and destroyed the provisions and clothing, so that nothing but a dismantled battery would fall into the hands of the enemy. After that, we did everything that could be done to render the battery useless.

In the evening, I, Mr. Brown, and the four Negroes took off in a small boat belonging to the Engineer. We departed and headed for New Bern. I took Captain Swindell's flag with me. I would not disgrace it by leaving it there.[112]

They ran into a severe thunderstorm on their way back to Newbern and took shelter on a small island along the shipping channel. The next morning, they continued their journey to Newbern and arrived there about dawn the following morning. They stayed with Henry Brown in his home at Newbern that night, and the next morning, Von Eberstein reported what had happened to General Gather at his headquarters at Gaston House. Eberstein's account is recorded as follows:

The next morning, I went down to Gaston House in New Bern to report to General Gather, whom I found there. I related to him the circumstances of the evacuation of Beacon Island. He listened very attentively. He then thanked me for remaining and destroying the guns. He pronounced Leith and Swindell not to be competent of having charge of a company. He also called them cowards. He told me to take the colors I had saved. "They belong to you." I gave the colors back to the company to which it belonged. There were many brave men in the company who had wanted to remain at the battery, but Captain Swindell would not let them.[113]

While Swindell and Leigh were meeting with Von Eberstein and the other senior noncommissioned officers at Beacon Island, another meeting was being held at Fort Oregon with Colonel Elwood Morris. A "council of war" was intent on abandoning that fort, located some forty miles north along the coast; removing all the guns and ordnance; and moving them to Roanoke Island. Colonel Morris argued that both forts, Oregon and especially Fort Ocracoke, were in strong positions that could only be attacked by ships of light draft and much inferior firepower. He also tried to reason that neither was even under threat of enemy attack as yet, but his opponents insisted that if Fort Ocracoke should fall, Union forces would command the sounds, and Oregon would not be able to hold out for any amount of time.

As Morris pondered the loss of the argument, the remaining men of Fort Oregon prepared the steamer *Raleigh* and four schooners to evacuate the soldiers, their gear, cannonballs and shells, company equipment and every piece of public property that could be removed. There were a number of attempts to remove the guns and load them on the ships, but after losing three of them overboard, the remaining guns were spiked and abandoned with the fort. The station barracks and all other useful structures were burned to the ground to prevent their reuse by the Yankees.[114]

REACTION TO VICTORY

On September 3, Commander Rowan, still on board the USS *Pawnee*, relayed this report about a probable fire at Fort Ocracoke (first burning of the fort as Confederate forces leave):

> *Report of Commander Rowan, U.S. Navy, commanding USS Pawnee, regarding affairs at Hatteras Inlet, North Carolina.*
>
> *U.S.S. Pawnee*
> *Hatteras Inlet, September 3, 1861*
> *To-day I learned from fugitives that Oregon Inlet and Ocracoke Inlet have been abandoned and the guns of the latter spiked. The forces at Oregon Inlet have moved over to Roanoke Island and are said to be fortifying the south end. Had I two or three well-armed tugs here now I could prevent it. We saw a large fire down the coast last night. The fugitives think it was Portsmouth, a small village at Ocracoke Inlet that has been burned by the enemy. I have communicated this intelligence to Captain Chauncey in the offing, that he might, if consistent with his*

instructions, go down and destroy the cannon and carriages before the enemy recovers from his panic and reoccupies the forts.

S.C. Rowan,
Commander, U. S. Navy.[115]
Hon. Gideon Wells,
Secretary of the Navy, Washington.

Rowan also sent the following letter to Flag Officer Stringham on the same date as above, concerning more information from the refugees:

Report of Commander Rowan, U.S. Navy, commanding U.S.S. Pawnee, giving information received from refugees.

U.S.S. Pawnee
Hatteras Inlet, September 3, 1861.
…Ten miles this side of Washington on the Pamlico River, at Mall's [Maul's] Point, they met three steamers full of soldiers, who hailed them and told them to return, as they had evacuated Ocracoke, spiked the guns, and destroyed the State property there.

There is a fort on Beacon Island (at Ocracoke) and a battery of six guns below it. There is no fort on the Portsmouth Island side of the inlet known of. They think the light to the westward last night came from Portsmouth Island or the forts…

They saw the fire last night and are sure that it was at Portsmouth or Beacon Island. Have heard that the forts at Ocracoke have been abandoned; passed near the island; saw no vessels or flags, nor any men…

S.C. Rowan,
Commander, U.S. Navy.
Flag-Officer S.H. Stringham
Commanding Atlantic Squadron.[116]

"The Destruction of the Fort Is Complete"

The Confederate soldiers who evacuated Fort Ocracoke knew that the Union would eventually come to Ocracoke Inlet, and the Union was obviously aware of the necessity of the fort's elimination. Plans were executed immediately on both sides to take action and limit the losses to their assets:

New Bern, September 14th, 1861
Lt. Col. Singleton, Cmdr. 9th Ba.

Dear Sir,

On the 13th last I read the following order—Special Order No. 24th:
That John D. Whitford is requested to fit out an expedition with a crew to
recover the guns and other property left at Ocracoke Inlet, for that purpose
the Dept. Quartermaster will place at his disposal the steamer Albemarle
& such other boats as he may require. Lt. Col. Singleton will furnish such
troops as Mr. Whitford may deem necessary.

By order Gen. Gatlin
R.H. Riddick

In accordance with the above order I would thank you to have ready to
embark on the steamer Albemarle at Fort Lane at the evening, fifty of
your men with such officers, you may think necessary to command them. As
it is impossible to get laborers, the men you send will be compelled to assist
in transferring the gins from the fort at Beacon Island to the boats, therefore
you would please instruct them accordingly. Capt. Sawyer will command the
steamer. Capt. David Sermmond, the men on shore engaged in the removal
of the guns & your own officers, your men while on duty on the steamer.

   I have denoted Ralph Daly as to return with the steamer and men to the
mouth of the river as agreed to prevent the possibility of being cut off by
the enemy.

   The expedition will probably be returned before Sunday night or Monday
morning. Rations will be furnished to the boat for 75 men for 3 days.

With high regard,
John D. Whitford

Steamer Albemarle Number 7
Newbern September 18th, 1861
John Whitford, Cmdr. C.S. Forces, New Bern

Sir,

Agreeably to your order after landing Maj. Halls Command in Hyde Co. on the night of the 17th, the following morning I crossed the sound for Beacon Island to tow up to Newbern the light boat which we were compelled to leave in the previous trip to that place.

While crossing the sound on the afternoon of the 17th, I discovered a dense smoke in the direction of Portsmouth. After sundown we could see the lights from the fire which led me to believe that that place had been fired by the enemy, but upon reaching Beacon Island I discovered that the light boat had been burned by the enemy and learned from Alford Dennis and William Mayo, citizens of Portsmouth that the steamer Fannie, *one of the states vessels with a crew of about seventy men reached the harbor of Ocracoke early on Monday morning the 16th and under the command of a Liet., the crew proceeded at once to destroy the bomb proof in the fort and to render the guns useless by blowing off the trunnions. They also fired a pile of wood on the land about the time the wind shifted to the northard which blew the fire into the Light House and destroyed the wood work of that building. They then visited Portsmouth and broke the trunnions off two sea coast howitzers which had been deposited there by our troops during the construct of Fort Ocracoke. The pilot of the steamer, Capt. Jacob Westervelt, who is well known in Newbern of the eastern counties and who sailed out of Newbern for 6 or 8 years previous to the commencement of the present disturbance in the county and who appears to be exceedingly active in his efforts to aid on the subjugation of our people who supported him for years—informed Capt. Dennis that they should next attack Fort Macon with their fleet and then in regular rotation each fortification on the southern coast and that they were merely waiting for the command to commence the work. Next in order Newbern & Washington would be attacked—He further stated that they would not trouble or molest in any way private property but would destroy all the public property that they could not take away—It was the design of the enemy to burn the Hospital at Portsmouth but in consequence of the direction of the wind they declined as it would have burned dwelling houses in its immediate vicinity.*

After obtaining this information I left the island and reached Newbern at 5½ o'clock. The steamer Fannie *remained in the harbor from Monday morning until Wednesday morning doubtedly the enemy had heard of the expedition sent from Newbern by you to recover the public property and were in search of our boat, which left the Light Boat just before night on Sunday previous to the appearance of the enemy's war vessels early on the morning of the Monday following.*

Very Respectfully
Samuel Sawyer
Cmdr. Steamer Albemarle

THE FLOATING BATTERY

The "light boat" mentioned in Sawyer's report is the same vessel "used as a store ship" as mentioned in Maxwell's report (see later in this section) and

Mortar rafts acting as similar floating batteries. *From* Civil War in Pictures *by Fletcher Pratt.*

was intended to be used as a floating battery or gun platform to support the fort. These "armed barges" were used quite commonly during the Civil War. It is not known exactly how the light boat would have been altered to act as a floating battery, but the search continues to find the remains of the vessel.

POLITICS OF THE UNION MILITARY

Many of the Union commanders saw an opportunity to carry on the momentum of their victories at Hatteras and looked for other forts to conquer. The U.S. Navy steamer *Monticello* forwarded this letter on its scouting missions at Ocracoke Inlet:

> *Major-General Wool, USA*
> *Commanding Fortress Monroe, U.S. Steamer* Monticello
> *Hampton Roads, Va. September 5, 1861*
>
> *Sir: Previous to our leaving Hatteras Inlet with the* Harriet Lane *in convoy we had cruised along and off the coast to the southward; ran close in to Ocracoke Inlet several times. The fort near the beacon-house had apparently no guns mounted and there was no evidence of its being occupied. In Portsmouth, a small town near by to the southward, a white flag was hoisted on one of the houses, and a number of Negroes came down to the beach waving another. Some two or three small schooners were seen in the sound. They left for the interior.*
>
> *This fort and inlet could readily be taken possession of and held by a small force.*
>
> *The steamer* Peabody, *with supplies, arrived at Fort Hatteras on the 4th instant.*
>
> *Very respectfully, your obedient servant,*
> *JNO. P. Gillis*
> *Commander.*

The Union blockading fleet in support of the U.S. Army landings at Forts Hatteras and Clark began planning to dispatch a small task force to venture down to Ocracoke Inlet to perhaps catch the Confederates off guard at Beacon Island. So preparations were set in motion. The commanding officer at the now Union Fort Clark mentions his suggestions for needed actions in a report dated September 7:

Major Gen. John E. Wool
Commanding Department of Virginia, Fort Monroe, VA
Hatteras Inlet, North Carolina
September 7, 1861
Suggestions:…Second. A small force should be stationed on Beacon Island,
which is in the mouth of the Ocracoke Inlet, and commands it.
Rush C. Hawkins, Colonel
Ninth Regiment NY Vol., Commanding Fort Clark

In a second letter, Colonel Hawkins emphasizes his urgent suggestion: "I still adhere to all of the suggestions contained in my former report and would most respectfully urge the importance of immediately occupying Roanoke and Beacon Islands." Others, too, had plans for Ocracoke Inlet and the valuable prize lying just inside the inlet:

Report of Flag-Officer Stringham, U.S. Navy, commanding Atlantic
Blockading Squadron, requesting directions regarding the occupation of the
fort on Ocracoke Inlet.

Hon. G. V. Fox,
Asst. Secretary of the Navy,
Washington,
U. S. Flagship Minnesota
Hampton Roads, September 11, 1861

Sir: I would respectfully call your attention to the second article of your
dispatch of the 3ᵈ instant, marked confidential, directing me to take
immediate possession of Ocracoke Inlet, but "not sink vessels at these inlets
inside, as was first contemplated."

The last dispatch from Captain Chauncey reports the fort at Ocracoke
abandoned, but I have sent to him for more explicit information.

The fort is situated on Beacon Island about 4 miles inside the bay, and
I have at this time no vessels of sufficient light draft to approach it either
from the sea or sound.

In case that I should soon be able to carry out your directions, will you
please inform me upon whom I am to call for troops to occupy it.

Respectfully, your obedient servant,
S.H. Stringham,
Commanding, Atlantic Blockading Squadron.

Photo of Silas H. Stringham. *Library of Congress.*

On September 16, preparations were made to send an expedition to the fort for the purpose of destroying it. Several letters that describe the strike force are recorded:

Letter from Commander Rowan, U.S. Navy, commanding U.S.S. Pawnee, *to Captain Chauncey, U.S. Navy, commanding U.S.S.* Susquehanna, *regarding the expedition to Beacon Island, NC.*

U.S.S. Pawnee
Hatteras Inlet, Monday Morning, September 16, 1861

Sir: The favorable appearance of the weather has decided [me] *to send my cooperating force outside. I have accordingly directed the officer in command of my force to proceed in the* Fanny *direct for Ocracoke Bar with our launch in tow, and to remain outside subject to your order. I send the* Tempest *with directions to report to you. This tug I commend to your care as she draws 9½ feet water and can not return through the sound.*

When you have fulfilled the object of the expedition will you be pleased to direct the Fanny *and our launch to return to this ship through the sound, unless in your good discretion you consider the weather sufficiently smooth, and the hour of departure appropriate to reach this bar and cross it in safety with the launch in tow.*

If the Tempest *can not cross the bar, will you be pleased to send her back, and if you wish it, she could bring your prize schooner with her. The* Tempest *has about two days' coal on board.*

I send all the sledges and chisels I have to break trunnions, etc., and shall, if possible, obtain from the fort a few round shot (32-pounder), which might be used in firing one gun against the trunnions of the other. I hope you have experienced men to use the sledges.

> *Hoping the expedition may be entirely successful,*
> *I am, very respectfully, your obedient servant,*
[S.C. Rowan]
Commander, U.S. Navy.
Captain Chauncey
Commanding U.S.S. Susquehanna.[117]

But a change in the weather and sea state altered Commander Rowan's plans, and he began to wonder about the safety of his men and machines. This was an important factor, and he was wise to take it into account, as the waters off and around Ocracoke Inlet are far from easy to navigate. The following memo was sent to Captain Chauncey later on the same day:

Letter from Commander Rowan, U.S. Navy, commanding U.S.S. Pawnee, *to Captain Chauncey, U.S. Navy, Commanding U.S.S.* Susquehanna *regarding the expedition to Beacon Island, N.C.*

U.S.S. Pawnee
Hatteras Inlet, September 16, 1861

Sir: I made all arrangements last night to send our cooperating force outside, but the surf is so bad on the bar this morning that I am compelled to change back to the original plan of going down to Ocracoke through the sound.

I send the Tempest *with directions to report to you. She has two or three days' coal, and water for the same time. I send my best pilot in the* Tempest *and hope she will be able to render good service. As this boat can not come back through the sound nor cross the bar when it is very rough, I fear you may have some trouble in taking care of her.*

I will hoist No. 0 at the mizzen when the Fanny *and launch leave the ship, and have directed them to meet your force and report to your commanding officer at Ocracoke. You will find them east of Beacon Island.*

Very respectfully, your obedient servant,
S.C. Rowan, Commander, U.S. Navy[118]

Lieutenant James Y. Maxwell, U.S. Navy, in a report dated September 18, 1861, chronicled the destruction of Fort Ocracoke. This report recorded the actions of a U.S. Navy landing party under his command that landed at the fort, as well as Portsmouth on September 16, 1861:

U.S.S. Pawnee
Hatteras Inlet, September 18, 1861

Sir: I have to report that, in compliance with your orders of the 16ᵗʰ, I started for Ocracoke on that day in the steamer Fanny, *towing the Pawnee's launch. Lieutenant Eastman had charge of the latter, with 22 men and 6 marines from the ship, the 12-pounder howitzer and I had on board 6 men and 61 soldiers of the naval brigade under Lieutenants Tillotson and Rowe.*

We arrived within 2 miles of the fort on Beacon Island at 11 a.m., when the Fanny *grounded. I sent Lieutenant Eastman in the launch to sound for the channel. While he was so occupied, a sailboat with two men put off from Portsmouth to cross the sound. A shot from the* Fanny *brought them alongside, and they piloted us to within a hundred yards of the fort. It is called Fort Ocracoke, and is situated on the seaward face of Beacon Island; it was entirely deserted. It is octagonal in shape, contains four shell rooms about 25 feet square, and in the center a large bombproof of 100 feet* square, with the magazine within it. Directly above the magazine on each side were four large tanks containing water.

The fort has been constructed with great care of sand barrace, covered with earth and turf. The inner framing of the bombproof was built of heavy pine timbers. There were platforms for twenty guns which had been partially destroyed by fire. The gun carriages had been all burned. There were 18 guns in the fort, viz, 4 8-inch shell guns and 14 long 32-pounders.

The steamer Albemarle left on Sunday afternoon, carrying off two guns. I found 150 barrels also, many of them filled with water; there being no water in the fort, they had brought it from Washington and New Berne.

I landed the men at 1:30 o'clock and commenced breaking off the trunnions of the guns.

While a portion of our men and naval brigade were so employed, I sent Lieutenant Eastman in the launch to Portsmouth, where he found three 8-inch navy shell guns lying on the beach and one mounted on a carriage. They had all been spiked. There was no battery erected there, although we were informed that one would have been built but for our coming.

There had been a camp at Portsmouth, called Camp Washington, but a portion of the troops were sent to Fort Hatteras when it was attacked on August 28, and the remainder retired to the mainland.

Portsmouth, which formerly contained 450 inhabitants, was nearly deserted, but the people are expected to return. Those remaining seem to be Union men, and expressed satisfaction at our coming.

Lieutenant Eastman assured them that they would not be molested by the Government and that they might return to their usual occupation. There are no entrenchments nor guns at Ocracoke. The fishermen and pilots who fled after our attack have generally returned. I tried to destroy the guns by breaking the trunions off with sledges and by dropping solid shot upon them from an elevation, with little success. I then fired solid shot from a 64-pounder at them, and in this manner disabled them.

Lieutenant Eastman disabled the guns at Portsmouth by breaking off the cascabels and leaving them in the salt water on the beach. After destroying the guns I collected all the lumber, barrace, and wheelbarrows and placed them in and about the bombproof, set fire to the pile and entirely destroyed it. A light-ship, which had been used as a storeship, and which was run upon the shore some distance from the fort, with the intention of subsequently towing off and arming, I also set fire to. At 6:30 this morning I started on our return. We met with no detention and arrived safely with all hands at 11:30 a.m. I am happy to report that the conduct of our men and the naval

brigade was excellent. Lieutenant Eastman, and Lieutenants Tillotson and
Rowe of the naval brigade, rendered me most efficient assistance.

I am, respectfully, your obedient servant,"
J.G. Maxwell
Lieutenant, U.S. Navy
Commander S.C. Rowan,
U.S.S. Pawnee.[119]

According to the account, Lieutenant Maxwell proceeded to Ocracoke Inlet, from the anchored Federal fleet lying off Hatteras Inlet, under orders from Commander S.C. Rowan, flag officer aboard the USS *Pawnee*. The U.S. steamer *Fanny*, though sailing with a temporarily repaired rudder, towed a launch from the *Pawnee* loaded with twenty-two men and six marines under command of Lieutenant Eastman, with Lieutenant Maxwell assigned as expedition leader. On board the *Fanny*, another "six men and sixty-one soldiers of the Naval Brigade," awaited their mission at Ocracoke Inlet.[120]

At 11:00 a.m., the *Fanny* grounded at Ocracoke Inlet, within two miles of Beacon Island. The launch was then dispatched to sound the channel, where they encountered and detained two men (presumably civilians on a fishing trip) in a small sailboat. These men piloted the *Fanny* to within one hundred yards of Fort Ocracoke. At 1:30 p.m., Lieutenant Maxwell dispatched the launch and Lieutenant Eastman to Portsmouth to search for and destroy any war materials left behind by Confederate forces. His own navy detachment disembarked from the *Fanny* and entered Fort Ocracoke.

In the fort, Maxwell reportedly found eighteen guns—fourteen thirty-two-pounders and four eight-inch navy shell guns—by his account and that of the newspaper reporter, Bennett. (See "October 1861" later in this chapter.) He learned from the two civilians that the Confederate steamer *Albemarle* recovered two guns just the day before their arrival. We now know that these were the two eight-inch columbiads and that they were taken to Fort Ellis, just below New Bern.[121] These guns originally came from Fort Macon, near Beaufort, and one of them eventually was moved back there and fell to Union forces when that fort was captured. (See "Fort Macon's Eight-inch Columbiads" later in this chapter.)

Maxwell's men set out immediately to destroy or finish destroying the remaining guns. They tried to remove the trunions (pivots that the cannons sit on while mounted in a carriage) with sledgehammers and by dropping solid shot on them. When this did not work, he said, "I then tried solid shot from a sixty-four at them, and in this manner disabled them." It is unclear as to how he accomplished this. Did he fire one gun against another? And what of the guns? Were they not spiked and, in that case, incapable of being fired? As to how spiked guns were fired one against another, *The Confederate Field Manual* also answers those questions:[122]

> *SPIKING AND UNSPIKING GUNS, AND RENDERING THEM UNSERVICEABLE*
> To spike a piece or to render it unserviceable—*Drive into the vent a jagged and hardened steel spike with a soft point, or a nail without a head; break it off flush with the outer surface, and clinch the point inside by means of a rammer.*

This is how the weapons were made useless, as they were sure to fall into Union hands, but how did Lieutenant Maxwell and his men make the guns serviceable to fire one against another?

> To unspike a piece—*If the spike is not screwed in or clinched, and the bore is not impeded, put in a charge of powder of one-third the weight of the shot, and ram junk wads over it with a handspike, laying on the bottom of the bore a strip of wood with a groove on the under side, containing a strand of quick-match, by which fire is communicated to the charge;…if this method is not successful…and if an iron gun, drill out the spike, or drill a new vent.* To use a piece which has been spiked—*Insert one end of a piece of quick-match in the cartridge, allowing the other to project out of the muzzle of the gun. Apply the fire to the quick-match and get out of the way. When quick-match of sufficient length is not at hand, insert one end in the cartridge, the other projecting in front of the shot; and after ramming the cartridge home, throw two or three pinches of powder into the bore. Place another piece of match in the muzzle, the end projecting out. The piece may be fired in this way without danger. Quick-match in the cartridge may be dispensed with by piercing three or four holes in the cartridge bag. In this manner the gun may be fired with great rapidity.*

We know from other reports concerning preparations for Maxwell's expedition that he did carry sledges, chisels, thirty-two-pound solid shot and seven-pound charges for the purpose of firing one gun against another.[123] This seemingly incredible feat sounds almost commonplace to these men and their rudimentary weapons. (See Commander Rowan's first letter to Captain Chauncey, dated September 16, 1861, and Commander Rowan's letter to Flag Officer Stringham, dated September 18, 1861.)

Meanwhile, Lieutenant Eastman had found the four eight-inch navy guns that were to be used in the Portsmouth battery. He destroyed them by breaking off the cascabels (the balls mounted on the breach ends of the gun used to pull the gun in and out of gun ports on a ship) and dragging them into the surf on the beach. The guns had already been spiked, and only one was mounted in a carriage. The other three were lying on the ground. Back at the fort, Maxwell had finished with the guns and proceeded to burn the fort. He gathered all the lumber and wooden materials, including wheelbarrows and water barrels; placed them in a great pile inside the bombproof; and set fire to it all. He also ordered a nearby vessel, a lightship recently removed from Diamond Shoals by Confederate soldiers, to be burned. This vessel had been grounded on a shoal a short distance away and was being used as a store ship, with the intention of being made into a floating battery later on. It should also be mentioned that Maxwell did not mean to burn the beacon along with the fort but that it had caught fire after the fort had been set ablaze due to an unexpected shift in the direction of the wind.[124]

On the morning of the eighteenth, at 6:30 a.m., Maxwell left Ocracoke Inlet and returned to the USS *Pawnee* with his men intact and having met no opposition of any kind, except for the unforgiving allies of the Confederacy, the shoals of Pamlico Sound.[125]

Commander Rowan's report of these activities was attached to Lieutenant Maxwell's report and is copied here:

U.S.S. Pawnee
Hatteras Inlet, September 18, 1861

Sir: On Saturday, the 14ᵗʰ instant, I gave a pass to one of the people on Hatteras Island to go to Ocracoke Inlet for the purpose of bringing his family from Portsmouth. I directed this person to examine the forts on Beacon Island and Portsmouth Island and bring me a true report of the condition of things, the number of guns mounted, if any, and the number dismounted, whether any troops were there, and whether the gun carriages had all been burned or not, and to report the result to me on his return.

On Sunday morning, the 15ᵗʰ instant, the boat came alongside, with the man and his wife and children in a destitute state; we gave them food, and the surgeon prescribed and furnished medicine for the sick of the family. The man reported that there are twenty guns in Fort Beacon and four 8-inch shell guns at Portsmouth; that the guns were spiked and the carriages burned on the 1ˢᵗ instant, as already reported to you. He also stated that a steamer came to Beacon Island before he left Portsmouth for the purpose of carrying off the guns. I immediately determined to use all the means at my command to prevent the removal of the guns, and forthwith got the steamer Fanny alongside to prepare for this service, and had the launch armed and equipped. I sent a request to Colonel Hawkins to give me as many of the naval brigade as could be spared, which he cheerfully complied with. When the Fanny was brought alongside, her iron rudder perch [post] was found so much injured that it would be impossible to send her without repairs; so the forge was gotten up, and the clink of hammers soon succeeded the voices of the crew in their responses to our usual Sunday morning service.

I dispatched the information to Captain Chauncey in the offing, who promptly informed me that he would send him the Tempest to tow his boats over the Ocracoke Bar.

At daylight on Monday morning the Fanny was towed alongside and her rudder temporarily fitted. The naval brigade was taken on board with four days' provisions and water; the launch similarly provided for.

The expedition being carefully organized and provided with sledge hammers to break off the trunnions, and 32-pounder shot and twenty 7-pound cartridges to be used in firing one gun against the trunnion of another, left his ship at half past 7 o'clock; the launch commanded by Lieutenant Eastman in tow of the Fanny; the expedition under command of Lieutenant Maxwell, the executive officer of this ship.

I dispatched the tug Tempest to Captain Chauncey, she drawing too much water to enter the sound. At 10 o'clock the Susquehanna and the tug started for the inlet. On the evening of the same day the tug and Susquehanna returned and anchored off Fort Clark. The tug came in next morning, and the pilot informed me that the force from the Susquehanna did not enter Ocracoke in consequence of the surf.

On the afternoon of the 17th instant I felt much anxiety for our expedition.

The Susquehanna remained at anchor in the offing and our force was left to take care of itself.

Early this morning the lookout at the masthead gave us the gratifying intelligence that our expedition was in sight, and it reached the ship about 11 o'clock.

Lieutenants Maxwell and Eastman performed the service with ability and energy and bore [have] my thanks.

The destruction of the fort is complete, and twenty-two guns disabled; these are all the guns that were there, with the exception of two taken off in the steamboat Albemarle on Sunday.

The destruction of the guns was with me a necessity. I had no means of transporting them nor defending them in their position. I therefore hope my course will meet your approval.

I enclose a copy of Lieutenant Maxwell's report, giving all the details of this important service, which was performed without an accident of any kind.

I have the honor to be, very respectfully, your obedient servant,
S.C. Rowan
Commander.
Flag-Officer S.H. Stringham,
Commanding Atlantic Squadron.[126]

Captain Chauncey, aboard the USS *Susquehanna*, seized his chance to gloat as well in the following letter, which conflicts the number of the weapons destroyed at Fort Ocracoke:

U.S.S. Susquehanna
Off Hatteras Inlet, September 19, 1861

Sir: Commander Rowan having received information that the rebels at Ocracoke were attempting to carry off the guns mounted on the fort at Beacon Island and at Portsmouth, an expedition was immediately prepared, consisting of the steamer Fanny *and the launch of the* Pawnee, *to go through the sound, while this ship should proceed to the nearest point off Ocracoke, with her boats fully prepared and armed, to support the part from the* Pawnee. *On Monday morning, the 16th instant, we were off the bar at Ocracoke, with the tug* Tempest *and a pilot for the purpose of taking in my boats, 2 launches, 2 cutters with 2 howitzers and 26 marines. In consequence of the late northerly and easterly winds, we found the bar utterly impassable, the surf breaking over the entire channel; consequently my boats were unable to enter, much to my regret. The launch from the* Fanny *landed at the fort at Beacon Island, hoisted the American flag, destroyed 1 8-inch 63-hundredweight and 13 32-pounders of 27 hundredweight, also the fort itself. They also destroyed 4 32-pounders of 27 hundredweight at the town of Portsmouth. No resistance was offered, as I understand, as the place has been comparatively deserted. The light-boat inside, with a quantity of stores on board, was burned. The expedition returned in safety on Wednesday, the 18th instant.*

It is rumored that there are 10,000 men at Beaufort, busily fortifying the place, being apprehensive of an attack…

I am sir, very respectfully, your obedient servant,
Jno. S. Chauncey,
Captain[127]

Even the army records show the destruction of the fort at Beacon Island and consider its potential strength had it not been abandoned and destroyed, but the records also show the disorganization that is so much associated with war, as Chauncey estimates the number of guns and type and the amount of ammunitions removed (the first mention of this), as well as the expedition's commanding officer:

Headquarters Fort Clark
Hatteras Inlet, North Carolina, September 19, 1861
Maj. Gen. John E. Wool,
Commanding Department of Virginia, Fort Monroe, Va.

On the 15th instant I learned through one of the citizens that the enemy were carrying off the guns from Beacon Island. On the morning of the 16th instant an expedition, consisting in part of the Union Coast Guard, under the charge of Lieutenants Rowe and Patten, and a detachment from the crew of the steamer Pawnee, under the charge of Lieutenant Maxwell, U.S. Navy, the whole under the command of Lieutenant Eastman, of the steamer Pawnee, *embarked on board the steamer* Fanny *and one of the launches belonging to the* Pawnee, *and proceeded immediately to Beacon Island, where they found a large battery, mounting twenty-two guns, four of which had been taken away the day previous on the steamer Washington to New Berne. Eighteen guns still remained, four 8-inch navy guns and fourteen navy 32's, all of which were destroyed and left in a perfectly useless condition by the men under the charge of Lieutenant Eastman. A boat's crew of the expedition then proceeded to the town of Portsmouth, where they found four more guns, one mounted and three buried in the sand on the beach. They were also destroyed.*

The bomb proofs at the battery, four in number, were then destroyed. All the wood work of the battery, together with a large pile of lumber, was then burned. A lightship, which had been towed from its moorings by the rebels, with the intention of taking it to Washington, was also burned. The expedition then returned, bringing with it some eighty shells taken from the battery.

While depreciating the loss of property, I rejoice in the belief that we have with little expense and labor inflicted another most serious blow upon the enemy, and too much credit cannot be awarded to the officers and men composing this expedition…

I am, most faithfully, your obedient servant,
Rush C. Hawkins,
Colonel Ninth Regiment N.Y. Volunteers, Commanding Post[128]

The commander of the Atlantic Blockading Squadron, Captain Silas Stringham, forwarded the following messages and touted the success of Maxwell's expedition in this letter to the secretary of the navy:

Report of Flag-officer Stringham, U.S. Navy, commanding Atlantic Blockading Squadron, transmitting reports of officers. From the U.S.S. Minnesota, dated September 22, 1861.

Sir: I have the honor, in my last official communication as flag-officer of the Atlantic Blockading Squadron, and pleasure of informing the Department, from reports herewith forwarded, of Commander S.C. Rowan, that by aid of the small steamer Fanny, *under command of Lieutenant James G. Maxwell, the property of the rebels at Ocracoke Inlet has been destroyed, and that point is ready to be closed up, as proposed by the Department, or being occupied as at Hatteras Inlet.*

If I may be permitted to offer advice or suggestion, I would respectfully say, do with Ocracoke what has been done at Hatteras, occupy, hold, use, and possess.

If these points are valuable to the rebels, they are only the more so under present circumstances to the Government.

I think 800 or 1,000 troops, with the assistance of the vessels, will be all-sufficient for this purpose.

Respectfully, your obedient servant,
S.H. Stringham, Flag-officer, Atlantic Blockading Squadron
Hon. Gideon Wells,
Secretary of Navy[129]

On September 25, 1861, a "proud" Gideon Wells, then the Union secretary of the navy, wrote this letter to Commander Rowan, praising his great accomplishment. One wonders what he wrote to Lieutenant Maxwell, or to Maxwell's troops, who actually did all the work.

Sir: Flag-Officer Stringham has forwarded to me your report dated the 18ᵗʰ instant, and enclosures, relative to the expedition dispatched by you to Ocracoke.

The Department is happy to express its appreciation and approval of your proceedings and of the conduct of the officers and men engaged in the expedition, who seem to have executed promptly and efficiently the duty assigned them. Navy Department, September 25, 1861.

Your communication of the 20ᵗʰ instant, respecting the Neuse River, ...
I am, respectfully, your obedient servant,
Gideon Wells
Commander S.C. Rowan,
Commanding U.S.S. Pawnee, *Hatteras Inlet.*[130]

October 1861

A newspaper report in the *Daily Progress* stated that the flames from the burning were visible thirty miles away and that the lighthouse was burned on Beacon Island along with the fort.[131] This information was gathered from an article in the *New York Herald*, and a humorous side note denounces the Unionist opinion of the article and the writer named Bennett:

Newbern Daily Progress, *Wednesday, October 2, 1861*
"The Enemy At Hatteras" (from the New York Herald, *September 22, 1861)*
Fortress Monroe, September 22:
I returned this morning by the S.R. Spaulding, *Captain Howes, from Hatteras Inlet, North Carolina, and bring advices up to last evening.*
On Monday last, the 16ᵗʰ, Inst., and expedition was sent to the Ocracoke Inlet to take and destroy the fort on Beacon Island, near the entrance to the sound. It was under command of Lieutenant Eastman, of the Pawnee, *and consisted of sixty five men from the Coast Guard, under Lieutenant Rowe, and a detachment of soldiers and marines from the* Pawnee, *in the ship's launch. The Coast Guard were on board the* Fanny, *which towed the launch down, taking the inside passage. The frigate* Susquehanna *and the* Tempest *went by sea to co-operate with the forces inside, but in consequence of their great draft, they were unable to approach near enough to the fort to be of service, and they returned to Hatteras Inlet without*

aiding in the work. The Fanny *was able to approach within a mile of the Fort, and the launch was sent ashore and carried the force which could be spared, which effected a landing with safety.*

The fort was found deserted, but the enemy had but a short time previous to our arrival visited the work, and successfully removed two heavy eight inch guns, and transported them to Newbern, where the rebels are erecting three strong batteries.

Monday and Tuesday were occupied in destroying the pieces of ordnance found in the fort and by Tuesday noon, we had destroyed or rendered unserviceable eighteen long 32's and four eight inch Navy guns. On Tuesday afternoon at a late hour, fires were built in various parts of the main bomb-proofs and magazine and three smaller bomb-proofs near the curtains of the work. The bomb-proofs which were constructed in the most substantial and skillful manner of heavy pine lumber and covered with sand and turf were soon in flames. The torch was also applied to the lighthouse, on the Island and this with the immense fort was soon wrapt in flames. The conflagration raged furiously all night, the light being plainly visible thirty miles distant.—The Fanny laid off at anchor until morning and on Wednesday, the fort having been completely destroyed, the expedition returned to this point without the loss of a man.

The destruction of the fort and armament was complete, and must involve the enemy in the loss of between two and three hundred thousand dollars. The fort was one of the largest on the coast and could have been held against any attack from our fleet, as it could not be approached within long range by vessels of deep draught.—But the enemy were terribly frightened by the capture of Forts Clark and Hatteras, and incontinently deserted their work the night following the loss of the latter fort.

While on the expedition some of the parties visited the small villages of Ocracoke and Portsmouth, and at the latter place discovered and destroyed two heavy guns which had been mounted there…

The privateers Coffee *and* Winslow *had visited Ocracoke inlet to carry off the rebel guns but left on the arrival of the* Fanny.

This article also states that the Confederate steamers *Coffee* and *Winslow* were run off by the presence of the *Fanny*. Though it is suggestive that the reporter, Bennett, was on the expedition, it seems odd that he did not know that the *Coffee* and *Winslow* were, in fact, the same ship. He also states that the *Fanny* and the launch made their way to Ocracoke via the Pamlico Sound and not on the ocean side of the Outer Banks.

After this, it seems that the war bypasses Beacon Island and Fort Ocracoke, as well as the adjoining town of Portsmouth. The losses of both forts at Hatteras allowed the Union forces to gain a foothold in North Carolina and endangered any further Confederate operations in the area. Later, the Confederate forces on Roanoke Island will be defeated and a besieged Fort Macon will also fall, just after one of the columbiads it loaned to Fort Ocracoke is returned after being rescued by the steamer *Albemarle* only a day before Maxwell's expedition invaded Beacon Island. (See Maxwell's account in this chapter.)

What of those guns? Where did they end up? The following series of correspondence tells the story, with the moral that even the Confederate States of America had its own bureaucracy. These weapons were originally mounted as part of the arsenal at Fort Macon but were later transferred to Fort Ocracoke as the primary battery for that installation. This series of events would be the source of much argument in the days to come and much heartburn for Oliver P. Dewey, who was the naval supply agent at New Bern, and John D. Whitford, who was commander of the fortifications there. It was quite an episode, as seen following.

FORT MACON'S EIGHT-INCH COLUMBIADS

Fort Macon, September 23, 1861
John Whitford Esq.

Dear Sir,
I supposed when I wrote that Gen. Gatlin had ordered one of the 8 in Columbiads, or both to this place—I have a carriage ready and would have been glad to have received one, thinking it highly probable that we might have a fight on hand—We stand in need of long range guns, no steamer will appear in les than 1¾ miles of us, and our 24 pdrs & 32's will be of no service at that distance.—The brand will be upon our Rifle 24—with only 4 shells, Rifle 32 with 7 shell, 1 10-inch Columbiad and 2 8-inch Columbiads with plenty of shot & shell—this will be a small armament to meet perhaps 10 times that number of guns with.

I fired one Rifle shell this morning with beautiful effect, but we have too few to experiment with, and I shall have to practice the balance on old Abe if he appears.—For your river battery the 32 pdr. Will be very effective, especially if you have them masked so that the enemy will be in ignorance of their whereabouts.—You will please let me know if there is any probability of getting one of the guns, as I may have to make some alterations here, in the disposition of battery needs, I am—

Truly yours,
H.T. Gavin
Capt. Arty & Eng.

Office Atlantic & No. Carolina RR
Newbern, NC 6 October, 1861
Gov. Clark, Raleigh

Dear Sir,
Were the two 8-inch Columbiads of Beacon Island transferred to the Confederate States? They are now mounted in Fort Ellis, on the Neuse below Newbern and I fear an effort will be made to have them moved to Fort Macon. In the first place I think they are greatly needed where they are as we have no rifled gun and furthermore I believe Rifled guns would not do more service at Fort Macon & require much less powder. I know our people and Col. Singletary would oppose their removal as they rely more on those two guns than all the others. Did you ever send for the Rifle machine—I have sent our Master Machinist to Portsmouth to get the necessary information to enable him to make Rifle shells. Nothing new this way.

Your obedient servant
John W. Whitford

State of North Carolina
Executive Department
Raleigh, October 16th, 1861
John D. Whitford Esq.

Sir,
I trust that Gen. Hill will not remove your Guns from the defense of Newbern without supplying their place with others equally as effective. I

can't say that they have been transferred for I don't know where they were or in what position when the transfer was made.

I have telegraphed letters to Charleston for the Rifling machine and no reply—telegraphed again to day.

I am never consulted about Coast Defenses now except in the last resort and then I believe only to shift the responsibility from other shoulders.

Would be glad to have from you a full return of all ordnance and ordnance stores at Newbern.

Very Respectfully
Henry S. Clark
Office Atlantic & North Carolina RR Co.

Newbern NC, October 13, 1861
Gov. Clark, Raleigh

Dear Sir:
Have the two 8 inch Columbiads at Beacon Island transferred to the Confederate States. They are now mounted in Fort Ellis, in the river below Newbern & I fear an effort will be made to have them moved to Fort Macon. In the first place I think they are greatly needed where they are as we have no rifled guns and further means I believe Rifle guns would be of great sacrifice on Fort Macon & use much less powder. I know our people and Col. Singleton would oppose the removal as they rely more on those two guns than all the others. Did you ever write for the Rifle Machines? I have sent our Master Machinist to Portsmouth to get the machinery information to enable him to make Rifle shells available near this way—

Your servant,
John D. Whitford
Goldsboro, October 27th, 1861

John D. Whitford Esq. Newbern, NC

Dear Whitford,
I regret that the Governor has seen fit to order away one of the Columbiads,
but I cannot interfere in the matter, as he is responsible for the defense of
this district. I hope he will soon have two others to replace it. One should go
down to-day and others are expected. The ammunition for the Howitzers
have been ordered—I would like to go down, but besides my duties do not
admit of it my health is very poor.

Your friend,
R.L. Guthrie

USS *PAWNEE*

Since the USS *Pawnee* was so instrumental in the ultimate end, it seems
fitting to list some of its history in this text. *Pawnee* weighed in at only 1,290
gross tons, yet its armament consisted of ten nine-inch Dahlgrens, one fifty-
pound Dahlgren rifle and a huge one-hundred-pounder rifled Parrott. This
formidable vessel was listed as a steamer sloop and spent its life assigned to
the South Atlantic Blockading Squadron.

The USS *Pawnee* was Commander Steven Clegg Rowan's ship and base of
operations while anchored off Hatteras Inlet in summer 1861. The *Pawnee*
witnessed the fall of Fort Sumter in April 1861, and Commander Rowan
had volunteered to run the vessel in to support the badly stricken fort, but
his request was denied by a "spineless" fleet commander, G.V. Fox, who
later became assistant secretary of the Union navy. On board that day was
Rear Admiral John Dahlgren, inventor of the Dahlgren cannon. By 1862,
Dahlgren was chief of the Bureau of Ordnance for the Union.

Opposite, top: The *Pawnee* was weighed at 1,289 tons. It was three masted and steam driven.
Courtesy of Drew Pullen, historian and author, Hatteras, North Carolina.

Opposite, bottom: The gun deck of the *Pawnee* while on blockade duty off Charleston, South
Carolina. Notice the huge weapons in the foreground are equipped with "navy" cascabels so
heavy hawser rope could pass through them on the rear of the gun. This huge "hawser," along
with the dual block and tackles, seen alongside the guns, were used to pull the guns back into
position after the recoil of firing the weapon displaces it. *Courtesy of the Library of Congress.*

The USS *Pawnee* in action against Confederate shore batteries in Aquiri Creek. This sketch was done by Lieutenant Le Rony, and his labels are seen above the battle.

On May 24, 1861, *Pawnee* worked in unison with Ellsworth's zouaves to drive the Confederate forces from Alexandria, Virginia. One of *Pawnee*'s junior officers, R.B. Lowry, landed with a complement of seamen and took formal possession of the city, establishing the first foothold of Union forces in Virginia.[132]

As the previous chapter documents, *Pawnee*'s first officer, Lieutenant Maxwell, was in command of the expedition against Fort Ocracoke.

THE FACES OF FORT OCRACOKE

Published version of the original engraving. *Courtesy of the Ocracoke Preservation Society; published in the* Illustrated London News, *dated October 19, 1861.*

ENGINEERING THE MOVEMENT OF THE GUNS

Top: How could such mammoth guns be moved about the fort like sticks of lumber? This photo shows a method of lifting using a tool called a garrison gin. It is mind-boggling to think that such huge weapons could be moved, positioned and removed with ease. This gun is being removed by Union victors after the fall of Fort McAllister, Georgia. *Courtesy of the Library of Congress.*

Right: Another garrison gin used to move medium to large weapons at Petersburg in 1864. *Courtesy of the Library of Congress.*

Sling cart used to transfer very large guns. This particular one was at the Tredegar Armory and was used to move the twelve-inch weapons being made there. Tredegar was captured when Richmond fell into Union hands. *Courtesy of the Library of Congress.*

CHAPTER 4

WHISPERS FROM OUR PAST

ARTIFACT RECOVERY, RESEARCH AND CONSERVATION

To some, the gathering of historic artifacts is a great hobby. To others, it is a method of free enterprise—the sale of these items from long ago, raking in great profits. To the archaeologist, the artifacts are the tangible pieces of information associated with the site. Most people who love archaeology can imagine they "feel" the history oozing out of each piece. Who was the last person to use this spoon? Who drank from this bottle last? What great eyewitnesses these pieces could be if only they could talk. The recovery of these items from our past is not just a gathering of souvenirs, it is a responsibility to preserve information regarding our history and to record the information held within. It is the opinion of the author that such responsibility does not allow selling of history's remaining instances or gathering of souvenirs.

SIDCO conserves, preserves and restores each and every artifact it recovers in a lab set up for that purpose. All of the artifacts now on display throughout eastern North Carolina, associated with SIDCO projects, have been conserved, drawn, photographed, recorded and numbered and then given back to state officials and placed in state ownership by SIDCO personnel and volunteers. Every single piece. It is our belief that they are truly more valuable if they can be viewed by the public and that no one person

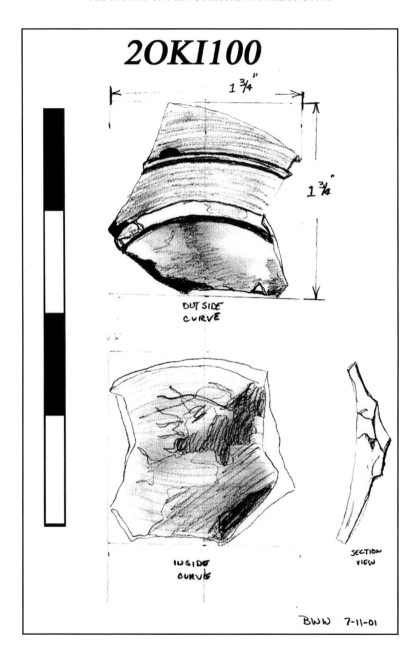

has the right to place history on their mantel for their enjoyment alone; that's SIDCO's prime directive and the basis of the entire organization.

The artifacts from Fort Ocracoke have been recorded here, by photograph, drawing or both, to illuminate the information stored in each piece of history.

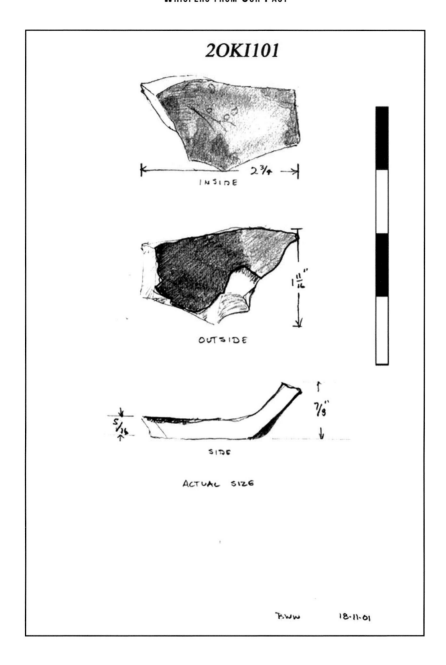

2OKI101

INSIDE

2 3/4

OUTSIDE

1 11/16"

SIDE

5/16

7/8"

ACTUAL SIZE

R.WW   18·11·01

Wherever possible, the research of the artifact is given in detail, such as the Park Scenery items, or dated, such as the black glass wine bottle pieces.

There are many, many pieces left on the site in order to avoid redundant recovery (fifty of the same item, etc.) and also to serve as the elements needed for an underwater museum at the site itself. They are a reminder of the human lives that were lived there throughout the decades and offer a sport diver the same chance to "feel" the history the way SIDCO divers did that fateful day in August 1998 and on every dive since.

The artifacts are presented here in numerical order by their artifact number whenever possible to make them easier to find when doing research, but they are more likely grouped according to type of material, especially when research has presented more information on that particular artifact and ones like it. Not every project artifact is seen here; it would be redundant to feature fourteen brass spikes, when only one would showcase the design. However, this chapter was well worth including in this text!

THE "FANCY FLOWERS" PRINT AND DESIGN

This Fancy Flowers design is extremely numerous on the fort site and certainly represents more than just a couple of item with this pattern. There are a number of pieces like butter dishes and small vanity boxes that have extravagant designs (see artifact 2OKI079 and others in this chapter).

THE STORY OF THE PARK SCENERY/ "RED COW" ARTIFACTS

In August 1998, during our initial dives on the fort site, one of the most noticeable artifacts was this large red design on cream-colored pottery, showing an ivy leaf on one side and the panoramic view of a farm with two cows standing in front. The design was nicknamed "the red bull." One of the best examples yet seen on the site was captured in a video taken by videographer Rick Allen. It features a rich red ivy design at the point of discovery, still on the ocean floor. The reverse side shows the red cows and the plantation yard. This very good example was lost during Hurricane Dennis, which hit two weeks after the discovery of the site. Since our recovery permit was not yet in place, we did not recover any artifacts during those first dives.

During the data recording, conservation, cataloguing and display processes in the years to follow, it was realized that there was also a "blue cow" design, which was a blue version of the red bull artifacts. What was even more

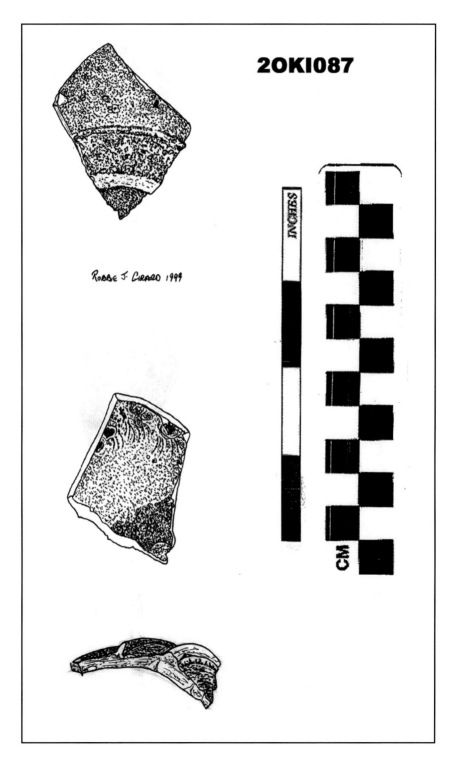

2OKI087

ROBBIE J. GIRARD 1999

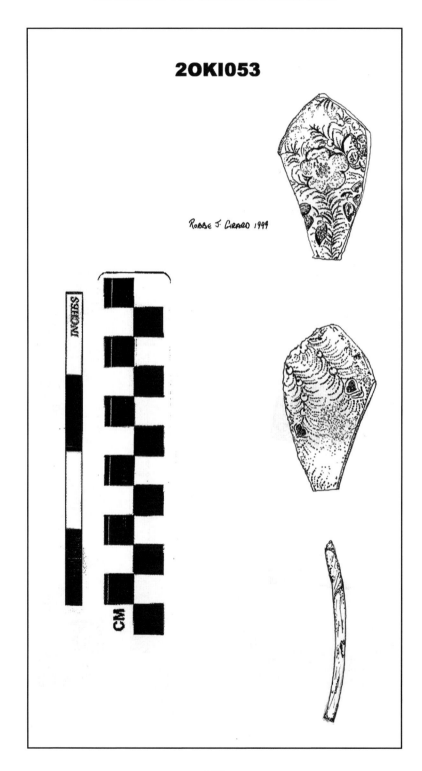

2OKI053

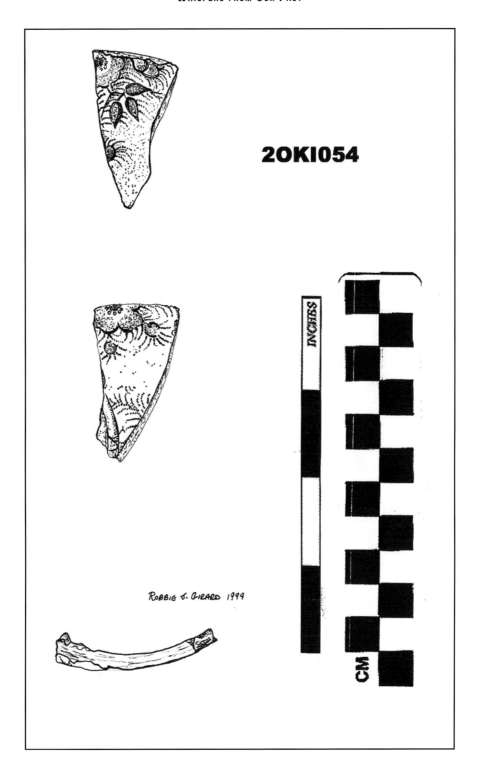

2OKI054

ROBBIE J. GIRARD 1999

2OKI059

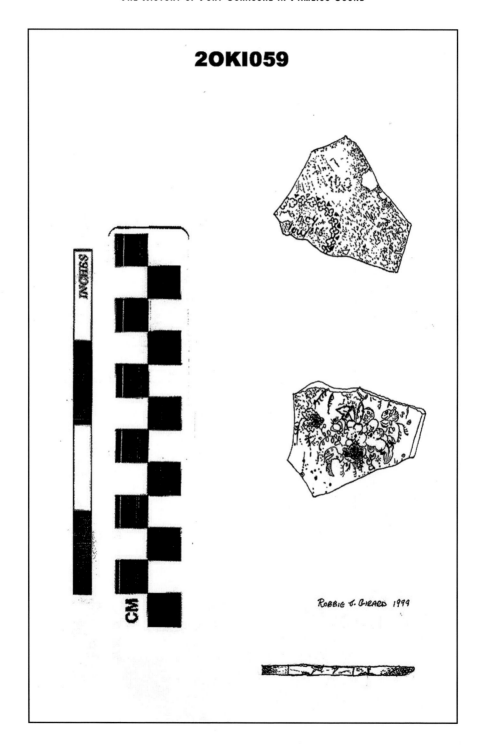

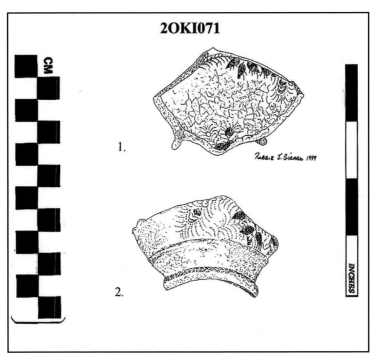

2OKI071

2OKI079

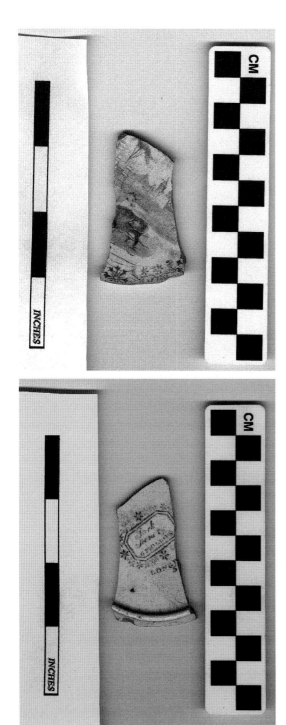

2OKI003 (front and back).

exciting is that the blue cow had a maker's mark on the reverse side. On early artifacts (1750–1920s), often the maker would print a mark or trademark on his product. This mark gives a wealth of information, including date, manufacture, location, number made and so forth.

SIDCO conservator Bobby Willis was able to track the maker's mark using the resources at www.thepotteries.org and finally gave the design a name. The design is called Park Scenery, and the maker is George Phillips. Phillips worked out of Burslem, Longport, and made the design from 1834 to 1848. He made it in three colors: blue, purple and plum. He also made items under the name G. Phillips or just Phillips. The fort site has yielded both blue and plum versions of the print. A close-up of the print shows a large "plantation" yard with grazing cattle and deer, as well as a huge manor house in the background and decorative gate and fountain in the foreground.

So far, all examples of this print have been recovered around or very near Datum 1, on the breakwater feature of the fort.

2OKI002 & 2OKI003 (FRONT)

Seen here are the front of 2OKI002 and 2OKI003, or the red version of the cow pattern and a close-up photo of the blue version of the same print.

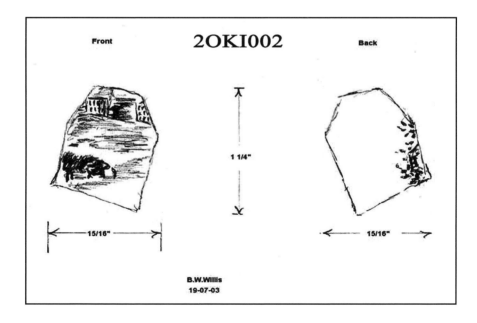

2OKI003

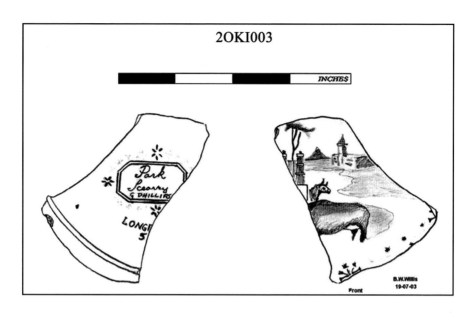

2OKI008

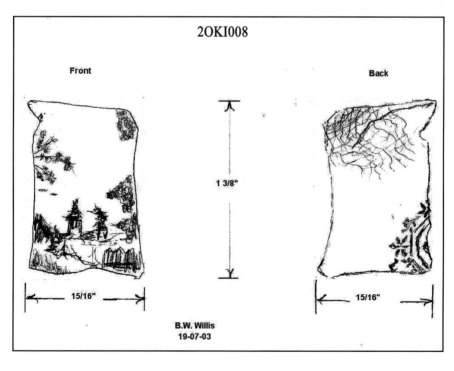

ARCHAEOLOGICAL LOCATION OF THE ARTIFACTS

If the reader does not learn any other thing in reading this text, please understand why, in archaeology, the location or provenience is recorded.

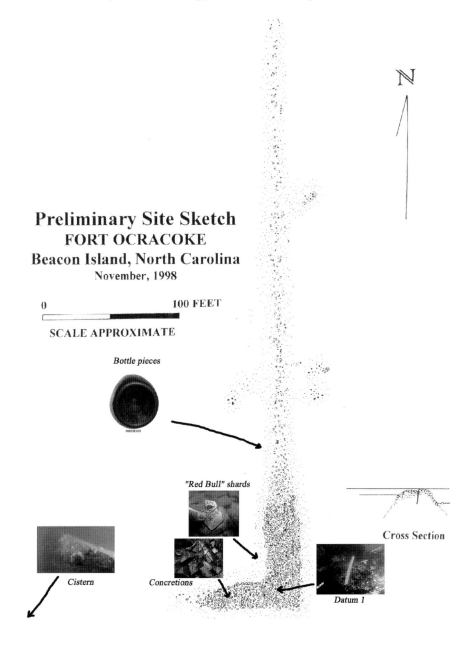

N

Preliminary Site Sketch
FORT OCRACOKE
Beacon Island, North Carolina
November, 1998

0   100 FEET

SCALE APPROXIMATE

Bottle pieces

"Red Bull" shards

Cross Section

Cistern

Concretions

Datum 1

The location of certain artifacts will tell much about the orientation of the wreck, the placement or existence of certain compartments and a wealth of other information not even begun to be touched on here. For instance, one would not find *all* the anchors amidships and *all* of the engine room on the bow; one would not find the captain's gear in the fo'c'sle area. The artifacts themselves are the "road signs" to the site. This is why it is so very important not to take artifacts home with you. Take only pictures…leave only bubbles.

There were some three hundred diagnostic artifacts recovered from this site, so to indicate the approximate location of a number of these, types and groups have been indicated on an overlay of the fort site map. This gives the reader some idea of the diagnostic value of each type.

Shown here are the locations of features like the Cistern, Datum 1 and the location of the two concretions, as well as other important general locations on the map. This gives the reader at least a working idea of the locations of the diagnostic artifacts and their importance.

2OKIOO4 OR "PEARLWARE"

This artifact is dated using a chart of period pottery compiled by Ivor Noel Hume, curator at Colonial Williamsburg. Though gray in appearance, the piece is called pearlware.

THE BLACK GLASS WINE BOTTLES FOUND NEAR DATUM 2

2OKI103

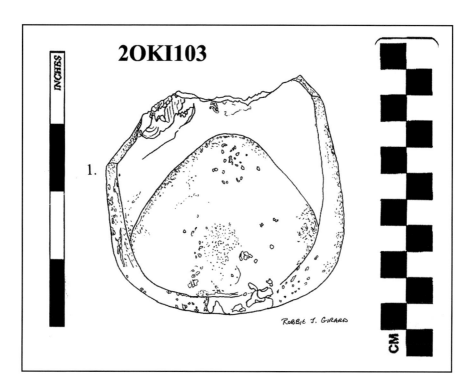

ROBBIE J. GIRARD

BLACK GLASS BOTTLES

A number of bottle components—either bottom or bases or an intact neck and lip—were discovered on the breakwater proper, mostly between Datum 2 and 3. Though no intact examples have yet been uncovered, the design of these items gives us many clues about the dates of their manufacture and the characteristics of the bottles themselves and their possible contents.

These pieces are often called "blacks" or black glass because of the dark coloring of the glass.[133] The basic glass color can vary from dark brown to an "olive" green. The glass turns black due to the use of charcoal to heat the material, which is handblown and manufactured one at a time. The result is that no two bottles are exactly alike.

2OKI105

The neck of a black glass bottle, recovered far to the north of the main concentration of bottle parts. Most of the black glass artifacts were discovered near the border between Datum 1 and 2. This artifact was recovered eighty feet away, near Datum 3.

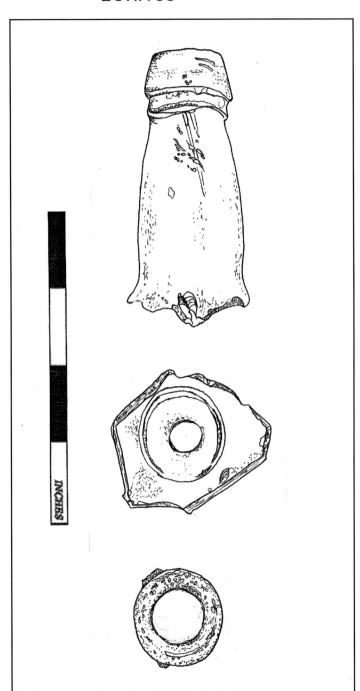

The nomenclature for the bottle type that is seen on the fort site is called cylinder. These had a longer body than the other types of this period and often had the maker's stamp embedded just below the neck of the bottle.

One important aspect of the dark color is that it will filter light and protect the contents of the bottle from sunlight, which is an important issue even today. Often simple milk jugs are manufactured today in colored plastic to prevent damage from light rays.

In the bottle base chart, the depth of the base nipple most closely matches the bottles made between 1798 and 1809. This "nipple" is formed in the bottom of the bottle during the glassblowing process, and in some cases, iron or graphite particles are left over on the bottom of the bottle from the iron tool (called a pontil) used to make it.

When you examine the design of the lip on 2OKI105, you will see that it most closely matches the example from 1850, as seen on the chart from Hume.[134] The combined evidence seen here suggests that we have examples found on Fort Ocracoke from both periods.

It is important to note that most of the bottle bottoms had been exposed to extremely high heat. This is noticeable in many of the artifacts recovered on or near Datum 1 and 2 of the breakwater, probably, as suggested, because they were exposed to the fire(s) that destroyed the fort.

As to these bottles' contents, it is suggested that wine was the most probable one, but until a more intact specimen is found, we may never know for sure.

CANNON QUOINS

During the Civil War, many large seacoast guns began the transition from the old "Napoleonic" warfare to the use of more improved weaponry with greater accuracy and more power. Often, this meant improving on the older version or modifying it to make the older design easier to use. We see this in the area of heavy seacoast defenses. Both guns and their carriages were made better and much more accurate. In the area of elevation adjustments, or the vertical angle of the cannon's aim, many carriages were equipped with elevating screws, jack screws built on the top of the carriage and fitted under the cascabel of the cannon to raise or lower the angle of the gun. Though these were the norm, once the war began, in the early stages, many gunners made do with what they had, especially in the Confederacy. Early guns used a different, simpler method of elevation adjustment: the quoin—basically a wooden wedge with a handle fashioned in the end of it. The wedges were very simply moved inward or added to lift the breach of the gun and lower the elevation.

Quoins were made of wood, usually oak or white oak, but even pine would do in a pinch. Some had increments of measure carved into the sides of them that matched up to a quoin bed, or a cradle the quoin slid in and out of. This would allow more exacting measurements, but often a gunner aimed by other means.

Quoins are more often associated with naval guns and carriages, and during the Civil War, many of the Confederate seacoast defense weapons

These one-hundred-pounder Parrott guns have elevation screws mounted directly below the cascabel or knob on the back of the gun tube; if you look closely, you can also see a wooden wedge or "quoin" just behind the elevation screw. *Courtesy of the Library of Congress.*

This gun has two quoins wedged under the breach of the gun, with the two handles sticking out. Note the arrow for reference. *Courtesy of the Library of Congress. Arrow by CC BY 2.0.*

were mounted on wooden carriages or even shipboard carriages, as often no other carriages could be found.

During the initial survey stages of the Fort Ocracoke project, several wedge-shaped pieces of wood were discovered near the Datum 1 marker and in the general vicinity of the top of the stone breakwater. Three of these were recovered, and immediately it was suggested that these might be quoins. They were found pointed end down in the sediment on top of the breakwater in about three feet of water. The exposed parts not buried

163

Arrow points to the quoin or wooden wedge used to adjust the elevation of the weapon by moving the wedge to change the angle of the gun. *Photo by author's daughter, Katie Smith. Arrow by CC BY 2.0.*

The arrow points to the iron screw elevation adjustment used on this thirty-two-pounder gun at Fort Macon State Park. *Photo by author's daughter, Katie Smith. Arrow by CC BY 2.0.*

were badly eaten by shipworms, but the parts buried were in very good shape. No handles were found, and they were all made from pinewood. Those that were not recovered soon washed out of the sediment and were lost to worms.

There were ten objects that could have been quoins found in all, somewhat evenly spaced along the breakwater from north to south. At this point, it was also suggested that they could be pilings used to support the beacon house or a dock, but no pilings or parts of pilings were found in the opposing areas. If they had been support pilings, there would most probably have been another set opposite the breakwater wall.

We will probably never know for sure if they are the quoins, but at the time of this publishing, several were undergoing conservation and stabilization.

CONCRETIONS

On September 19, 1998, divers recovered two "concretions," or clusters of artifacts suspended in a common media. The two concretions were

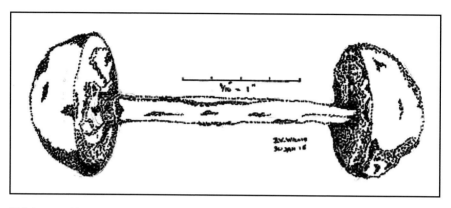

This is an artifact drawing of a piece of bar shot (two cannonballs separated by an iron bar welded between them, used to cut away sails and rigging as it tumbled end over end through the air). It was recovered by Robert Fowler O'Neal, of Ocracoke, in the late 1950s. He spotted the piece lying on the bottom, completely uncovered, during a flounder fishing trip. He found the artifact very near the shoaling area west of Datum 1.

found near Datum 1 and recovered as two whole pieces. They consisted of various types of artifacts, including pottery, glass and slate, all held together by masonry that had become pliable and had resolidified, trapping them in a cluster of history. The masonry was semihardened, and part of Concretion 1 broke away in transit. Concretion 2 held together long enough to be photographed and documented. Concretion 1 contained, in all, some two hundred separate artifacts, most of which were pottery. The concretion media was removed using an air scribe, or "engraver," which vibrated the loose particles away without damage to the artifacts trapped inside.

ORDNANCE

Comparatively, we recovered very little ordnance during the project. One would think bullets and cannonballs would be lying everywhere on a sunken fort, but that was not the case. We suspect that any ordnance left at the site today would have been tests shots from gunnery practice and would not be left directly on the site, but have been shot all over the area surrounding the fort. Anything of use left in the immediate area of the fort would have been collected up by iron salvagers right after the Civil War and sold for scrap.

This is most likely what happened to the gun tubes themselves, since we did not find any during the project. To date, these are the only two artifacts we know about in existence. Perhaps more will be discovered in the future and turned over to the proper authorities for proper conservation and display in an accredited museum.

0002OKI262

Inches

0002OKI262 was a .58-caliber Minié ball that had been fired during rifle practice and was found lodged in a timber used to make the training target. This particular round was fired by the British-made Enfield rifle, widely used by Confederate troops. These weapons were purchased from the British and secretly shipped to the Confederate states on blockade-running steamers, sneaking into ports like Wilmington and Charleston in the dead of night.

CHAPTER 5

ARCHAEOLOGY

METHOD, EQUIPMENT, MAPPING AND CONCLUSIONS

Method, Equipment and Preliminary Mapping

In this chapter we will discuss the conclusions and explain how they were deduced and what it took to get there. We will explain the equipment used and in what manner and why. A great deal of the information is based on circumstantial evidence, which is, of course, normal for archaeological investigations.

Where does one begin an archaeological project? This is dependent on where you start (at what phase of the project itself) and the information gathered before you get to the given starting point. Of course, this information must have some level of accuracy and probably needs to be something more substantial than what you heard in the local bar. There will be plenty of time to chase wild geese later. Primary source documents—information based on original archived documents that provide data from period eyewitnesses—are the only information sources one should use. If you listen to what is being said by those who witnessed the incident, they will give you the circumstances of the subject of the survey. One should always avoid secondhand stories; they are useless.

This is not an instruction booklet on proper archaeology beyond touching on the correct research methodology; remote sensing is the focus here. Let's jump ahead a little, as our concern here is location of cultural deposits underwater. In nearly all cases, only electronics will do this job, but one cannot just simply throw the sensors overboard; all systems must complement each other and do it in the right place, at the right time.

Remote Sensing Methods and Equipment

Remote sensing is simply the search for a given target—in our case, shipwrecks—by use of electronic or other systematic means. The electronic devices used here all have sensors or implements that focus or direct the units' ability to "see" though the medium below, be it water, sandy bottom, etc. This equipment, depending on the type, could be described in general as a large "metal detector," though this term is used here very loosely. Metal detectors are certainly one tool used to detect cultural deposits, but there are a great number of others, including the magnetometer/gradiometer, sub-bottom profiler, towed-video systems, side-scan and down-looking sonar and even boat-towed diver vehicles. Ground-penetrating radar is also beginning to be used in certain conditions.

Mowing the Lawn

Imagine dropping your wristwatch into a dark swimming pool late at night. You get into the water and begin to randomly walk around on the bottom, hoping to step on the watch. It might take all night to find it…and that's in a swimming pool. Now imagine the same scenario, but instead of random movements, you record your movements and search in a well-planned pattern of parallel tracks, much like mowing a yard with a lawn mower. Logic holds that, unless you make a mistake, you can't miss stepping on the wristwatch.

Our remote sensing operations are very much like working in a huge swimming pool that has to be cut up into smaller squares, and the electronics we use are much more accurate than stomping around in the dark. Using our boats or work platforms as mowers and towing the sensors of our electronics like blades, we "mow the lawn" of our search areas in a systematic pattern and record the areas we have already searched using the software explained above (see following graphic). In order to do this properly, you must know where you are, which is why we use the DGPS system and its great accuracy (more on that later). You also must be able to "see" what you are looking for. Our best tool for this is the magnetometer.

A magnetometer is a device that looks at or senses the patterns of the earth's magnetic field and "sees" deviations in that field. Since all fernery metals (iron, steel) have magnetic properties, they act like magnets, possessing a north and a south pole, just like a bar magnet. They also cause interruptions in the earth's magnetic field, interruptions that our device can detect. An iron-hulled shipwreck is obviously going to give us quite a target as our magnetometer's sensor or "towfish" passes over it, but even a wooden-hull vessel built with iron fasteners will create a large disturbance in the earth's existing magnetic field, thus setting off the device.

SIDCO uses one of the world's best magnetometers: the Schonstedt Instruments model GAU-30 magnetometer/gradiometer. This particular device is also a gradiometer, or a magnetometer with two sensors in the same towfish. The device gives its readings by recording the difference in the two sensor measurements. The gradiometer feature also allows us to use the device with pinpoint accuracy. By positioning the towfish in a certain manner, the sensor will look right past a huge iron cannon to see the cannonball lying underneath it. The device is so sensitive it will detect a shipwreck lying thirty feet below the bottom of the ocean sediment or sand. On some other models, the towfish is a quite elaborate piece of equipment; with fins and an odd cone-shaped nose, it rather looks like a fish. The "fish" on the GAU-30 is the silver pipe seen below the control box. This makes it easy to handle while doing gradiometer work, yet rugged and dependable while being towed over the bottom, behind a boat, for magnetometer work. The sensor must be towed at a forty-five-degree angle relative to the ocean bottom. This is accomplished using lead counterweights placed in different positions on the towfish/sensor and temporarily attached to hold the towfish at the needed angle while being pulled though the water column. A towrope is used to attach the towfish to the stern of the boat so as not to stress the cable between the fish and the control unit. Duct tape is used to secure the cable to the rope every couple of feet to keep the tension off the delicate electronic cable. The towfish may be rugged, but the cable is not.

For shallow-water work, in areas where the towfish or sensor may come in contact with the bottom or even cultural materials such as wrecks or old navigational beacons or geological obstacles like rocks or coral formations, the equipment is placed in a long piece of PVC pipe to protect it. The pipe must be nonferrous material yet strong enough to handle the impact. If the remaining pipe section is extended up, toward the interior of the boat, beyond its mount bracket, it will allow the boat crew to observe the angle at which the sensor is towed and ensure the proper altitude to the bottom. This pipe also makes a suitable platform on which to mount other equipment packages, such as the underwater video systems.

The graphic of Beacon Island shows the results of the magnetometer survey SIDCO completed in the area of the island, the purpose of which was to look for remaining cannons or ordnance associated with the fort. As with the other forts in the area, all shot, cannons and shell were removed when the fort was abandoned (also as recorded at Fort Oregon; see Chapter 3), according to the data from the magazine survey. There *had* been a number of smaller targets located during the search that could have been the odd shell or shot or a practice shot or two and even today fishermen still find an occasional remaining projectile, but there is also a huge amount of crab pots and associated debris, all made of iron and steel-mesh chicken wire, which makes locating a single cannonball nearly impossible. On the magnetometer, a dense iron ball and a wad of chicken wire would give about the same reading. Also on the graphic, the reader will notice that the dark track of the electronics did not reach the southernmost side of the island. This is where the water was so shallow that boats could not go there, and the survey had to be finished using handheld detectors.

The lanes around Beacon Island, as recorded, look rather haphazard and disorganized, but there are several reasons for this. The original plan was to survey in lanes about forty feet apart, this to give the magnetometer enough overlap from one lane to the next, to "see" any substantial iron objects or deposits of cultural materials. Wind, tide and currents always affect the survey vessels and make more exact lanes impossible. It is much more important to cover all the territory than for it to be "pretty."

NAVIGATION AND POSITION FINDING

Mapping of the site is a paramount concern and is ultimately one of the primary goals of any archaeological project. Due to the massive size of the Fort Ocracoke site, mapping had to be split into two operations: feature location and feature mapping. In feature location, each feature must be located in relation to a central marker or datum and coordinated as closely as possible in latitude and longitude. Feature mapping is the more exact drawing of each feature and then placing that drawing into perspective with the other features of the site. Think of it as locating each important piece on a large map, like a state on a map of the United States, and then mapping and drawing each county contained in that state and placed in relation to the rest of the map.

Global Positioning Systems, or GPS, uses a network of twenty-four satellites orbiting the earth to find a point or position on the surface of the planet. These satellites transmit a high-frequency radio signal to the individual GPS receiver, providing it with data that allows it to calculate its distance from the given satellite. The receiver must acquire at least three satellites to determine latitude and longitude or location of the receiver. Most acquire twelve or more at one time, giving it even more accuracy. The system was conceived by the U.S. Department of Defense to guide missiles and other ordnance to enemy targets with unprecedented accuracy, but the government soon realized the vast number of possible uses for this system for needs other than military. The system of satellites took years to implement, starting in the mid-1970s with rocket launches and, later, top-secret military payloads carried into space by space shuttle. The shuttle *Challenger* is said to have had two GPS satellites onboard when it exploded in flight in 1986.

The system today is accurate to between thirty and one hundred feet, but this is, in most cases, not accurate enough for archaeological measurements, so a more expensive system was also used to boost the accuracy of the GPS. A differential beacon receiver was mated with the GPS receiver, making it a DGPS. This differential device uses radio beacon signals transmitted by various Coast Guard bases to improve the accuracy of the GPS position to between one and five feet, which is mandatory for better archaeological mapping. The nonmoving differential transmitter stations are land based and are given the exact location of the GPS satellites. They recompute the signal from the satellites and add their given land locations to "correct" the satellite data and pass it on to the DGPS receiver.

The system we used initially was a middle-of-the-price-range unit made by Lowrance Electronics, Inc. The GlobalNav 310 and Eagle DGPS beacon receiver were the mainstays of our mapping work. The 310 gives exceptional accuracy and a wealth of information including position and a plotting screen showing a bird's-eye view of the known features and their relative position to one another as well as distance. The unit is also extremely useful in remote sensing operations, as it records the boat's track and allows the operator to keep track of areas already searched. The data collected by this instrument can be saved in memory and analyzed by special mapping software called Fugawi 3.1. This program will overlay the gathered data on a NOAA nautical chart (in BSB format) and reference the navigational data to other nearby geographical features such as shoals, channels and markers. The GPS instrument uses a small self-contained memory to record targets or waypoints and track plots or "bread-crumb" trail markers to show where the survey vessel has already been. This data can be downloaded from the instrument memory to a computer and displayed on the Fugawi software.

The software integrates the navigational chart most appropriate to the information downloaded from the GPS instrument, giving the reader a clear picture of the track plots, targets located, existing targets, landmarks and mapping features. Also shown are surrounding geographical features such as shoals, navigational beacons and the depth of the nearby waters. The graphic is taken from NOAA Chart No. 11550 (see the earlier chart with the track plots). In the chart, you can see several important items, including the shallow water surrounding the fort site, the depth of the water, datum markers, possible magnetometer targets and the track plot of the particular remote sensing survey, accurate to within five to fifteen feet.

This also gives an idea of the size of the Fort Ocracoke site and the relation of Beacon Island to the rest of the area. The sandy shoal to the south of the island could possibly be the remains of the earthen walls, suspected of washing away during a hurricane in either 1899 or 1933. If so, the remains of many cultural features could lie underneath the sand, visible only to our electronic remote sensing equipment. This method makes it easy to plan the next remote sensing mission without resensing any areas. It also gives the reader a permanent record of the area searched and any targets found during that search.

For all the advantages and dividends this equipment produces, the sheer size of the fort site adds greatly to the complexity of managing this equipment, especially while using a variety of vessels ranging from small johnboats to a twenty-four-foot SeaOx. Both the GlobalNav 310 and the accompanying differential receiver were designed to be permanently mounted to the uppermost surfaces of the boat, just like any other marine electronic device of this size. Various modifications were made to the systems (SIDCO has several systems) to allow them to be used on a variety of platforms, including cars and trucks.

Not long after the completion of the Fort Ocracoke project, Lowrance donated several new units that overshadow the capabilities of the GlobalNav 310 GPS, three- to fourfold. These newer units were like stepping up to a fully

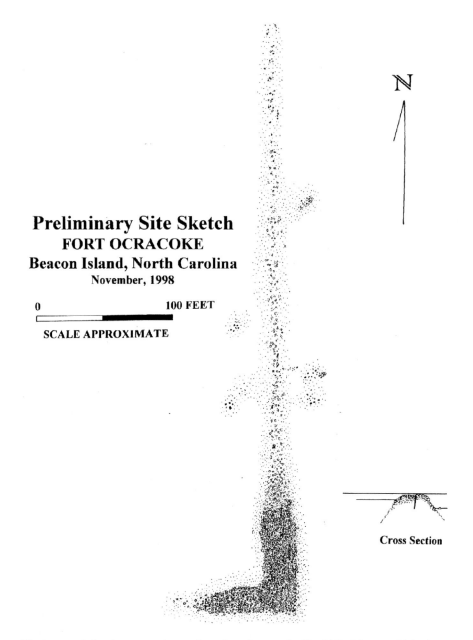

Preliminary Site Sketch
FORT OCRACOKE
Beacon Island, North Carolina
November, 1998

0   100 FEET

SCALE APPROXIMATE

N

Cross Section

The layout of the site proper is seen here in a site map by David D. Moore, which gives an excellent view of the breakwater. The beacon most probably stood in the corner of the "L."

loaded Cadillac from a VW Beetle with features installed that accomplish what we had to do by hand before. If you have it, it's silly not to use today's advanced technology. If it's there, use it! The newer systems also use WAAS (advanced navigation system used for commercial airlines) instead of the differential beacon receiver, and this is accuracy for free, without the extra expense of the DGPS or differential beacon antenna. In brief, the WAAS satellites were installed by a program funded by the Federal Aviation Administration (FAA) to increase the accuracy of commercial aircraft. This system increases GPS accuracy to around seven feet inside the Continental United States and Canada. This rivals the performance of differential and comes free with all modern GPS units.

THE SITE MAP AND INTERMEDIATE MAPPING

One of the most important pieces of any archaeological report is the site map, which gives the reader a bird's-eye view of the site proper. Normally this would include the entire site, its features and archaeological items and labels of each. The Fort Ocracoke site is so huge that the main site map includes only the relatively small area included in this project. Even the site features are far enough away from the main area that they are shown on the NOAA chart graphic. In this manner, each feature is described separately from the main map.

THE SITE TODAY

The mapping of such a huge site can only be done in parts and stages. In order to show all the features of this site, we use layers to show the various parts. The exact boundaries of the Fort Ocracoke site have never been completely determined, and the info in Chapter 2 makes it quite obvious why. The dynamic constant changing of the terrain in the area of the fort makes exact coordinates impossible, and the perimeter of the site can only be a matter of speculation. Because of this we worked where we had exact features and accurate measurements to use.

VISUALIZING THE PAST...
DESCRIBING THE SITE TODAY

Describing anything while inspiring an image in the mind's eye is a daunting task without some kind of sketch, drawing or photograph. We have a handful of graphics left behind for us from the past (see Chapter 3), the best of which was the black-and-white engraving of the scene of the fort in flames, for the second time, after Lieutenant Maxwell and his expeditionary force had finished destroying the remaining structure and were leaving to return to USS *Pawnee*. The engraving based on a sketch drawn by a Union officer named Le Rony is the clearest, richest image known. This shows quite well many of the features of the fort, as well as the placement and orientation of the walls, palisades, some of the gun platforms and associated parapets and other important facets of the site.

If you examine the *London Illustrated News* engraving of the fort burning, which is one of the best visual records of the fort remaining today, one can see the beacon for Beacon Island. This large building stands near the southeast corner of the eastern wall, along with what looks like the sally port (door of a fort) at the inshore or western end of a dock. This and the fact that divers recovered many pieces of gray- and green-slate shingles suggest that the beacon stood right over the inside walls of the "L," directly above Datum 1. This is indicated because such a building would need the strongest possible roofing materials due to the severe maritime environment, and the heavy slate shingles would have fallen into the water below and ended up at Datum 1, where they were recovered, some of them with the nail holes still intact. The beacon is also probably the "large house" described in Von Eberstein's description of the officers' quarters in the fort proper:

> *By early afternoon of the following day, the guns at Fort Hatteras had been silenced and the Fort surrendered. When Captains Leith and Swindell heard of this, they called a conference of their officers to be held in a big house which was on the island, and which they used as officer's quarters. I was invited by Captains Leith and Swindell and the other officers to take part in the deliberations.*[135]

The breakwater is the most notable and visual feature of the site. For many years, the corner of the breakwater (the corner of the "L" portion of the breakwater as seen in the site map) was considered a menace to navigation by the local fishermen because the stone is piled to within four inches of surface. The "pipe" feature often caught unwary boaters unprepared to see an eight-inch-diameter iron pipe sticking nearly vertical off the bottom and only twelve inches under the surface. It remains a dangerous area for the uninformed boat captain. When initial survey work was done in the summer of 1998, many pieces of modern running gear were found in the "L," including a skeg from an outboard motor, two aluminum propeller blades and a complete stainless propeller with the broken drive shaft still inside. It is this point that we chose for Datum 1, the point from which all the other features were measured.

It should be noted here as a reminder that if you the reader were looking into the picture, Ocracoke would be behind you, Ocracoke Inlet to your left and Portsmouth lies just opposite and can be seen left of the southernmost point of the fort.

SIDCO uses two types of markers in the field, a datum stake and a survey stake. The datum stake is much more permanent in nature and needs to remain in position. It also must have magnetic properties so its signature can be seen on a magnetometer/gradiometer survey map and these magnetic points can be matched up to their position on a hand-drawn site map. The survey stake is a visual marker only and is generally made of PVC plastic and graduated black and white in feet for use as photographic scales.

On the inner edge of the "L," as close to the highest point on the breakwater as possible, a datum stake was driven down between the stones to a depth of about 3.75 feet. It is tagged "D1" with a white plastic tag to mark it as Datum 1. This marker is the keystone and reference point of the entire site.

In the two maps shown for reference, we see Beacon Island overall, and in the blowup we see actual features on the island itself, including a lighthouse of some type. The lighthouse drawing is very similar to other lighthouses drawn on other charts of the period including the Shell Castle Lighthouse, which stood only about a mile or so to the west of Beacon Island, so this may be an icon. The various buildings seen offer no identification as to what they represent, but the "Site of Fort, 1812" certainly puts us in the right location with little doubt. There is also what looks like a pier or dockage of some kind very close to the dock structure seen in the *London Illustrated Times* engraving. This structure is also presumably very close to the "L" in the breakwater and the datum point placed in 1998 called Datum 1. Comparing the charts in Chapter 2, the engraving, eyewitness descriptions, historical facts and every other scrap of information we can assemble, we can put together a facsimile of how the fort appeared in 1861. We cannot duplicate exact features because the descriptions are sketchy and full of holes, giving us only pieces of the picture of the fort on Beacon Island.

FORT OCRACOKE COMPOSITE MAP
ASSEMBLED IN 2006 ROBERT K. SMITH SIDCO

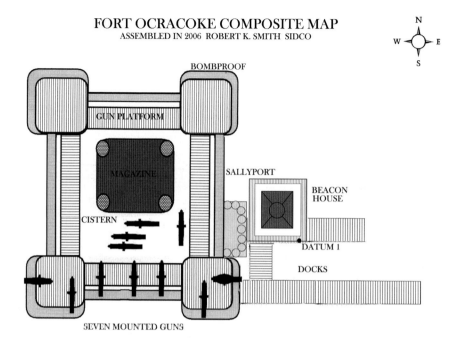

A composite graphic of the fort as it was described by a number of sources, including the *London Illustrated Times* engraving and the Le Rony sketch. Lieutenant Maxwell's description is probably the most useful, and ironically, he is the one who ordered the destruction of the installation itself. Though rudimentary, this graphic gives one at least an idea as to what Fort Ocracoke looked like. Note: Use the site map on page 174 to match up the location of "Datum 1" to see the placement of the fort features. Be sure to pay attention to the North Pointers, since the charts are shown in right angles to each other in the text.

Also, we cannot duplicate some features because we have no real description of the item, but we can see represented features in the engraving. One example of this is the palisade wall at the water's edge (see Chapter 3) and the placement of the beacon itself. The location of the guns is only speculative and based on small observations made by Von Eberstein in his notes. Maxwell also missed a good opportunity to give us a location of the guns he helped destroy. Based on these and other items in the following engraving picture, we will try to assemble a graphic of the fort, as it exists in our imaginations and as close as possible to how the proud fort actually existed.

This very well-done diorama, on display at Fort Fisher State Park, shows how big mounds of sand were converted into active military installations. Note the skidways for sliding heavy loads up and down the walls of the gun platforms and the placement of the bombproofs with their narrow doorways.

THE DIVER'S VIEW OF THE SITE TODAY

(See Site Map on page 174)

Starting at Datum 1, on the upper corner of the southernmost wall section, there is a pinnacle of the rock pile and the intersection of the "L," plus small outcroppings farther to the south and east. This structure stands some eight to twelve feet off the bottom and comes to within eighteen inches of the surface.

GRANITE BLOCKS

If the diver swims north along the upper crest of the wall, he would run into fourteen granite blocks some three feet by eighteen inches by eighteen inches, both green and gray in color. It has been suggested that these may have come from the base of the lighthouse at Shell Castle, as it is obvious that the fort builders added whatever was available to the breakwater to keep the walls from washing down with the tide (see Chapter 3).

CONCRETIONS NO. 1 AND NO. 2

Very near Datum 1, just to the west and only about six feet away, SIDCO diver Wayne Willis discovered two massive (some fifty pounds each) conglomerations of various types of artifacts—including pottery, black glass, ornate earthenware and other pieces—all concreted together by mortar and marine growth.

SKEGS ON THE SLOPE

The western slope of this feature was peppered with modern outboard motor parts, including skegs, prop blades and broken shafts. One intact stainless steel propeller with the sheared drive shaft still inside was located here. This area was also inundated by pieces of broken green and gray slate shingles.

SHINGLES

The full-size pieces are twelve to fourteen inches long and six inches high and have two holes cut or drilled in the upper edge to hold the shingle in place. These beautiful slate shingles protected the beacon's roof. In those days, the slate shingle is the only type that would have stood up to the harsh marine environment. There were many shingles, and the roof of the beacon must have been large; these may also be several layers of shingles and older shingles, thrown overboard once they were changed out on the roof above.

We see here also a huge amount of red and orange handmade brick, which may have been a large double-level fireplace and cooking facilities contained inside the beacon house.

POTTERY

As the diver descends to the base of the wall in the crook of the "L," a large amount of pottery is found, some in single pieces, some in large piles or caches of many pieces and patterns. Moving north along the base, SIDCO divers found a barrel bottom, slightly buried in the bottom; underneath was a collection of fifty to sixty assorted pieces of pottery. One of the primary designs found here was the Park Scenery print (see Chapter 4).

Black Glass (Blacks)

Farther to the west along datum marker 2 (fifty feet due north of Datum 1), at the base of the wall, a large number of black glass shards and pieces was found, some of them bottle bases, and even one bottle neck was found. These dated to the early 1800s (see Chapter 4). As the diver swims north, the pile gradually levels off until it disappears under the sand.

The Discovery of the Fort

The discovery and identification of the Fort Ocracoke site was very much a comedy of successful events, all leading up to a most logical conclusion. Take a mysterious pile of ballast stone and rock on a sandy bottom, a whole community of commercial fishermen who knew the stone wall was simply a menace to navigation, several very talented local historians and our dive team, and add them all together. The result could be every element needed to create a real "whodunit" novel, but this is not fiction. Having already evaluated several possible archaeological and historical targets in the areas of Ocracoke Inlet and Pamlico Sound, there was a knowledge database of what sites might be there for us to encounter. One was Fort Ocracoke:

> *Discovery of sunken Civil War Fort made near Ocracoke, Press Conference to be held!*

> *Divers have discovered the sunken remains of what is believed to be the Civil War era fortress: Fort Ocracoke. A press conference will be held at the North Carolina Maritime Museum in Beaufort, on Friday, Feb. 26 at 9:30 AM, in the auditorium. Speakers will be President and Vice President of Surface Interval Diving Company as well as Trustees of SIDCO and several state organizers.*

Fort "Ocracoke" or "Morgan" was a 20-gun Confederate stronghold built near Portsmouth NC, and designed to protect Ocracoke Inlet from Union invaders.

The fort was abandoned after the battle of Forts Hatteras and Clark and was destroyed by fire, by a Union naval detachment from the USS Fanny.

The fort remains were discovered by divers from Surface Interval Diving Co. a nonprofit archaeological corporation operating out of Beaufort NC after a tip came from a local charter boat captain.

SPECIAL NOTE TO THE READERS

This is the best time to explain that the sheer size and magnitude of this project was staggering, preventing examination of every aspect of the site to the extent that we would have liked. We spent seven years of time and resources on a survey that was much more than just "preliminary" yet much less than a complete excavation. The area involved with this site is at least one square mile or more, and even the best-funded entity would have had to pick and choose which facets of the project were more important than others. This also makes it very hard to determine when the end of the project should come.

LISTING THE EVIDENCE: THE CONCLUSIONS

Each of the items listed in the following pages is seen elsewhere in the text, so its location will be given for review. Artifact information pertaining to the proof seen will also reference back to the location and chapter for the reader's evaluation.

In modern archaeology, barely 10 percent of *all* projects done in a given year, worldwide, will produce that single artifact, document or eyewitness that would prove the exact identity of the site. This means, and is academically accepted, that the given project must be proven with circumstantial evidence, as best as possible and to the most logical conclusion of their work. This conclusion should never be based on finances, unscrupulous leadership or any other reasons other than to support the archaeological integrity of the preservation of the site.

In order to present the proof best, we will list each part of the story:

- *Period glass artifacts*: Black glass wine bottles are present on the site, especially near Datum 2. These "blacks" are dated by the measurements of the base of the bottles found (see Chapter 5). These bottles date to very close to 1848 as compared to the Hume charts.
- *Period earthenware*: The blue-banded gray pottery found near Datum 1 date, according to the Hume chart, to 1795. Both of these items predate the Civil War site and date well within some of the earlier forts, which leads credence that one fort was built on top of another, as suggested.
- *Slate shingles*: These pieces are most probably shingles (by the nail holes), which suggest a roof of a building, probably the roof of the beacon itself.
- *Lieutenant Le Rony's drawing and the resulting engraving of the burning fort*: The drawing shows features of the fort proper and relays possible locations for each, including the beacon, palisade wall, eastern fort wall, northern fort wall, several gun barbettes, long dock and sally

port, possible breakwater placement along the eastern wall and location of USS *Fanny* during Maxwell's expedition and its position relative to Portsmouth, seen in the distance.

- *Position, location and earlier charts*: Many of the earlier charts of Beacon Island show varying types, sizes and states of repair of several fort structures as they evolved through the years (Chapter 2). Their locations correspond nearly exactly, one on top of another, owing to differences between early navigation and positioning methods as compared to modern differential DGPS and Fugawi moving map software. Their methods were somewhat in error, where our method is exact within three feet anywhere on the planet, which leaves considerable yet acceptable differences.

- *Eyewitness accounts*: Several people remember playing on the remnants of the fort walls (Chapter 2), and their memories support theoretical locations of the fort sites. In eastern North Carolina, the coastal communities are close-knit and small. Often it is possible to see your neighbors in the boat anchored beside you while on a fishing trip or summer outing. Features such as the fort walls would be used for navigation, and their locations would be passed down through the years.

- *No shipwreck site*: There are no shipwreck-related materials like ships fittings, anchors, sail rings, etc. and, especially, no fuel. Only a few small pieces of coal were found on the site, and much, much more would be required to even suggest the leftovers from the coal bins of a small steamship.

- *No ordnance (cannonballs or grapeshot) found*: The missing ordnance was an issue of great disappointment to the team. If one can imagine the huge amount of ammunition that each weapon in a twenty-gun fort would require, both solid shot and canister, grape- or shell shot, the lack of remaining artifacts seems impossible. Especially after you factor in the presence of two or three forts on almost the same site, as well as the shifting sands of Pamlico Sound, which cover and uncover *anything* left lying in the water from one season to the next. Also, in the Civil War abandonment, Von Eberstein states that only he, four black men who were working on the fort and Henry Brown were left after Lieutenants Swindell and Leigh boarded vessels headed for New Bern as quickly as possible and in great fear for their lives. These six men had only a small sailboat in which to travel to Washington, hardly big enough to carry the men, much less the ammunition for twenty battle-ready seacoast weapons, and the six of them could not have loaded and saved all that shot and shell, even if they had had a battleship.

A tremendous effort was expended in an attempt to find the abandoned ordnance at Fort Ocracoke, using some of the most sophisticated electronic remote sensing equipment ever made, and still no ordnance was located. (See "Mowing the Lawn" earlier in this chapter.) It is of popular belief that, due to the tremendous magnetic signature surrounding Beacon Island itself, most of the ordnance must be beneath the grassy marsh island. This is further complicated by the fact that fishermen have, for years, been throwing old crab pots on the island and even stacking new ones there between seasons. The older ones, rusting to dust, are discarded on the island proper. There is no way to determine if the items making the electronics "sing" are Federal period ordnance or last year's decaying crab pots.

WHAT HAPPENED TO THE CANNON LEFT AT FORT OCRACOKE?

After the Confederate withdrawal from Fort Ocracoke and the quiet recovery of the two columbiads by CSS *Albemarle* a day before Lieutenant Maxwell's U.S. Navy expedition finished destroying the fort, the grand total of heavy weapons left at the fort includes one eight-inch navy gun, three eight-inch seacoast howitzers and fourteen thirty-two-pounder seacoast guns. Maxwell explains in his report that he had neither equipment nor time to recover these guns, so he ordered them destroyed by spiking, beating off the trunions and/or firing one gun against another. We know that this was Plan A, based on the materials issued to his detail when he departed from USS *Pawnee*.

Here we see Plan A and the tools to do it:

I send all the sledges and chisels I have to break trunions, etc., and shall, if possible, obtain from the fort a few round shot (32-pounder), which might be used in firing one gun against the trunions of the other. I hope you have experienced men to use the sledges.[136]

The expedition being carefully organized and provided with sledge hammers to break off the trunions, and 32-pounder shot and twenty 7-pound cartridges to be used in firing one gun against the trunions of another.[137]

What Maxwell found in the fort:

There were platforms for twenty guns, which had been partially destroyed by fire. The gun carriages had been all burned. There were 18 guns in the fort, viz, 4 8-inch shell guns and 14 long 32-pounders.[138]

The results and why:

I tried to destroy the guns by breaking the trunions off with sledges and by dropping solid shot upon them from an elevation, with little success. I then fired solid shot from a 64-pounder at them, and in this manner disabled them…

The destruction of the fort is complete, and twenty-two guns disabled; these are all the guns that were there, with the exception of two taken off in the steamboat Albemarle *on Sunday.*

The destruction of the guns was with me a necessity. I had no means of transporting them nor defending them in their position. I therefore hope my course will meet your approval.[139]

So, eighteen seacoast guns were left to the elements and waters of Pamlico Sound. So where are the cannons today? During the reconstruction of the nation, after the end of the Civil War, there was a tremendous need for scrap iron. Sites like this had tons of iron was lying about, just waiting to be picked up by someone who had the proper heavy equipment. Normally, the U.S. Army Corps of Engineers kept records of Civil War forts, their contents and what was salvaged by junk dealers. However, Fort Ocracoke was not recorded here, and no salvage records exist to tell us if any of the eighteen guns were recovered. Also, if a salvage company *did* take the guns to market, as scrap iron, how did they find them in the shifting sands of Ocracoke Inlet? It was tough enough relocating features of the site with modern electronics, much less if the items were buried.

Another facet of this story is that in such an operation, several sizable boats, a barge, etc., would have been seen by local fishermen, and the story of "the time they took the guns off Beacon Island" would have been an occurrence that many of the older fishermen would have remembered. Once again, very few people had even heard of Fort Ocracoke, much less of the recovery of any guns. Nothing happens in Core/Pamlico Sound without someone seeing it. The most probable location of the guns is directly below the remainder of Beacon Island, which is now a marine bird sanctuary, which makes any kind of test excavations impossible. It is also very probable that the guns were recovered by postwar salvors and are gone forever.

WHY ARE THERE NO BUTTONS, MESS KITS OR OTHER ITEMS MARKED "CSA"?

This is an important question, yet easy to explain. When war was declared between the states, the South was very far from ready. There was no Confederate navy; there was little more than rabble for an organized army. When men joined the Confederate army, most had no uniforms to wear (some did, given by local ladies' groups, but there were many different uniforms based on the ideas of the seamstress; this explains the many colors in the Confederate lines: light blue, butternut, light gray, dark gray, etc.), and commanders had no mess kits to issue. For the most part, any equipment issued was marked "US," taken from local armories. Often, a soldier who was a farmer yesterday fell in dressed and equipped in his best field clothing and gear, as though he were going on a camping or hunting trip. It took some time for the Confederate authorities to secure the proper gear for their military. A Confederate soldier was usually relegated to a tin cup, some old, bent spoons, his field knife and a china dish or bowl from his wife's setting at home. Since the majority of action in the area of Fort Ocracoke took place in the early months of the war, there would have been little official issue equipment left here. This also explains the huge amount of broken pottery in the area, either dumped there as trash or burned in the beacon when the fort was destroyed. To better illustrate this, reexamine the list of missing gear needed by the Washington Grays when they mustered out to Portsmouth:

Washington Greys
10 Tents & fixtures
1 Capt. Marquee
3500 Rounds Ball Cartridges
1500 Caps
5 Camp Chests & furniture
99 Muskets Sharp. late patent "Springfield" 1850 with lock, bayonets attached
99 Canteens & Haversacks
The above except the muskets, were furnished by the Magistrates of

Beaufort Co.
Articles needed
Body Belts
Cartridge Boxes
Knapsacks
Side Arms for officers
Bayonet scabbards
Cap Pouches
Bullet & Ball Moulds
Hospital Stores
Lead
Stationary
Powder
Camp Stools
Drum & Fife

Remarks *The tents are of very inferior material, too small for service, do not shed rain and will not stand the severe winds of the sea coast, they are now pitched at Fort Ocracoke, in double of one upon another, that they may shed rain. The camp chests are sufficient for the Co.*[140]

THE CISTERN

In July 1999, divers found a circular brick-and-mortar feature in 10 feet of water, (298' X 260 degrees from Datum 1). This item lies at N35 05'.798 W76 02'.660, which is 5 feet, 5 inches wide (outside diameter) and 8 inches thick, or (approximately) two rows of brick. Several of the brick were laid flat with angles cut, while others were laid whole and uncut. The workmanship of this feature was unbelievable, and it was built with great care. Completely hand laid and set by rack of eye, it was quite beautiful and an unexpected find.

A cistern is a large water storage tank usually connected to a gutter system so that rainwater will collect inside the cistern tank. In some places in eastern North Carolina, especially on the Outer Banks, they were the only source of fresh water, as wells were often contaminated by salt water or heavy mineral content. There were four very large cisterns located beside the magazine in Fort Ocracoke. The cisterns in Fort Ocracoke were huge. One source says nineteen thousand gallons each! (See Chapter 3.)

An example of a cistern (or rainwater tank) made from brick and mortar; this is one of the huge cisterns at Fort Macon State Park in Atlantic Beach, North Carolina. *Photo by the author.*

> *And in the center a large bombproof of 100 feet square, with the magazine within it. Directly above the magazine on each side were four large tanks containing water.*[141]

To be sure, most modern-day shallow wells driven in the area are terribly laced with heavy sulfur and iron minerals to the point of being undrinkable and must be treated with softeners. Untreated wells on the Outer Banks are worse. One taste of this water makes the thought of rainwater much more preferable. The cistern feature found at Fort Ocracoke was possibly the opening to a potential "trove" of period diagnostic artifacts, as it is probable that retreating Confederate soldiers might be more apt to "dispose" of hard-to-move items in a large freshwater tank, just in case they come back. However, for us working in ten feet of water, in a "killer" 1.5-knot current, it is quite an undertaking. Several attempts succeeded in moving only a few feet of sediment, uncovering a few pieces of trash and modern items. One other concern at this point became the possibility of a cave-in as more sand was removed and less sand remained to counter the sand pushing in on the brick structure from the outside. With this concern and also after a hurricane deposited eight feet of sand on top of the feature, the job was abandoned.

Reverberations of a Civil War Find at Ocracoke

For nearly a century, North Carolina's Civil War history had been recorded, published and preserved by private groups, small museums and the state's vast army of competent historians, many of whom are self-taught and avocational. Many tried desperately to publicize the importance of coastal North Carolina during the first part of the War Between the States, yet somehow Ocracoke was completely ignored. With the discovery of Fort Ocracoke, Ocracoke and the surrounding areas finally got the recognition they deserved. In 2000, Ocracoke was added to the North Carolina Civil War Trails.

One of the greatest accomplishments of SIDCO's career is the placement of the Fort Ocracoke Monument on Ocracoke Island, near the Ocracoke Preservation Society Museum. This monument not only commemorates the fort site, but it also follows the charter of SIDCO's nonprofit standing in the publication of North Carolina's long-forgotten sunken archaeological sites and the promotion of our state's underwater history as an attraction of the tourism industry. It was wonderful to see Ocracoke added to the North Carolina Civil War Trails, finally, after so many generations.

Bonny Blue Flag

For several years, SIDCO attempted to make the fort more visible to the public, particularly to those on the Cedar Island and Swan Quarter ferries. Though the fort, at that time, had not been made public, people could at least have an idea of where the site was if they could see some kind of marker. This also had to be done in such a manner that potential looters would not be able to find the main archaeological site proper, so it was decided to erect a flagpole and fly one or, sometimes, two flags to mark the site.

This would be quite an undertaking for a number of reasons, the largest of which was probably the weather. In the maritime environment, it does not take long to blow a flag to stitches, no matter what it is made of. One would have to change the flags out on a weekly basis, which could get expensive.

SIDCO pumped down a converted fiberglass flagpole some seven hundred yards northwest of the actual dig site and rigged it to fly two three- by five-foot banners. As the sun went down in the west, the shadows

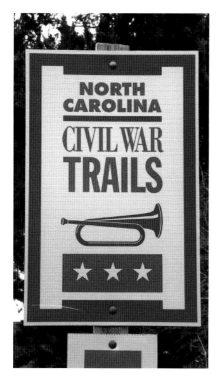

Left: As a direct result of SIDCO's Fort Ocracoke Project, Ocracoke was finally placed on the official Civil War Trails map and given its rightful place in North Carolina's Civil War history. *Photo by author.*

Below: Monument in remembrance of Fort Ocracoke and those who built, garrisoned and lived there on display near National Park Service dock on Ocracoke Island. The reverse side lists those who served in the Civil War from Hyde County, both Union and Confederate.

Two initial exhibits were at the Ocracoke Preservation Society Museum on Ocracoke Island and the North Carolina Maritime Museum in Beaufort. An exhibit can now be seen in the Graveyard of the Atlantic Museum in Hatteras, as well as other accredited museums.

made Beacon Island look like a ghostly apparition of the fort with the flag flying high above the marsh grass bastions, but then the question had to be answered: which flags to fly? One suggestion was the U.S. flag, but historically that flag never flew over the site. The current state flag was also suggested, but there were a number of similar reasons that eliminated it from the running. The "diver down" flag was also thought of, but it is considered a navigational aid and should never be used in this manner. Historically, there are two probable flags: the First National Confederate, and the First North Carolina Secession flag (see The Flags of Fort Ocracoke in Chapter 3), so these were chosen to make the site visible to both the ferries and the general public. SIDCO maintained these flags and the pole for the next two years until 2001, when workload and logistics prevented the upkeep of the flagpole assembly and it was removed.

THE FUTURE OF THE FORT

Is there anything that can be done, at this point, to further preserve Fort Ocracoke? Probably not. With the dynamic environment of Pamlico Sound, a feature that is uncovered one week ends up lying under several feet of sand after a hard nor'easter the next. The shifting sands themselves are probably the best guardian for the remaining cultural resources at Fort Ocracoke, and any further organized attempt to secure the site, as such, would be fruitless. On the contrary, the possibilities of an underwater museum might be one of the best ideas for the site's future. A self-guided tour of the submerged features of the site using underwater signs and "downlines" to lead the divers to each one might be just the way to not only preserve it but also keep it accessible to the public. New features would wash out periodically, and others would be covered, as well as the guidelines and signs, which would require some maintenance. This would need some upkeep, but the first underwater museum in North Carolina would be the result—a small price to pay. There would be some inevitable looting, but all this would be worth the trouble for such a wonderful asset.

With the size of the site proper, it is most probable that further information could be learned from future archaeological projects by other state entities, East Carolina University, graduate students and other accredited archaeological organizations. The site is huge, and much can be learned by parting the territory out to many associated projects. There are still many associated archaeological interests, such as the remaining mysteries of and including the Stone Fleet, Shell Castle, the Battle Galleys and CSS *Warren Winslow*—the list goes on of the incredible and massive collections of submerged history in the rich waters of Pamlico Sound.

THE WASHINGTON GRAYS

Though four other North Carolina/Confederate companies were "assigned" to the garrisoning of Fort Ocracoke, the information available suggests that the Washington Grays, banded in Washington, North Carolina, had enough to do with the fort and its daily operations to earn an honorable mention in this text, not to mention that three members of its ranks leave behind records that directly describe the fort and its history.[142]

This battery of heavy artillery, called the "Washington Grays," was accepted in State service for twelve months on April 22, 1861 and assigned to the 7th Regiment N.C. State Troops as Company A on May 29, 1861 and ordered to Ocracoke. On June 22, 1861 it was mustered into State service as Company K, 10th Regiment N.C. State Troops (1st Regiment N.C. Artillery), and on August 20 it was transferred to the Confederate States service. Originally known as "Sparrow's Company," after its first Captain, it later became known as "Shaw's Company" when 1st Lieutenant William Shaw succeeded Captain Thomas Sparrow, who was promoted to Major on January 9, 1863.

On August 29, 1861 this battery was captured at Fort Hatteras and confined at Fort Warren, Boston Harbor, Massachusetts, until paroled and exchanged. By the end of January 1862 the entire company had been exchanged and re-formed at Wilmington where it was detailed on garrison duty at Fort French. It remained at Fort French through June 1863 when it was transferred to Fort Lee, near the same city. It remained on garrison duty at Fort Lee until May 8–9, 1864. On May 8 a detachment was sent to Weldon under Lieutenant John M. Blount. The rest of the battery was transferred to Smithville on May 9, where it remained on guard duty until June 20 when it was ordered to North East. After spending three days at North East, the battery returned to Smithville where on June 26, 1864 it was further divided. Forty-one men were sent to Wilmington, and the balance of the battery remained at Smithville. Muster rolls indicate battery headquarters were located at Wilmington for July–October 1864. On November 10, 1864 the battery was included in a detachment sent to Masonboro Sound where it remained until recalled to Wilmington on December 16. From Wilmington it was sent to Fort Fisher where it participated in the action on December 24–25, 1864 and was captured when the fort fell on January 15, 1865. The men captured at Fort Fisher were confined at Elmira, New York, while the officers were sent to Fort Columbus, New York Harbor. All were confined until paroled for exchange or released after the war had ended.

The detachment at Weldon remained there from May 1864 until General Lawrence Baker withdrew to join General Johnston on April 12, 1865. Failing to penetrate the Federal lines, General Baker surrendered his command at Bunn's House, Nash County, on April 20, 1865. Lieutenant Blount's detachment was not listed on the parole rolls; consequently it must have left General Baker's command before he surrendered. The other detachments of the battery, on duty at Wilmington, were absorbed by other commands, and as infantry, after the evacuation of Wilmington; they participated in the subsequent operations below Kinston, at Bentonville, and were surrendered by General Johnston April 26, 1865.

The information contained in the following roster of the battery was compiled principally from the company muster rolls, which cover from the date of muster in through October 1864, less the rolls for November–December 1862 and March–April 1863 which were not found. Although there are no Roll of Honor records for this battery, useful information was obtained from receipt rolls, hospital records, prisoner of war records, and other primary records, supplemented by State pension applications, United Daughters of the Confederacy records, and post war rosters and histories.

Here we show the roster of the Grays at the time of their assignment at Fort Ocracoke and Portsmouth:

Washington Grays/Co. A, 7th North Carolina Volunteers, Heavy Artillery—Captain Thomas Sparrow, *Commanding*

SPARROW, THOMAS

Resided in Beaufort County where he enlisted at age 42, April 22, 1861 for twelve months.

Appointed Captain by Governor Ellis to rank from May 16, 1861. Captured at Fort Hatteras August 29, 1861 and confined at Fort Warren, Massachusetts until paroled and exchanged at Fort Monroe, Virginia about February 3, 1862. Promoted to Major January 9, 1863 and transferred to the Field and Staff of this regiment.

BLOUNT, JOHN M. *1st Lieutenant*

Resided in Beaufort County where he enlisted at age 21, April 22, 1861 for twelve months. Mustered in as Corporal. Captured at Fort Hatteras August 29, 1861 and confined at Fort Warren, Massachusetts until paroled and exchanged at Fort Monroe, Virginia about February 3, 1862. Appointed 2nd Lieutenant April 30, 1863 and promoted to 1st Lieutenant September 2, 1863. Detailed at Weldon May 8, 1864 where he remained through October 1864.

COLLINS, JOSIAH, JR. *1st Lieutenant*

Appointed 1st Lieutenant by Governor Ellis to rank from May 16, 1861. Detailed to Raleigh in June 1861 as State Ordnance Officer and attached to the State Adjutant General's Department.

FULFORD, IRVIN *2nd Lieutenant*

Resided in Beaufort County where he enlisted at age 22, April 24, 1861 for twelve months.

Mustered in as Private. Captured at Fort Hatteras August 29, 1861 and confined at Fort Warren, Massachusetts until paroled and exchanged at Fort Monroe, Virginia about February 3, 1862. Appointed Sergeant February 1862 and promoted to 1st Sergeant July–August 1863. Promoted to 2nd Lieutenant September 23, 1863. Captured at Fort Fisher January 15, 1865 and confined at Fort Columbus, New York Harbor until paroled and exchanged at City Point, Virginia, February 25–March 5, 1865.

PRIMROSE, CICERO S. *1st Lieutenant*

Temporarily attached to this company after his company, Company F of this regiment was captured at Fort Macon on April 26, 1862. Returned to Company F in August 1862 after it was exchanged.

THOMAS, ANTHONY J. *1st Lieutenant*

Resided in Beaufort County where he enlisted at age 22, April 22, 1861 for twelve months.

Appointed 2nd Lieutenant by Governor Ellis to rank from May 16, 1861. Captured at Fort Hatteras August 29, 1861 and confined to Fort Warren, Massachusetts until paroled and exchanged about February 3, 1862. Promoted to 1st Lieutenant January 9, 1863. Detailed at Wilmington in charge of military prison from July–August 1863 through October 1864.

WHITEHURST, JAMES J. *1st Lieutenant*

Enlisted in Beaufort County at age 24, April 22, 1861 for twelve months.

Appointed 2nd Lieutenant by Governor Ellis to rank from May 16, 1861. Captured at Fort Hatteras August 29, 1861 and confined at Fort Warren, Massachusetts until paroled and exchanged January 21, 1862. Promoted to 1st Lieutenant January

9, 1863. Transferred to 66th Regiment N.C. Troops upon promotion to Captain August 18, 1863.

NON-COMMISSIONED OFFICERS AND PRIVATES

ATKINSON, WILLIAM E. *Private*
Enlisted in Wake County April 15, 1864 for the war. Severely wounded and captured at Fort Fisher January 15, 1865.

ATTMORE, SITGREAVES *Private*
Enlisted in Wake County at age 34, March 22, 1864 for the war. Captured at Fort Fisher January 15, 1865 and confined at Elmira, New York until paroled and exchanged February 28, 1865. Admitted to hospital at Richmond, Virginia March 4, 1865 with debility where he was captured April 3, 1865. Transferred to hospital at Point Lookout, Maryland Mary 12, 1865 where he died May 22, 1865 of chronic diarrhea.

BARDUE, W.J. *Private*
Paroled at Goldsboro, North Carolina May 23, 1865.

BATTLE, GEORGE C. *Private*
Re-enlisted in Wake County April 14, 1864 for the war after having served in Company I 15th Regiment N.C. Troops (5th Regiment N.C. Volunteers). Detailed at Weldon through October 1864.

BAYNOR, WILLIAM W. *Corporal*
Enlisted in Beaufort County July 24, 1861 for the war. Mustered in as Private. Captured at Fort Hatteras August 29, 1861 and confined to Fort Warren, Massachusetts until paroled for exchange February 3, 1862. Appointed Corporal May–June 1863. Transferred to Company C, 40th Regiment N.C. Troops (3rd Regiment N.C. Artillery) June 9, 1864.

BELL, PATRICK H. *Private*
Enlisted in Edgecombe County April 1, 1862 for the war. Present until detailed at Weldon on May 8, 1864. Absent detailed through October 1864.

BLOUNT, CALVIN F. *Private*
Enlisted in Wake County March 25, 1864 for the war. Died at Wilmington April 28, 1864 of meningitis.

BOND, JOHN F. *Private*
Enlisted in Beaufort County April 22, 1861 for the war. Captured at Fort Hatteras August 29, 1861 and confined to Fort Warren, Massachusetts until paroled for

exchange February 3, 1862. Present or accounted for through October 1864. Captured at Fort Fisher January 15, 1865 and confined at Elmira, New York where he died February 18, 1865 of chronic diarrhea.

BORDEAUX, JAMES *Private*
Enlisted in New Hanover County May 1, 1864 for the war. Present or accounted for through August 1864.

BRIDGMAN, SETH *Private*
Born in Beaufort County where he resided as a merchant and enlisted at age 19, April 22, 1861 for twelve months. Assigned to duty in Captain Henry Harding's Company before being mustered into this company. Mustered into Captain Harding's Company, which became Company B, 61st Regiment N.C. Troops, November 9, 1861 as a Sergeant.

BRIMER, ANTHONY T. *Private*
Enlisted in New Hanover County March 26, 1863 for the war. Present until detailed at Weldon May 8, 1864. Absent detailed through October 1864.

BRINSON, WILLIAM C. *Sergeant*
Enlisted in New Hanover County July 8, 1862 for the war. Mustered in as Private. Appointed Sergeant November–December 1863. Present or accounted for through October 1864. Captured at Fort Fisher January 15, 1865 and confined at Elmira, New York until paroled for exchange February 25, 1865.

BROOKS, WILLIAM A. *Private*
Enlisted in Wake County April 16, 1864 for the war. Detailed at Weldon May 8, 1864. Absent detailed through October 1864.

BROWN, DAVID *Private*
Enlisted in Gaston County March 22, 1863 for the war. Discharged July 24, 1864 by reason of "incipient cataract of both eyes."

BROWN, J.L. *Private*
Enlisted in Beaufort County at age 26, April 22, 1861 for twelve months. Captured at Fort Hatteras August 29, 1861.

BURKHARDT, AMON *Private*
Enlisted in Beaufort County at age 25, April 22, 1961 for the war. Captured at Fort Hatteras August 29, 1861 and confined at Fort Warren, Massachusetts until paroled for exchange February 3, 1862. Absent sick throughout 1863 and reported as a deserter January 10, 1864.

BUXTORF, FREDERICK *Private*
Born in Berne, Switzerland, and was by occupation a merchant prior to enlisting in Beaufort County at age 26, April 22, 1861 for twelve months. Transferred to Company C, 40th Regiment N.C. Troops (3rd Regiment N.C. Artillery) October 6, 1861.

CANOY, JOHN H. *Private*
Resided in Randolph County where he enlisted March 23, 1863 for the war. Present or accounted for through October 1864. Captured at Fort Fisher January 15, 1865 and confined to Elmira, New York until released after taking Oath of Allegiance August 7, 1865.

CARNEY, JOHN N. *Private*
Enlisted in New Hanover County July 19, 1863 for the war. Deserted October 26, 1863.

CARVER, ALFRED B. *Private*
Born in Haywood County and was by occupation a farmer prior to enlistment in Wake County at age 33, March 27, 1864 for the war. Discharged at Fort Pender, Brunswick County, July 25, 1864 by reason of "chronic ulcers of both legs."

CASON, BENJAMIN F. *Private*
Enlisted in Pitt County May 14, 1862 for the war. Present until detailed at Weldon May 8, 1864. Absent detailed through October 1864.

CHAMBERS, JAMES G. *Private*
Enlisted in New Hanover County October 4, 1864 for the war. Captured at Fort Fisher January 15, 1865 and confined at Elmira, New York until paroled for exchange February 20, 1865. Died on route before exchanged.

CHISINHALL, JAMES R. *Private*
Born in Orange County and was by occupation a farmer prior to enlistment in Wake County at age 21, April 7, 1864 for the war. Discharged at Fort Pender, Brunswick County, July 25, 1864 by reason of physical disability.

CLARK, HENRY S. *Musician*
Enlisted in New Hanover County January 1, 1863 for the war. Mustered in as a Musician. Present or accounted for through October 1864. Captured at Fort Fisher January 15, 1865 and confined at Elmira, New York until paroled for exchange February 13, 1865. Detailed at Camp Lee near Richmond, Virginia after exchanged.

CLARK, ROBERT H. *Corporal*
Enlisted in Beaufort County at age 21, April 22, 1861 for twelve months. Mustered in as Private. Captured at Fort Hatteras August 29, 1861 and confined at Fort

Warren, Massachusetts until paroled for exchange December 17, 1861. Appointed Corporal December 1, 1863. Present until detailed at Weldon May 8, 1864. Absent detailed through October 1864.

COER, S.O. *Private*
Died at Point Lookout, Maryland November 1, 1863 and buried in Confederate Cemetery, Point Lookout.

COKER, JOHN L. *Private*
Transferred from Company H of this regiment November 12, 1863. Present or accounted for through October 1864. Captured at Fort Fisher January 15, 1865 and confined at Elmira, New York until released after taking Oath of Allegiance May 15, 1865.

CONGLETON, OWEN *Private*
Enlisted in New Hanover County at age 17, May 8, 1864 for the war. Captured at Fort Fisher January 15, 1865 and confined at Elmira, New York where he died February 24, 1865 of typhoid fever.

CORBIN, EDWARD *Private*
Enlisted in Beaufort County May 1, 1862 for the war. Detailed as a pile driver June 1862. Transferred to Company A, 2nd Regiment Confederate Engineer Troops October 1, 1863.

CORDON, WILLIAM W. *1st Sergeant*
Enlisted in Beaufort County at age 21, April 22, 1861 for twelve months. Mustered in as Corporal. Captured at Fort Hatteras August 29, 1861 and confined at Fort Warren, Massachusetts until paroled for exchange December 17, 1861. Promoted to Sergeant January–February 1863 and to 1st Sergeant November–December 1863. Present or accounted for through October 1864. Captured at Fort Fisher January 15, 1865 and confined at Elmira, New York until released after taking Oath of Allegiance July 11, 1865.

CORNELL, EZRA E. *Private*
Enlisted in Beaufort County at age 23, April 24, 1861 for twelve months. Captured at Fort Hatteras August 29, 1861 and confined at Fort Warren, Massachusetts until released on parole November 2, 1861.

CORNELL, JOHN W. *Private*
Enlisted in Beaufort County at age 21, April 22, 1861 for twelve months. Captured at Fort Hatteras August 29, 1861.

COWELL, WILLIAM B. *Private*
Enlisted in Beaufort County at age 28, April 22, 1861 for twelve months. Mustered in as Private. Captured at Fort Hatteras August 29, 1861 and confined at Fort Warren, Massachusetts until paroled for exchange December 17, 1861. Appointed Sergeant February–June 1862. Reduced to ranks when detailed to work on gunboats at Wilmington September 4, 1862. Absent detailed through April 1864. Detailed at Weldon May 8, 1864. Absent detailed through October 1864.

CULBERSON, JOSEPH J. *Private*
Born in Moore County and enlisted in Wake County at age 30, April 2, 1864 for the war. Discharged at Fort Pender, Brunswick County, June 10, 1864, by reason of "maiming of the hands produced by machines."

CUTHBERTSON, DAVID B. *Private*
Enlisted in Randolph County March 23, 1863 for the war. Admitted to hospital at Wilmington with intermittent fever October 30, 1863. After recovering he was detailed as a nurse at the hospital. Remained on detail through December 1864.

DANIEL, J.W. *Private*
Captured in Virginia and confined at Fort Warren, Massachusetts, November 1, 1861. Released February 3, 1862 on parole to be exchanged.

DAVIDSON, J.G. *Private*
Captured in Virginia and confined at Fort Warren, Massachusetts, November 1, 1861. Released February 3, 1862 on parole to be exchanged.

DAVIS, JOSEPH W. *Private*
Enlisted in Beaufort County at age 22, April 22, 1861 for twelve months. Captured at Fort Hatteras August 29, 1861 and confined at Fort Warren, Massachusetts until paroled for exchange February 3, 1862. Transferred to Company A, 17th Regiment N.C. Troops (2nd Organization) April 4, 1864.

DILL, SAMUEL L. *Private*
Enlisted in New Hanover County July 1, 1863 for the war. Present or accounted for through October 1864. Captured at Fort Fisher January 15, 1865 and confined at Elmira, New York until paroled and sent to James River, Virginia for exchange March 14, 1865.

DOUGHTY, CHARLES H. *Private*
Resided in Beaufort County where he enlisted at age 18, April 22, 1861 for twelve months. Assigned to duty in Captain William B. Rodman's Company before being mustered into this company. Mustered into Captain Rodman's Company, which

became Company C, 40th Regiment N.C. Troops (3rd Regiment N.C. Artillery) October 5, 1861 as a Corporal.

DOWNS, BRITTON E. *Private*
Transferred from C.S. Navy July 19, 1863. Deserted October 26, 1863.

DYMOTT, ROBERT E. *Private*
Enlisted in Beaufort County April 10, 1862 for the war. Present until detailed at Weldon May 8, 1864. Absent detailed through October 1864.

EARLS, DANIEL *Private*
Enlisted in Cleveland County February 26, 1863 for the war. Present or accounted for through October 1864. Captured at Fort Fisher January 15, 1865 and confined at Elmira, New York where he died April 1, 1865 of an "ulcer around the neck." Buried in Woodlawn National Cemetery, Elmira, New York.

EBORN, NYMPHAS O. *Private*
Born in Beaufort County where he resided as a farmer and enlisted at age 29, April 24, 1861 for twelve months. Assigned to duty in Captain James J. Leith's Company before mustered into this company. Mustered into Captain Leith's Company which became Company B, 17th Regiment N.C. Troops (1st Organization) August 18, 1861.

ELLIS, CHARLES T. *Private*
Enlisted in New Hanover County March 17, 1864 for the war. Present or accounted for through October 1864. Captured at Fort Fisher January 15, 1865 and confined at Elmira, New York where he died March 28, 1865 of diarrhea.

ELLISON, JOHN E. *Private*
Enlisted in Beaufort County at age 23, April 22, 1861 for twelve months. Assigned to duty in Captain James J. Leith's Company before being mustered into this company. Mustered into Captain Leith's Company, which became Company B, 17th Regiment N.C. Troops (1st Organization) August 18, 1861.

ELLISON, THOMAS H. *Private*
Born in Craven County and was by occupation a merchant prior to enlistment in Beaufort County at age 31, April 22, 1861 for twelve months. Discharged at Washington March 1862. Re-enlisted February 10, 1863 in Company G of this regiment.

ENGLISH, ROBERT L. *Private*
Enlisted in New Hanover County April 14, 1863 for the war. Present or accounted for until dropped from rolls October 21, 1864. Paroled at Greensboro May 24, 1865.

ETHERIDGE, ROSCOE *Private*
Enlisted in New Hanover County February 27, 1864 for the war. Present or accounted for through January 1865.

EVANS, STEPHEN *Private*
Enlisted in Wake County March 9, 1863 for the war. Died at Wilmington September 15, 1863 of chronic diarrhea.

FLOYD, HUGH H. *Private*
Born in Gaston County and was by occupation a farmer prior to enlistment in Wake County at age 30, March 30, 1864 for the war. Discharged at Fort Pender, Brunswick County, July 25, 1864 by reason of "division of extensor muscles of right leg interfering materially with locomotion."

FRAZIER, MURDOCK *Private*
Enlisted in New Hanover County February 14, 1863 for the war. Present until detailed at Fayetteville Arsenal May 1, 1864 and attached to Company G, 2nd Battalion N.C. Local Defense Troops at Fayetteville.

FRENCH, GEORGE R. *Private*
Enlisted in New Hanover County January 17, 1862 for the war. Present until detailed as clerk in General W.H.C. Whiting's headquarters May–June 1864. Absent detailed through October 1864.

FRY, JOHNSTON *Private*
Enlisted in New Hanover County December 25, 1863 for the war. Died at Wilmington January 3, 1864 of typhoid fever.

FURR, JOHN B. *Private*
Enlisted in New Hanover County March 24, 1864 for the war. Present or accounted for through October 1864. Captured at Fort Fisher January 15, 1865 and confined at Elmira, New York where he died March 3, 1865 of variola. Buried in Woodlawn National Cemetery, Elmira, New York.

GAINOR, WILLIAM T. *Private*
Enlisted in Pitt County May 14, 1862 for the war. Present or accounted for through October 1864. Captured at Fort Fisher January 15, 1865 and confined at Elmira, New York where he died March 4, 1865 of chronic diarrhea. Buried in Woodlawn National Cemetery, Elmira, New York.

GALLAGHER, C.K. *Private*
Enlisted in Beaufort County at age 36, April 22, 1861 for twelve months. Captured at Fort Hatteras August 29, 1861.

GAUTIER, ENDIMEON A. *Private*
Enlisted in Beaufort County at age 20, April 22, 1861 for twelve months. Mustered in as Sergeant. Reduced to ranks when detailed in Quartermaster Depot at Tarboro February–June 1862. Absent detailed through September 1862 when he was reported as a deserter.

GEER, EDWIN, JR. *Private*
Born in New Hanover County where he resided as a student and enlisted at age 19, July 10, 1862 for the war. Transferred to Company B, 61st Regiment N.C. Troops September 29, 1862.

GIBBS, WILLIAM *Private*
Transferred from Company K, 17th Regiment N.C. Troops (2nd Organization) April 11, 1862. Discharged at Wilmington May 29, 1863 by reason of disability caused by a wound.

GODFREY, OTT H. *Private*
Enlisted in Beaufort County April 22, 1861 for twelve months. Captured at Fort Hatteras August 29, 1861 and confined at Fort Warren, Massachusetts until paroled for exchange February 3, 1862.

GOFFIN, WILLIAM *Private*
Enlisted in Beaufort County at age 36, April 22, 1861 for twelve months. Captured at Fort Hatteras August 29, 1861 and confined at Fort Warren, Massachusetts until paroled for exchange February 3, 1862. Died January 2–5, 1864 of disease.

GRANT, SOLOMAN E. *Private*
Enlisted in New Hanover County April 16, 1864 for the war. Captured at Fort Fisher January 15, 1865 and confined at Elmira, New York where he died March 6, 1865 of diarrhea. Buried in Woodlawn National Cemetery, Elmira, New York.

GRIMMER, W.L. *Private*
Born in Pitt County and was by occupation a merchant and clerk prior to enlistment in Beaufort County at age 18, April 22, 1861 for twelve months. Captured at Fort Hatteras August 29, 1861 and confined at Fort Warren, Massachusetts until paroled for exchange December 17, 1861. Discharged from company upon appointment as 2nd Lieutenant of Company C, 13th Battalion N.C. Infantry January 28, 1862.

GRIST, ALLEN, JR. *Corporal*
Enlisted in Beaufort County at age 22, April 22, 1861 for twelve months. Mustered in as Corporal. Present or accounted for through October 1862 when he transferred to Company K, 41st Regiment N.C. Troops (3rd Regiment N.C. Cavalry).

GRIST, SAMUEL L. *Private*
Born in Beaufort County where he resided as a farmer and enlisted at age 21, April 22, 1862 for the war. Transferred to Company C, 61st Regiment N.C. Troops September 10, 1862.

GRIST, WILEY G. *Private*
Enlisted in New Hanover County September 28, 1862 for the war. Transferred to Company G, 41st Regiment N.C. Troops (3rd Regiment N.C. Cavalry) October 1862.

GURGANUS, JAMES R. *Private*
Enlisted in Edgecombe County October 20, 1864 for the war. Captured at Fort Fisher January 15, 1865 and confined at Elmira, New York until released after taking Oath of Allegiance July 7, 1865.

HALL, HARRISON *Sergeant*
Resided in Beaufort County where he enlisted at age 22, April 22, 1861 for twelve months. Mustered in as Corporal. Captured at Fort Hatteras August 29, 1861 and confined at Fort Warren, Massachusetts until paroled for exchange February 3, 1862. Appointed Sergeant February 1862. Present until appointed Acting Hospital Steward March 10, 1863, and assigned to Company H, 49th Regiment N.C. Troops.

HANCOCK, JAMES B. *Private*
Enlisted in Beaufort County at age 22, April 22, 1861 for twelve months. Assigned to duty in Captain William B. Rodman's Company before being mustered into this company. Mustered into Captain Rodman's Company, which became Company C, 40th Regiment N.C. Troops (3rd Regiment N.C. Artillery) October 5, 1861.

HANCOCK, JEREMIAH *Private*
Enlisted in New Hanover County October 8, 1864 for the war.

HANCOCK, WILLIAM H. *Private*
Enlisted in Beaufort County at age 20, April 22, 1861 for twelve months. Assigned to duty in Captain William B. Rodman's Company before being mustered into this company. Mustered into Captain Rodman's Company which became Company C, 40th Regiment N.C. Troops (3rd Regiment N.C. Artillery) October 5, 1861.

HANCOCK, ZUMARIAH *Private*
Resided in Guilford County and enlisted in New Hanover County July 18, 1863 for the war. Deserted August 20, 1863 and returned October 8, 1864. Captured at Fort Fisher January 15, 1865 and confined at Elmira, New York until released after taking Oath of Allegiance July 11, 1865.

HANKS, WILLIAM H. *Private*
Enlisted in Beaufort County at age 24, April 22, 1861 for twelve months. Transferred to C.S. Navy July 1861.

HARDENBERGH, SELBY *Private*
Resided in Beaufort County where he enlisted at age 19, April 22, 1861 for twelve months. Assigned to duty in Captain William H. Tripp's Company before being mustered into this company. Mustered into Captain Tripp's Company which later became Company B, 40th Regiment N.C. Troops (3rd Regiment N.C. Artillery) upon appointment as 1st Lieutenant October 1, 1861.

HARDENBERGH, THOMAS H. *Private*
Enlisted in Beaufort County at age 21, April 22, 1862 for twelve months. Discharged upon furnishing a substitute February–June 1862.

HARDISON, JAMES B. *Private*
Enlisted in Pitt County May 14, 1862 for the war. Present or accounted for through October 1864.

HARDISON, WILLIAM S. *Private*
Enlisted in Pitt County May 14, 1862 for the war. Present or accounted for through October 1864. Wounded and captured at Fort Fisher January 15, 1865. Died of wound at hospital in Morehead City January 21, 1865.

HARRELL, SAMUEL M. *Private*
Resided in Lenoir County and enlisted in Beaufort County at age 18, April 22, 1861 for twelve months. Captured at Fort Hatteras August 29, 1861 and confined at Fort Warren, Massachusetts until paroled for exchange February 3, 1862. Detailed at military prison at Wilmington from June 1863 through February 1865.

HARRELSON, BRICE *Private*
Resided in Caswell County and enlisted in New Hanover County March 17, 1864 for the war. Present or accounted for through October 1864. Wounded and captured at Fort Fisher January 15, 1865 and confined at Point Lookout, Maryland until released after taking Oath of Allegiance June 28, 1865.

HARRISON, THOMAS *Private*
Enlisted in Beaufort County at age 25, April 22, 1861 for twelve months. Captured at Fort Hatteras August 29, 1861.

HARVEY, EDWARD *Private*
Enlisted in Carteret County July 22, 1861 for the war. Detailed as clerk in office of Atlantic & North Carolina Railroad April–September 1862. Detailed as clerk in Adjutant's office, this regiment, in October 1862. Remained on detail and appointed Sergeant-Major August 20, 1863 and transferred to the Field and Staff of this regiment.

HARVEY, WILLIAM H. *Private*
Enlisted in Beaufort County at age 21, April 22, 1861 for twelve months. Captured at Fort Hatteras August 29, 1861 and confined at Fort Warren, Massachusetts until paroled for exchange February 3, 1862. Present until detailed at Weldon May 8, 1864. Absent detailed through October 1864.

HAWES, BEE *Private*
Enlisted in New Hanover County June 19, 1863 for the war. Deserted August 20, 1863.

HAWKINS, JOSPEH M. *Private*
Enlisted in Beaufort County at age 21, April 22, 1861 for twelve months. Mustered in as Private. Captured at Fort Hatteras August 29, 1861 and confined at Fort Warren, Massachusetts until paroled for exchange December 17, 1861. Appointed Corporal February–June 1862. Reduced to ranks November–December 1862. Present until detailed at Weldon May 8, 1864. Absent detailed through October 1864.

HAYDOCK, JAMES M. *Private*
Enlisted in Randolph County March 23, 1863 for the war. Deserted August 20, 1863.

HICKS, ELIAS F. *Private*
Enlisted in New Hanover County April 16, 1864 for the war. Killed in action at Fort Fisher January 15, 1865.

HOBBS, GEORGE A. *Corporal*
Transferred from Company A, 17th Regiment N.C. Troops (2nd Organization) April 4, 1864 as a Private. Appointed Corporal October 19, 1864. Captured at Fort Fisher January 15, 1865 and confined at Elmira, New York where he died March 21, 1865 of phthisis. Buried in Woodlawn National Cemetery, Elmira, New York.

HOLT, JAMES H. *Private*
Born in Alamance County and was by occupation a cashier prior to enlistment in Wake County at age 31, April 27, 1864 for the war. Discharged at Fort Pender,

Brunswick County, December 22, 1864 by reason of "having received a commission as Captain and Assistant Quartermaster of the Military Institute at Fayetteville, N.C."

IRELAND, HENRY BIZZELL *Private*
Born in Duplin County where he resided prior to enlistment in New Hanover County April 16, 1864 for the war. Detailed at Weldon May 8, 1864. Absent detailed through October 1864. Paroled April 14, 1864.

JARVIS, OLIVER *Private*
Enlisted in Beaufort County at age 31, April 22, 1861 for twelve months. Transferred to Company G, 19th Regiment N.C. Troops (2nd Regiment N.C. Cavalry) June 21, 1861 upon appointment as Lieutenant of Commissary.

JENKINS, WILLIAM H. *Private*
Enlisted in Beaufort County at age 20, April 22, 1861 for twelve months. Captured at Fort Hatteras August 29, 1861 and confined at Fort Warren, Massachusetts until paroled for exchange February 3, 1862. Present until transferred to Company B, 40th Regiment N.C. Troops (3rd Regiment N.C. Artillery) November 1, 1862.

JOHNSON, JOHN H. *Musician*
Born in Baltimore, Maryland and was by occupation a painter prior to enlistment in Beaufort County at age 20, April 22, 1861 for twelve months. Mustered in as Musician. Captured at Fort Hatteras August 29, 1861 and confined at Fort Warren, Massachusetts until paroled for exchange February 3, 1862. Transferred to Company B, 61st Regiment N.C. Troops September 15, 1862.

JONES, DANIEL S. *Private*
Resided in Guilford County and enlisted in New Hanover County June 17, 1863 for the war. Captured at Fort Fisher January 15, 1865 and confined to Elmira, New York until released after taking Oath of Allegiance June 23, 1865.

JONES, LAFEYETTE J. *Assistant Surgeon*
Temporarily attached by the Confederate Surgeon General to this company from September 1863 through January 26, 1864 when he was ordered back to Richmond. A Virginian, he had been commissioned Assistant Surgeon, Provisional Army of the Confederate States, to rank from August 16, 1862.

KELLY, JOHN T. *Private*
Born in Chatham County and was by occupation a hatter prior to enlistment in Wake County at age 26, April 15, 1864 for the war. Discharged at Fort Pender, Brunswick County by reason of "contraction of tendons of the right hand induced by a burn received in infancy."

KENNEDY, LEVI B. *Private*
Enlisted in Wake County April 15, 1864 for the war. Present or accounted for through October 1864. Captured at Fort Fisher January 15, 1865 and confined at Elmira, New York where he died February 6, 1865 of chronic diarrhea. Buried in Woodlawn National Cemetery, Elmira, New York.

KING, JAMES A. *Private*
Resided in Wake County where he enlisted at age 34, April 23, 1864 for the war. Present or accounted for through December 7, 1864 when he was furloughed from hospital at Wilmington for sixty days.

KIRBY, DIXON *Private*
Enlisted in Wake County March 29, 1864 for the war. Captured at Fort Fisher January 15, 1865 and confined at Elmira, New York where he died April 13, 1865 of variola. Buried in Woodlawn National Cemetery, Elmira, New York.

LABARBE, LEWIS J. *Private*
Enlisted in Beaufort County at age 32, April 22, 1861 for twelve months. Detailed in Quartermaster Department at Tarboro as clerk from July 1861 through October 1864.

LANIER, SAMUEL T. *Private*
Enlisted in Beaufort County at age 18, April 22, 1861 for twelve months. Captured at Fort Hatteras August 29, 1861 and confined at Fort Warren, Massachusetts where he died January 25, 1862 of typhoid fever.

LATHAM, JESSE G. *Sergeant*
Enlisted in Beaufort County at age 21, April 22, 1861 for twelve months. Mustered in as Private. Captured at Fort Hatteras August 29, 1861 and confined at Fort Warren, Massachusetts until paroled for exchange February 3, 1862. Appointed Corporal January–February 1863 and promoted to Sergeant May–June 1863. Present or accounted for through October 1864.

LATHAM, T.J., JR. *Private*
Enlisted in Beaufort County at age 25, April 22, 1861 for twelve months. Captured at Fort Hatteras August 29, 1861 and confined at Fort Warren, Massachusetts until paroled for exchange December 17, 1861.

LAWSON, WILLIAM *Private*
Captured at Fort Fisher January 15, 865 and confined at Elmira, New York where he died February 20, 1865 of diarrhea. Buried in Woodlawn National Cemetery, Elmira, New York.

LEACH, HUGH *Private*
Enlisted in Randolph County March 16, 1863 for the war. Present or accounted for through October 1864. Captured at Fort Fisher January 15, 1865 and confined at Elmira, New York where he died March 30, 1865 of diarrhea. Buried in Woodlawn National Cemetery, Elmira, New York.

LEDWELL, DAVID *Private*
Transferred from C.S. Navy July 19, 1863. Deserted September 21, 1863.

LEGGETT, URIAH S. *Private*
Enlisted in Pitt County May 14, 1862 for the war. Present or accounted for through October 1864.

LEMLY, ITHIEL T. *Private*
Enlisted in New Hanover County July 11, 1862 for the war. Present or accounted for until transferred to Company H of this regiment November 12, 1863.

LEMONS, JOHN A. *Private*
Enlisted in Union County March 23, 1863 for the war. Present or accounted for through October 1864. Captured at Fort Fisher January 15, 1865 and confined at Elmira, New York where he died May 20, 1865 of pneumonia. Buried in Woodlawn National Cemetery, Elmira, New York.

LIDDON, DAVID S. *Private*
Resided in Beaufort County where he enlisted at age 21, April 22, 1861 for twelve months. Captured at Fort Hatteras August 29, 1861 and confined at Fort Warren, Massachusetts until paroled for exchange February 3, 1862. Present or accounted for through October 1864. Captured at Fort Fisher January 15, 1865 and confined at Elmira, New York until released after taking Oath of Allegiance May 29, 1865.

LILLY, WILLIAM B. *Private*
Transferred from Company C, 40th Regiment N.C. Troops (3rd Regiment N.C. Artillery) June 9, 1864. Captured at Fort Fisher January 15, 1865 and confined at Elmira, New York until released after taking Oath of Allegiance July 19, 1865.

LITTLE, ALEXANDER H. *Private*
Enlisted in Beaufort County April 22, 1861 for twelve months. Captured at Fort Hatteras August 29, 1861 and confined at Fort Warren, Massachusetts until paroled for exchange December 17, 1861. Present or accounted for through October 1864. Wounded and captured at Fort Fisher January 15, 1865.

LIVERMAN, JESSE *Private*
Captured at Fort Hatteras August 29, 1861 and confined at Fort Warren, Massachusetts until paroled for exchange November 2, 1861. Enlisted in Pitt County May 8, 1862 for the war. Present or accounted for through October 1864.

LONGMAN, JAMES *Private*
Enlisted in Beaufort County at age 48, April 22, 1861 for twelve months. Assigned to duty in Captain Charles P. Jones' Company, which became 2nd Company G, 36th Regiment N.C. Troops (2nd Regiment N.C. Artillery). Never mustered into service.

MALLICOTE, JOHN *Private*
Died at Camp Douglas, Illinois March 19, 1865 and buried at Oak Woods Cemetery, Chicago, Illinois.

MALLISON, DAVID B. *Private*
Resided in Beaufort County and enlisted in New Hanover County at age 17, January 1, 1863 for the war. Present or accounted for through October 1864. Captured at Fort Fisher January 15, 1965 and confined at Elmira, New York until released after taking Oath of Allegiance May 19, 1865.

MALLISON, JAMES C. *Private*
Enlisted in Beaufort County at age 19, April 22, 1861 for twelve months. Captured at Fort Hatteras August 29, 1861 and confined at Fort Warren, Massachusetts until paroled for exchange February 3, 1862. Present until detailed at Weldon May 8, 1864. Absent detailed through October 1864.

MALLISON, WILLIAM CHARLES *Private*
Born in Beaufort County where he resided as a sail maker and enlisted at age 18, April 24, 1861 for twelve months. Escaped capture at Fort Hatteras August 29, 1861 and joined Company C, 61st Regiment N.C. Troops until his company was exchanged in April 1862. Returned to company about April 11, 1862. Present or accounted for through October 1864.

MANESS, ALFRED W. *Private*
May–June 1863 muster roll carries the remark that he deserted April 22, 1863. Returned from desertion February 16, 1864 and re-enlisted on that date in New Hanover County for the war. Deserted July 11, 1864.

MANESS, LEWIS W. *Private*
Enlisted in New Hanover County March 14, 1863 for the war. Present or accounted for through October 1864. Wounded and captured at Fort Fisher January 15, 1865 and confined at Point Lookout, Maryland where he died of wound February 15, 1865.

MANESS, MARSHALL G. *Private*
Enlisted in New Hanover County March 25, 1864 for the war. Detailed at Weldon through October 1864.

MASTERS, SAMUEL *Private*
Enlisted in New Hanover County July 11, 1862 for the war. Discharged at Wilson October 13, 1863 by reason of "disease of heart."

MASTIN, C.H. *Corporal*
Enlisted in Beaufort County at age 44, April 22, 1861 for twelve months. Appears as Corporal on muster roll dated July 23, 1861; however, he was discharged before the company was mustered in.

McCULLOUGH, J.A. *Private*
Enlisted in Beaufort County at age 22, April 22, 1861 for twelve months. Never mustered into company.

McDONALD, JOHN *Surgeon*
Enlisted in Beaufort County April 22, 1861 for twelve months. Before being mustered into this company he contracted with the Surgeon General of the Confederate Government as a surgeon and was assigned to General Hospital, Orange Court House, Virginia. Later appointed Assistant Surgeon, Provisional Army of the Confederate States.

McINTOSH, DANIEL *Private*
Enlisted in Wake County April 12, 1864 for the war. Captured at Fort Fisher January 15, 1865 and confined at Elmira, New York where he died April 2, 1865 of diarrhea. Buried in Woodlawn National Cemetery, Elmira, New York.

McLOUGHLIN, MALCOLM *Private*
Enlisted in Beaufort County at age 19, April 22, 1861 for twelve months. Captured at Fort Hatteras August 29, 1861 and confined at Fort Warren, Massachusetts until paroled for exchange February 2, 1862. Deserted at Washington in April 1862.

McWILLIAMS, PETER *Private*
Born in Beaufort County where he resided as a coach trimmer and enlisted at age 17, April 22, 1861 for twelve months. Captured at Fort Hatteras August 29, 1861 and confined at Fort Warren, Massachusetts until paroled for exchange December 17, 1861. Transferred to Company B, 61st Regiment N.C. Troops September 13–17, 1862.

MELVIN, WILLIAM *Private*
Resided in Alamance County where he enlisted March 14, 1863 for the war. Present or accounted for through October 1864. Captured at Fort Fisher January 15, 1865 and confined at Elmira, New York until released after taking Oath of Allegiance June 12, 1865.

MOORE, WILSON E. *Private*
Resided in New Hanover County where he enlisted April 13, 1863 for the war. Present or accounted for through October 1864. Wounded and captured at Fort Fisher January 15, 1865 and confined at Fort Delaware, Delaware until released after taking Oath of Allegiance May 9, 1865.

MOORING, WILLIAM B. *Private*
Born in Beaufort County where he resided as a farmer and merchant and enlisted at age 22, April 22, 1861 for twelve months. Assigned to duty in Captain William B. Rodman's Company before being mustered into this company. Mustered into Captain Rodman's Company, which became Company C, 40th Regiment N.C. Troops (3rd Regiment N.C. Artillery) October 23, 1862.

MORHN, CHARLES *Private*
Enlisted in Beaufort County at age 27, April 22, 1861 for twelve months. Captured at Fort Hatteras August 29, 1861 and confined at Fort Warren, Massachusetts until paroled for exchange February 3, 1862. Died of yellow fever October 23, 1862.

MORTON, VALENTINE R. *Private*
Enlisted in Beaufort County at age 27, April 22, 1861 for twelve months. Discharged on furnishing a substitute February 28–June 30, 1862.

MOZINGO, JOHN W. *Private*
Enlisted in Wake County March 23, 1864 for the war. Deserted August 5, 1864.

MURPH, DANIEL WASHINGTON *Private*
Enlisted in Lincoln County March 12, 1863 for the war. Present or accounted for through September 9, 1864 when he was furloughed from hospital at Charlotte. Killed in action at Fort Fisher December 25, 1864.

MURPHY, MILES *Private*
Enlisted in Randolph County March 23, 1863 for the war. Captured at Fort Fisher January 15, 1865 and confined at Elmira, New York until transferred for exchange March 2, 1865.

MURPHY, WILLIAM T. *Private*
Enlisted in Randolph County March 29, 1864 for the war. Deserted July 18, 1863 and returned October 8, 1864. Wounded and captured at Fort Fisher January 15, 1865 and confined at Point Lookout, Maryland until released after taking Oath of Allegiance June 3, 1865.

MYERS, W.B. *Private*
Enlisted in Beaufort County at age 43, April 22, 1861 for twelve months. Detailed as Commissary of Fort Ocracoke before being mustered in. Appointed Captain, Commissary of Subsistence, November 11, 1861 and assigned to post at Tarboro.

NICHOLS, HAZARD *Private*
Transferred from 2nd Company C, 36th Regiment N.C. Troops (2nd Regiment N.C. Artillery) February 1, 1863. Present or accounted for through October 1864. Captured at Fort Fisher January 15, 1865 and confined at Elmira, New York where he died March 20, 1965 of chronic diarrhea. Buried in Woodlawn National Cemetery, Elmira, New York.

NORMAN, JAMES S. *Corporal*
Resided in Beaufort County where he enlisted April 16, 1862 for the war. Mustered in as Private and appointed Corporal November–December 1863. Present or accounted for through October 1864. Captured at Fort Fisher January 15, 1865 and confined at Elmira, New York until released after taking Oath of Allegiance July 11, 1865.

OLIVER, GEORGE W. *Private*
Born in Bertie County and was by occupation a farmer prior to enlistment in Beaufort County at age 18, July 10, 1861 for the war. Captured at Fort Hatteras August 29, 1861 and confined at Fort Warren, Massachusetts until paroled for exchange February 3, 1862. Deserted September 12, 1863 and enlisted in Company E, 2nd Regiment N.C. Infantry (Union) October 6, 1863.

ORISON, J.L. *Private*
Captured in Virginia and confined at Fort Warren, Massachusetts November 1, 1861. Paroled for exchange January 6, 1862.

OTT, GODFREY *Private*
Enlisted in Beaufort County at age 24, April 22, 1861 for twelve months. Captured at Fort Hatteras August 29, 1861 and confined at Fort Warren, Massachusetts until paroled for exchange February 3, 1862. Present or accounted for through October 1864.

OWEN, JAMES *Private*
Re-enlisted November 19, 1862 in New Hanover County for the war after having served in Company A, 1st Regiment N.C. Infantry (6 months, 1861). Transferred to 2nd Company C 36th Regiment N.C. Troops (2nd Regiment N.C. Artillery) February 1, 1863.

PARVIN, WILLIAM AUGUSTUS *Private*
Enlisted in Beaufort County at age 22, May 8, 1861 for twelve months. Captured at Fort Hatteras August 29, 1861 and confined at Fort Warren, Massachusetts until paroled for exchange February 3, 1862. Detailed as crew member of a government transport, Samuel Hines, June 5, 1863. Absent detailed through October 1864.

PATE, JAMES *Private*
Enlisted in Pitt County May 8, 1862 for the war. Present or accounted for through October 1864.

PATE, JOSEPH *Private*
Born in Beaufort County where he resided as a seaman and enlisted at age 21, May 8, 1861 for twelve months. Temporarily attached to Company B, 61st Regiment N.C. Troops when this company was captured at Fort Hatteras August 29, 1861. Present or accounted for until transferred to C.S. Navy July 19, 1863.

PATRICK, WILLIAM H. *Private*
Born in Beaufort County where he resided as a farmer and enlisted at age 24, April 22, 1861 for twelve months. Captured at Fort Hatteras August 29, 1861 and confined at Fort Warren, Massachusetts until paroled for exchange February 3, 1862. Transferred to Company B, 61st Regiment N.C. Troops September 8, 1862, having been elected 2nd Lieutenant of that company September 5, 1862.

PEDRICK, WILLIAM J. *Private*
Enlisted in Beaufort County at age 22, April 22, 1861 for twelve months. Present or accounted for until detailed as a crew member of the government transport Samuel Hines June 5, 1863. Absent detailed through October 1864.

PERRY, LEWIS H. *Private*
Resided in Edgecombe County and enlisted in New Hanover County October 20, 1864 for the war. Captured at Fort Fisher January 15, 1865 and confined at Elmira, New York until released after taking Oath of Allegiance July 9, 1865.

PHILIPS, J.B. *Private*
Resided in Nash County where he enlisted in December 1864 for the war.

POTTS, J.R. *Sergeant*
Enlisted in Beaufort County at age 21, April 22, 1861 for twelve months. Mustered in as Sergeant. Captured at Fort Hatteras August 29, 1861 and confined to Fort Warren, Massachusetts until paroled for exchange December 17, 1861.

PRESNELL, WILLIAM *Private*
Appears on May–June 1863 muster roll with the remark that he was discharged June 1, 1863 by reason of disability.

PUGH, ALEXANDER H. *Private*
Enlisted in Randolph County April 6, 1863 for the war. Deserted January 10, 1864. Paroled at Greensboro May 10, 1865.

PUGH, WILLIAM WASHINGTON *Private*
Enlisted in Beaufort County at age 19, April 22, 1861 for twelve months. Captured at Fort Hatteras August 29, 1861 and confined at Fort Warren, Massachusetts until paroled for exchange February 3, 1862. Present or accounted for through October 1864. Captured at Fort Fisher January 15, 1865 and confined at Elmira, New York until transferred for exchange February 20, 1965. Furloughed from hospital at Richmond, Virginia March 15, 1865 for thirty days.

QUINN, LEWIS C. *Private*
Resided in Beaufort County where he enlisted at age 19, April 22, 1861 for twelve months. Temporarily attached to Company I, 3rd Regiment N.C. State Troops when this company was captured at Fort Hatteras August 29, 1861. Returned to company after it was exchanged in February 1862. Present until detailed at the military prison at Wilmington January–February 1864. Absent detailed through October 1864.

RAWLS, JOSPEH J. *Private*
Enlisted in Pitt County May 14, 1862 for the war. Present or accounted for through October 1864. Wounded at Fort Fisher December 25, 1864. Captured at Fort Fisher January 15, 1865 and confined at Elmira, New York until released after taking Oath of Allegiance July 26, 1865.

RAYFIELD, EDWARD J. *Private*
Resided in Beaufort County where he enlisted May 8, 1862 for the war. Present or accounted for through October 1864. Wounded and captured at Fort Fisher January 15, 1865 and confined at Fort Delaware, Delaware until released after taking Oath of Allegiance June 7, 1865.

REANEY, HENRY J. *Private*
Enlisted in Beaufort County at age 19, April 22, 1861 for twelve months. Captured at Fort Hatteras August 29, 1861 and confined at Fort Warren, Massachusetts until paroled for exchange February 3, 1862. Died at Wilmington June 28, 1863 of typhoid fever.

REANEY, JOHN E. *Sergeant*
Enlisted in Beaufort County January 27, 1862 for the war. Mustered in as Private and appointed Corporal May–June 1863. Promoted to Sergeant September–October 1863. Present or accounted for through October 1864.

REDDITT, DAVID F. *Sergeant*
Resided in Beaufort County where he enlisted as age 26, April 22, 1861 for twelve months. Mustered in as Sergeant. Temporarily attached to Company B, 61st Regiment N.C. Troops when this company was captured at Fort Hatteras August 29, 1861. Served as 1st Sergeant in Company B, 61st Regiment N.C. Troops. Returned to company after it was exchanged in February 1862. Transferred to Company B, 61st Regiment N.C. Troops September 1, 1862 having been elected 1st Lieutenant of that company September 5, 1862.

REID, LOUIS H. *Private*
Enlisted in Beaufort County at age 21, April 22, 1861 for twelve months. Assigned to duty in Captain Charles P. Jones' Company before being mustered into this company. Mustered into Captain Jones' Company, which became 2nd Company G, 36th Regiment N.C. Troops (2nd Regiment N.C. Artillery) September 23, 1861 as a Sergeant.

RESPESS, HENRY *Private*
Enlisted in Beaufort County at age 18, April 22, 1861 for twelve months. Present or accounted for through May 1863. Died at Wilmington June 2–3, 1863 of typhoid fever.

RESPESS, JOHN J. *Private*
Born in Beaufort County where he resided as a farmer and enlisted at age 17, April 22, 1861 for twelve months. Assigned to Company B, 61st Regiment N.C. Troops before being mustered into this company. Mustered into Company B, 61st Regiment N.C. Troops November 9, 1861.

RESPESS, WILLIAM O. *Private*
Transferred from Company I, 3rd Regiment N.C. State Troops May 5, 1862. Wounded at Washington October 1862. Discharged at Wilson April 13, 1863 by reason of wound.

RICHARDSON, GEORGE W. *Private*
Enlisted in Beaufort County at age 19, April 22, 1861 for twelve months. Captured at Fort Hatteras August 29, 1861 and confined at Fort Warren, Massachusetts until paroled for exchange February 3, 1862. Present until detailed in Ordnance Department at Wilmington August 23, 1863. Absent detailed through October 1864. Paroled at Greensboro May 1865.

ROBBINS, THOMAS A. *1st Sergeant*
Enlisted in Beaufort County at age 21, April 22, 1861 for twelve months. Mustered in as 1st Sergeant. Captured at Fort Hatteras August 29, 1861 and confined at Fort Warren, Massachusetts until paroled for exchange February 3, 1862. Discharged April 16, 1862 on furnishing a substitute.

ROBERSON, HARRISON *Private*
Transferred from Company F, 17th Regiment N.C. Troops (2nd Organization) April 27, 1864. Captured at Fort Fisher January 15, 1965 and confined at Elmira, New York where he died March 7, 1865 of pneumonia. Buried in Woodlawn National Cemetery, Elmira, New York.

ROGERSON, SAMUEL *Private*
Enlisted in Beaufort County at age 24, April 22, 1861 for twelve months. Captured at Fort Hatteras August 29, 1861 and confined at Fort Warren, Massachusetts until paroled for exchange February 3, 1862. Died March 10, 1862 of typhoid pneumonia.

ROSLER, J.A. *Private*
Enlisted in Pasquotank County at age 21, April 22, 1861 for twelve months. Transferred to the C.S. Navy July 1861 for service on the Forest.

SANFORD, JOHN L. *Private*
Enlisted in Beaufort County August 10, 1861 for the war. Captured at Fort Hatteras August 29, 1861 and confined at Fort Warren, Massachusetts until paroled for exchange February 3, 1862. Present or accounted for through October 1864.

SATTERTHWAITE, THOMAS H. *Corporal*
Resided in Beaufort County where he enlisted at age 21, April 24, 1861 for twelve months. Appointed Corporal and assigned to duty in Company B, 61st Regiment N.C. Troops November 9, 1861 as 1st Lieutenant.

SCHENCK, SAMUEL G. *Sergeant*
Enlisted in Beaufort County at age 28, April 22, 1861 for twelve months. Mustered in as Private. Captured at Fort Hatteras August 29, 1861 and confined at Fort Warren,

Massachusetts until paroled for exchange February 3, 1862. Appointed Sergeant February–June 1862. Transferred to Company G of this regiment September 27, 1862.

SECREST, LAFAYETTE A. *Private*
Enlisted in New Hanover County May 11, 1864 for the war. Present or accounted for through October 1864. Captured at Fort Fisher January 15, 1865 and confined at Elmira, New York where he died April 13, 1865 of "spasm of glottis." Buried in Woodlawn National Cemetery, Elmira, New York.

SHAW, EDWARD B. *Corporal*
Enlisted in Beaufort County at age 28, April 22, 1861 for twelve months. Mustered in as Private. Appointed Corporal January–February 1863. Present or accounted for through February 1863.

SHAW, R.B. *Private*
Enlisted in Beaufort County at age 19, April 22, 1861 for twelve months. Never mustered into service.

SINNETT, ASA R. *Private*
Enlisted in Beaufort County August 10, 1861 for the war. Captured at Fort Hatteras August 29, 1861 and confined at Fort Warren, Boston Harbor, Massachusetts until paroled for exchange December 17, 1861. Died at Wilmington March 16–19, 1863 of disease.

SMITH, A.R. *Private*
Captured at Fort Hatteras August 29, 1861 and confined at Fort Warren, Massachusetts until paroled for exchange December 17, 1861. Furloughed from hospital at Richmond, Virginia January 20, 1864 for seven days.

SMITH, JAMES M. *Private*
Enlisted in New Hanover County April 16, 1864 for the war. Transferred to Captain W.R. Bass' Company N.C. Troops July–August 1864.

SPARROW, ALONZO J. *Private*
Enlisted in New Hanover County November 25, 1862 for the war. Present or accounted for through October 1864.

SPARROW, GEORGE A. *Private*
Transferred from 2nd Company G, 36th Regiment N.C. Troops (2nd Regiment N.C. Artillery) May 3, 1862. Later discharged from this company and re-enlisted in 2nd Company G, 36th Regiment N.C. Troops (2nd Regiment N.C. Artillery).

SPARROW, STEPHEN D. *Sergeant*
Enlisted in Pitt County May 1, 1862 for the war. Mustered in as Private and appointed Sergeant September–October 1862. Transferred to the Engineer Corps August 16, 1863.

STALLINGS, JOHN E. *Private*
Enlisted in Beaufort County at age 20, April 22, 1861 for twelve months. Captured at Fort Hatteras August 29, 1861 and confined to Fort Warren, Massachusetts until paroled for exchange February 3, 1862. Present or accounted for through October 1864.

STALLINGS, SLADE R. *Private*
Enlisted in Beaufort County at age 26, April 2, 1861 for twelve months. Mustered in as Private. Captured at Fort Hatteras August 29, 1861 and confined at Fort Warren, Massachusetts until paroled for exchange February 3, 1862. Appointed Corporal September–October 1863 and reduced to ranks January–February 1864 for being absent without leave for two months. Present or accounted for through October 1864. Captured at Fort Fisher January 15, 1865 and confined at Elmira, New York where he died March 10, 1865 of pneumonia. Buried at Woodlawn National Cemetery, Elmira, New York.

STANCIL, GODFREY A. *Private*
Enlisted in New Hanover County May 2, 1864 for the war. Detailed at Weldon through October 1864.

STANLEY, THEODORE H. *Private*
Enlisted in New Hanover County March 8, 1863 for the war. Present until detailed at Weldon May 8, 1864. Absent detailed through October 1864.

STEVENSON, WILLIAM M. *Sergeant*
Born in Beaufort County where he resided as a merchant and enlisted at age 21, April 22, 1861 for twelve months. Mustered in as Sergeant. Transferred to Company B, 61st Regiment N.C. Troops in October 1861 upon being elected 2nd Lieutenant.

STOUT, JAMES A. *Private*
Enlisted in Randolph County March 23, 1863 for the war. Present or accounted for through October 1864.

STUART, J.E. *Private*
Appears on May–June 1863 muster roll with the remark that he "deserted from company on the 22 April 1863."

SUMNER, BRIGHT *Private*
Enlisted in Randolph County March 3, 1863 for the war. Deserted August 20, 1863 and returned December 14, 1863. Died at Smithville June 29, 1864 of disease.

SWINDELL, FRANCIS M. *Private*
Enlisted in Beaufort County at age 19, April 22, 1861 for twelve months. Captured at Fort Hatteras August 29, 1861 and confined at Fort Warren, Massachusetts until paroled for exchange December 17, 1861. Discharged April 10, 1862 on furnishing a substitute.

THOMAS, CHRISTOPHER C. *Private*
Enlisted in Beaufort County at age 22, April 22, 1861 for the war. Captured at Fort Hatteras August 29, 1861 and confined at Fort Warren, Massachusetts until paroled for exchange February 3, 1862. Present until transferred to Company F, 17th Regiment N.C. Troops (2nd Organization).

THOMAS, JOHN A., JR. *Private*
Enlisted in Beaufort County at age 19, April 22, 1861 for twelve months. Assigned to Captain William H. Tripp's Company before being mustered into this company. Mustered into Captain Tripp's Company which became Company B, 40th Regiment N.C. Troops (3rd Regiment N.C. Artillery) December 9, 1861 as Sergeant.

TURNER, RANDOLPH R. *Corporal*
Enlisted in Beaufort County August 10, 1861 for the war. Mustered in as Private. Captured at Fort Hatteras August 29, 1861 and confined at Fort Warren, Massachusetts until paroled for exchange February 3, 1862. Died at Wilmington November 13, 1863 of acute dysentery.

TURNER, THOMAS *Private*
Enlisted in Caswell County March 7, 1863 for the war. Deserted November–December 1863.

UTLEY, MIRABEAU *Private*
Enlisted in New Hanover County April 6, 1864 for the war. Present of accounted for through October 1864.

VAUGHN, JAMES W. *Private*
Enlisted in New Hanover County April 22, 1863 for the war. Present or accounted for through October 1864.

VINCENT, BENJAMIN W. *Private*
Enlisted in Wayne County March 18, 1864 for the war. Transferred to Company H of this regiment September 17, 1864.

VOLIVA, JOSEPH P. *Private*
Enlisted in Beaufort County at age 20, May 8, 1861 for twelve months. Captured at Fort Hatteras August 29, 1861 and confined at Fort Warren, Massachusetts until paroled for exchange February 3, 1862. Present or accounted for through October 1864.

VON EBERSTEIN, WILLIAM H. *Sergeant*
Born in St. Servan, France, and was by occupation an engineer prior to enlistment in Beaufort County at age 40, April 22, 1861 for twelve months. Mustered in as Sergeant. Present or accounted for until transferred to Field and Staff, 61st Regiment N.C. Troops July 3, 1863 on promotion to Sergeant-Major. Discharged near Richmond, Virginia October 15, 1864 due to wounds.

WALKER, CHARLES *Private*
Died at Wilmington June 10, 1863 of typhoid fever.

WALLACE, JAMES M. *Private*
Enlisted in Beaufort County at age 18, April 22, 1861 for twelve months. Transferred to Company H, 17th Regiment N.C. Troops (1st Organization) before being mustered into this company.

WALLCOTT, STEPHEN F. *Private*
Enlisted in Beaufort County August 10, 1861 for the war. Captured at Fort Hatteras August 29, 1861 and confined at Fort Warren, Massachusetts until paroled for exchange February 3, 1862. Present until transferred to C.S. Navy July 19, 1863.

WATERS, ASA *Private*
Enlisted in Beaufort County at age 18, April 22, 1861 for twelve months. Captured at Fort Hatteras August 29, 1861 and confined at Fort Warren, Massachusetts until paroled for exchange February 3, 1862. Present through December 1863 and detailed as a nurse at Wilmington from January through October 1864.

WATERS, BARTEMUS *Private*
Enlisted in Beaufort County at age 22, April 4, 1861 for twelve months. Captured at Fort Hatteras August 29, 1861 and confined at Fort Warren, Massachusetts until paroled for exchange February 3, 1862. Present until detailed at Weldon May 8, 1864. Absent detailed through October 1864.

WATERS, JAMES C. *Private*
Enlisted in Beaufort County at age 28, April 24, 1861 for twelve months. Captured at Fort Hatteras August 20, 1861 and confined at Fort Warren, Massachusetts until paroled for exchange February 3, 1862. Present or accounted for through October 1864. Captured at Fort Fisher January 15, 1865 and confined at Elmira, New York until paroled for exchange February 20, 1865. Furloughed from hospital at Richmond, Virginia March 16, 1865 for thirty days.

WATERS, JOHN *Private*
Enlisted in New Hanover County September 22, 1863 for the war. Deserted September 23, 1863.

WATSON, WILLIAM J. *Private*
Enlisted in New Hanover County March 10, 1864 for the war. Paroled at High Point May 2, 1865.

WHITAKER, JAMES REID *Private*
Enlisted in Beaufort County at age 20, April 22, 1861 for twelve months. Captured at Fort Hatteras August 29, 1861 and confined at Fort Warren, Massachusetts until paroled for exchange February 3, 1862. Present or accounted for through October 1864.

WHITEHEAD, JAMES S. *Private*
Born in Pitt County where he resided as a lawyer prior to enlistment in Beaufort County at age 24, May 8, 1861 for twelve months. Captured at Fort Hatteras August 29, 1861 and confined at Fort Warren, Massachusetts until paroled for exchange February 3, 1862. Transferred to Company E, 55th Regiment N.C. Troops on being appointed Captain April 1, 1862.

WHITLEY, THOMAS L. *Private*
Resided in Martin County and enlisted in New Hanover County October 20, 1864 for the war. Wounded and captured at Fort Fisher January 15, 1865 and confined at Fort Delaware, Delaware until released after taking Oath of Allegiance June 8, 1865.

WILLIAM, J.W. *Private*
Appears on May–June 1863 muster roll with the remark that he "deserted from company on the 22 April 1863."

WILLIAMS, DORSON M. *Private*
Enlisted in Wake County April 16, 1864 for the war. Present or accounted for through October 1864.

WILLIAMS, SAMUEL W. *Private*
Enlisted in Beaufort County at age 25, April 23, 1861 for twelve months. Captured at Fort Hatteras August 29, 1861 and confined at Fort Warren, Massachusetts until paroled for exchange February 3, 1862. Present or accounted for through October 1864.

WILLIAMS, S.M. *Private*
Enlisted in New Hanover County September 1, 1862 for the war.

WILLIAMS, WILLIAM *Private*
Deserted from company April 22, 1863 and returned February 16, 1864. Deserted a second time July 11, 1864.

WILLIS, CHARLES T. *Private*
Resided in Carteret County and enlisted in New Hanover County July 1, 1862 for the war. Present or accounted for through October 1864. Captured at Fort Fisher January 15, 1865 and confined at Elmira, New York until released after taking Oath of Allegiance June 16, 1865.

WILLIS, WILLIAM B. *Private*
Enlisted in Beaufort County at age 22, April 22, 1861 for twelve months. Captured at Fort Hatteras August 29, 1861 and confined at Fort Warren, Massachusetts until paroled for exchange November 1861. Present until detailed in Navy Yard at Wilmington September 4, 1862. Absent detailed through October 1864.

WILSON, CHARLES *Private*
Enlisted in Beaufort County at age 23, May 8, 1861 for twelve months. Transferred to C.S. Navy May 8–July 25, 1961.

WOODLEY, WILLIAM T. *Private*
Enlisted in Beaufort County at age 19, October 27, 1861 for twelve months. Never mustered into this company and joined Company K, 41st Regiment N.C. Troops (3rd Regiment N.C. Cavalry.) Mustered into that company November 6, 1861.

WOOLARD, HENRY R. *Corporal*
Enlisted in Beaufort County at age 23, April 22, 1861 for twelve months. Mustered in as Private. Captured at Fort Hatteras August 29, 1861 and confined at Fort Warren, Massachusetts until paroled for exchange February 3, 1862. Appointed Corporal October 1, 1863. Present or accounted for through October 1864.

WOOLARD, JACOB B. *Sergeant*
Enlisted in Beaufort County at age 23, April 22, 1861 for twelve months. Mustered in as Private. Captured at Fort Hatteras August 29, 1861 and confined at Fort

Warren, Massachusetts until paroled for exchange February 3, 1862. Appointed Corporal May–June 1863 and promoted to Sergeant September–October 1863. Present or accounted for through October 1864.

WRIGHT, JAMES L. *Private*
Enlisted in Wake County April 10, 1864 for the war. Present or accounted for through October 1864. Captured at Fort Fisher January 15, 1865 and confined at Elmira, New York where he died April 18, 1865 of variola. Buried in Woodlawn National Cemetery, Elmira, New York.

WROTON, THOMAS O. *Private*
Enlisted in Beaufort County at age 22, April 22, 1861 for twelve months. Captured at Fort Hatteras August 29, 1861 and confined at Fort Warren, Massachusetts until paroled for exchange February 3, 1862. Present until transferred to C.S. Navy July 19, 1863.

MISCELLANEOUS

The following list of men was compiled from primary records that record the unit as the 10th Regiment N.C. State Troops (1st Regiment N.C. Artillery) but do not give the company to which they belonged. As the names do not appear on any of the surviving muster rolls of any company in the regiment, they have not been checked for possible misspelling or incorrect unit designation. Some men appear on records created in areas where the regiment did not serve. It is possible the individual either gave an assumed name or purposely gave an incorrect unit designation. Since it is impossible to identify them with any company, they are recorded separately.

ANDERSON, BENJAMIN *Private*
Appears on a register of refugees and rebel deserters sent from City Point, Virginia to Washington, D.C. April 12, 1865. Furnished transportation to Wilmington.

BALD, F.T. *Private*
Paroled at Salisbury May 27, 1865.

BATE, ELIAS *Private*
Died at Wilmington January 2, 1863 of typhoid fever.

BRINDLE, WILLIAM *Private*
Claim filed by widow January 9, 1865 for balance of pay due. Date of death not recorded.

BRYANT, JAMES *Private*
Confined at Camp Distribution, Camp Hamilton, Virginia December 17, 1864 and sent to Military Prison, Norfolk, Virginia December 18, 1864.

Appendix A

HALL, HENRY A. *Private*
Reported dead August 2, 1862.

LOFLIN, G.C. *Private*
Resided in Anne Arundel County, Maryland and surrendered at Richmond, Virginia April 3, 1865. Took Oath of Allegiance April 16, 1865.

MAHONEY, JOHN *Private*

McDONALD, J.D. *Private*
Appears on a register headed: "Record of Transportation issued by the Provost Marshal General, Defenses North of the Potomac." Carried a deserter with the remark that he took the Oath of Allegiance and was sent to Indiana December 27, 1864.

MEYERS, M. *Private*
Captured in Virginia and confined at Fort Warren, Massachusetts November 1, 1861. Paroled for exchange February 3, 1862.

SHAW, WILLIAM, JR.
Resided in Beaufort County where he enlisted at age 33, April 22, 1861 for twelve months. Appointed 1st Lieutenant by Governor Ellis to rank from May 16, 1861. Captured at Fort Hatteras August 29, 1861 and confined to Fort Warren, Massachusetts until paroled to be exchanged January 3, 1862. Promoted to Captain January 9, 1863. Captured at Fort Fisher January 15, 1865 and confined at Fort Columbus, New York Harbor until paroled and exchanged at City Point, Virginia, February 25–March 5, 1865.

SMALL, A. *Private*
Confined at Military Prison, Camp Hamilton, Virginia November 25, 1864 and sent to Norfolk, Virginia the next day.

STEARNS, C.C. *Private*
Deserted near Richmond, Virginia October 12, 1864 and surrendered to Federal authorities.

After the captured members of the Grays were repatriated to North Carolina, Captain Sparrow was promoted to major, and the company was commanded by Captain William Shaw.

LIST OF RECOVERED ARTIFACTS AND PROVENIENCE INFORMATION

SIDCO Artifact Inventory—0002OKI

Artifact Number	Entry Number	Description & Medium	State of Preservation	Recovery Date	Recovered By	Exact Provenience	Present Location	Samples	X-ray	Cataloguer
0002OKI001	1	custard glass bottom	Finished	5/22/1999	RKS	26' X 350 Deg, Datum 2	OPS Exhibit	NA	No	Smith
0002OKI002	2	red bull pottery	Finished	5/22/1999	RKS	16' X 90 Deg, Datum 2	OPS	NA	No	Smith
0002OKI003	3	blue bull pottery	Finished	5/22/1999	RKS	2' X 220 Deg, Datum 1	OPS	NA	No	Smith
0002OKI004	4	blue edge, "sun" design, earthen	Finished	5/22/1999	DDP	16' X 358 Deg, Datum 2	OPS	NA	No	Smith
0002OKI005	5	wht/blu crosshatch design pottery	Finished	5/22/1999	DDP	1' X 356 Deg, Datum 2	OPS	NA	No	Smith
0002OKI006	6	cup btm, pink/ grn flower design	Finished	5/22/1999	RKS	38' X 0 Deg, Datum 2	OPS	NA	No	Smith
0002OKI007	7	red grape design on wht china	Finished	5/22/1999	RKS	11' X 60 Deg, Datum 2	OPS	NA	No	Smith

0002OKI008	8	blue cow/ building in background	Finished	5/22/1999	JWG	2' X 218 Deg, Datum 2	OPS	NA	No	Smith
0002OKI011	11	cup btm pink/ grn flwr design	Finished	5/22/1999	JWW	2' X 218 Deg, Datum 2	OPS	NA	No	Smith
0002OKI012	12	top of lamp chimney	Finished	5/22/1999	JWG/ JG	15' X 120 Deg, Datum 1	OPS	NA	No	Smith
0002OKI013	13	starburst design bl/gry	Finished	5/22/1999	RKS	26' X 358 Deg, Datum 2	OPS	NA	No	Smith
0002OKI014	14	cup btm pink/ grn design brn/gry	Finished	5/22/1999	JWG	2' X 220 Deg, Datum1	OPS	NA	No	Smith
0002OKI015	15	bowl btm peacock fthr design	Finished	5/22/1999	DEP/JWW	22' X 42 Deg, Datum 1	OPS	NA	No	Smith
0002OKI016	16	wh/bl crosshatch design pottery	Finished	5/22/1999	RKS	10.5" X 358 Deg, Datum 2	OPS	NA	No	Smith
0002OKI017	17	starburst design bl/gry triang shp	Finished	5/22/1999	RKS	11' X 60 Deg, Datum 2	OPS	NA	No	Smith

SIDCO Artifact Inventory—0002OKI

Artifact Number	Entry Number	Description & Medium	State of Preservation	Recovery Date	Recovered By	Exact Provenience	Present Location	Samples	X-ray	Cataloguer
0002OKI018	18	pink flowrs, wht/grn design edge at top	Finished	5/22/1999	RKS	2' X 220 Deg, Datum 2	OPS	NA	No	Smith
0002OKI019	19	bl/wht peacock feather design	Finished	5/22/1999	JWG	1' X 218 Deg, Datum 1	OPS	NA	No	Smith
0002OKI020	20	bl/wht peacock feather design	Finished	5/22/1999	RKS	2.5' X 219 Deg, Datum 1	OPS	NA	No	Smith
0002OKI021	21	pink flowr on sides, lt grn curved	Finished	5/22/1999	DDP	2' X 225 Deg, Datum 1	OPS	NA	No	Smith
0002OKI022	22	glass lt blu btl bottom	Finished	5/22/1999	RKS/ JWW	20' X 358 Deg, Datum 2	OPS	NA	No	Smith
0002OKI023	23	btl btm amber with light	Finished	5/22/1999	RKS	26' X 59 Deg, Datum 2	OPS	NA	No	Smith

0002OKI024	24	peacock feather design crvd piece	Finished	5/22/1999	DDP	2' X 216 Deg, Datum 1	OPS	NA	No	Smith
0002OKI025	25	pink flowrs on sides & on back	Finished	5/22/1999	JG	2' X 210 Deg, Datum 1	OPS	NA	No	Smith
0002OKI026	26	rnbw clr 1 shape pottery	Finished	5/22/1999	JG	1.5' X 221 Deg, Datum 1	OPS	NA	No	Smith
0002OKI027	27	burg/wht design wavy design sw	Finished	5/22/1999	DG	2' X 218 Deg, Datum 1	OPS	NA	No	Smith
0002OKI028	28	cup btm wavy design seaweed	Finished	5/22/1999	JG	1.75' X 217 Deg, Datum 1	OPS	NA	No	Smith
0002OKI029	29	burnt ptry pnk/ grn design	Finished	5/22/1999	DG	3' X 225 Deg, Datum 1	OPS	NA	No	Smith
0002OKI030	30	china bwl edge pnk colored	Finished	5/22/1999	DG	2' X 224 Deg, Datum 1	OPS	NA	No	Smith
0002OKI031	31	brn wavy design sldr	Finished	5/22/1999	RKS	3' X 160 Deg, Datum 1	OPS	NA	No	Smith

SIDCO Artifact Inventory—0002OKI

Artifact Number	Entry Number	Description & Medium	State of Preservation	Recovery Date	Recovered By	Exact Provenience	Present Location	Samples	X-ray	Cataloguer
0002OKI032	32	pf design gray color	Finished	5/22/1999	JG	2' X 229 Deg, Datum 1	OPS	NA	No	Smith
0002OKI033	33	crosshatch design red color	Finished	5/22/1999	JG	2' X 195 Deg, Datum 1	OPS	NA	No	Smith
0002OKI034	34	bl/wh design of snowflake	Finished	5/22/1999	DG	3' X 215 Deg, Datum 1	OPS	NA	No	Smith
0002OKI035	35	grooved wh/bl pottery	Finished	5/22/1999	DG	2' X 210 Deg, Datum 1	OPS	NA	No	Smith
0002OKI036	36	starburst design bl/wht china	Finished	5/22/1999	DDP	5' X80 Deg, Datum 1	OPS	NA	No	Smith
0002OKI038	38	amber glass bottom	Finished	5/22/1999	RKS	37' X 358 Deg, Datum2	OPS	NA	No	Smith
0002OKI039	39	peacock feather bl/wht design	Finished	9/19/1998	DDP	22' X 42 Deg, Datum 1	OPS	NA	No	Smith

ID	Num	Description	Status	Date	Initials	Measurement	OPS	NA	No	Smith
0002OKI040	40	bl/wht crosshatch design	Finished	5/22/1999	RKS	2' X 210 Deg, Datum 1	OPS	NA	No	Smith
0002OKI041	41	bl/wht design distorted by fire	Finished	5/22/1999	JG	2.5' X 230 Deg, Datum 1	OPS	NA	No	Smith
0002OKI042	42	pnk/grn flwr design on beige	Finished	5/22/1999	DDP	2.5' X 234 Deg, Datum 1	OPS	NA	No	Smith
0002OKI043	43	bl crosshatch design lip edge	Finished	5/22/1999	DDP	16' X 358 Deg, Datum 2	OPS	NA	No	Smith
0002OKI044	44	red/blk/wht btm w/rim	Finished	5/22/1999	DDP	2.5' X215 Deg, Datum 1	OPS	NA	No	Smith
0002OKI045	45	peacock feather pointed piece	Finished	5/22/1999	DDP	4' X 215 Deg, Datum 1	OPS	NA	No	Smith
0002OKI046	46	wh/blk pottery chard w/ crazing	Finished	5/22/1999	DDP	5' X 80 Deg, Datum 1	OPS	NA	No	Smith
0002OKI047	47	bl/wht starburst design	Finished	5/22/1999	DG	3' X 225 Deg, Datum1	OPS	NA	No	Smith

SIDCO Artifact Inventory—0002OKI

Artifact Number	Entry Number	Description & Medium	State of Preservation	Recovery Date	Recovered By	Exact Provenience	Present Location	Samples	X-ray	Cataloguer
0002OKI048	48	cup base pottery piece	Finished	5/22/1999	DDP	6' X 70 Deg., Datum 1	OPS	NA	No	Smith
0002OKI049	49	bl/wht oriental design fire dmge	Finished	5/22/1999	DDP	2' X 40 Deg., Datum 1	OPS	NA	No	Smith
0002OKI050	50	glass partial base green color	Finished	10/16/1998	LB	40' X 350 Deg., Datum 1	OPS	NA	No	Smith
0002OKI051	51	plate, coat of arms underside	Finished	10/16/1998	LB	40'x340 deg, Datum 1	OPS	NA	No	BWW
0002OKI052	52	gn glass shard	Finished	10/16/1998	LB	40'x350 deg, Datum 1	OPS	NA	No	BWW
0002OKI053	53	pink/green bowl lip	Finished	9/19/1998	DP	22'x042 deg, Datum 1	OPS	NA	No	BWW
0002OKI054	54	pink/green sm base	Finished	9/19/1998	DP	22'x042 deg, Datum 1	OPS	NA	No	BWW

0002OKI055	55	rosebud pottery	Finished	9/19/1998	DP	22'x042 Deg., Datum 1	OPS	NA	No	BWW
0002OKI056	56	plate piece blue pat	Finished	9/19/1998	DP	22'x042 Deg., Datum 1	OPS	NA	No	BWW
0002OKI057	57	pottery piece blue/pink flowers	Finished	9/19/1998	DP	22'x042 deg., Datum 1	OPS	NA	No	BWW
0002OKI058	58	pottery red/ white	Finished	9/19/1998	DP	22'x042 deg., Datum 1	OPS	NA	No	BWW
0002OKI059	59	pottery pink/ green	Finished	9/19/1998	DP	22'x042 deg., Datum 1	OPS	NA	No	BWW
0002OKI060	60	pottery piece no pat	Finished	9/19/1998	DP	22'x042 deg., Datum 1	OPS	NA	No	BWW
0002OKI061	61	pottery piece base	Finished	9/19/1998	DP	22'x042 deg., Datum 1	OPS	NA	No	BWW
0002OKI062	62	pottery piece w/ rim blue/ bronze	Finished	9/19/1998	DP	22'x042 deg., Datum 1	OPS	NA	No	BWW

SIDCO Artifact Inventory—0002OKI

Artifact Number	Entry Number	Description & Medium	State of Preservation	Recovery Date	Recovered By	Exact Provenience	Present Location	Samples	X-ray	Cataloguer
0002OKI063	63	pottery w/ rim blue	Finished	9/19/1998	DP	22'x042 deg, Datum 1	OPS	NA	No	BWW
0002OKI064	64	pottery crosshatch purple/green	Finished	9/19/1998	DP	22'x042 deg, Datum 1	OPS	NA	No	BWW
0002OKI065	65	pottery w/ rim pink/green	Finished	9/19/1998	DP	22'x042 deg, Datum 1	OPS	NA	No	BWW
0002OKI066	66	pottery piece brown/black	Finished	9/19/1998	DP	22'x042 deg, Datum 1	OPS	NA	No	BWW
0002OKI067	67	pottery cream w/ blue print	Finished	9/19/1998	DP	22'x042 deg, Datum 1	OPS	NA	No	BWW
0002OKI068	68	pottery rim piece green	Finished	9/19/1998	DP	22'x042 deg, Datum 1	OPS	NA	No	BWW
0002OKI069	69	pottery piece brown pattern	Finished	9/19/1998	DP	22'x042 deg, Datum 1	OPS	NA	No	BWW

0002OKI070	70	pottery piece brown pattern	Finished	9/19/1998	DP	22'X042 deg, Datum 1	OPS	NA	No	BWW
0002OKI071	71	cup pink/ green heart pat	Finished	9/19/1998	DP	22'x042 deg, Datum 1	OPS	NA	No	BWW
0002OKI072	72	slate piece gray green	Finished	10/16/1998	LB	15'x300 deg, Datum 1	OPS	NA	No	BWW
0002OKI073	73	slate piece dk gray	Finished	10/16/1998	LB	10'x280 deg, Datum 1	OPS	NA	No	BWW
0002OKI074	74	plate lip green	Finished	9/19/1998	DP	22'x042 deg, Datum 1	OPS	NA	No	BWW
0002OKI075	75	pottery piece green pat	Finished	9/19/1998	DP	22'x042 deg, Datum 1	OPS	NA	No	BWW
0002OKI076	76	pot piece blue/ green pat	Finished	9/19/1998	DP	22'x042 deg, Datum 1	Ops	NA	No	BWW
0002OKI077	77	pottery piece blue heart pink/blue	Finished	9/19/1998	DP	22'x042 deg, Datum 1	OPS	NA	No	BWW

SIDCO Artifact Inventory—0002OKI

Artifact Number	Entry Number	Description & Medium	State of Preservation	Recovery Date	Recovered By	Exact Provenience	Present Location	Samples	X-ray	Cataloguer
0002OKI078	78	pottery piece partial base pink/green	Finished	9/19/1998	DP	22'x042 deg, Datum 1	OPS	NA	No	BWW
0002OKI079	79	pot rec base pink/green pat	Finished	9/19/1998	DP	22'x042 deg, Datum 1	OPS	NA	No	BWW
0002OKI082	82	pot piece green/white burned	Finished	9/19/1998	DP	22'x042 deg, Datum 1	OPS	NA	No	BWW
0002OKI083	83	pot piece with red-brown hearts/flowers	Finished	9/19/1998	DP	22'x042 deg, Datum 1	OPS	NA	No	BWW
0002OKI084	84	pot piece white burned 1 side	Finished	9/19/1998	DP	22'x042 deg, Datum 1	OPS	NA	No	BWW
0002OKI085	85	pot piece pink burned	Finished	9/19/1998	DP	22'x042 deg, Datum 1	OPS	NA	No	BWW

0002OKI086	86	pot piece pink/ green burned	Finished	9/19/1998	DP	22'x042 deg, Datum 1	OPS	NA	No	BWW
0002OKI087	87	pot piece pink/ green burned	Finished	9/19/1998	DP	22'x042 deg, Datum 1	OPS	NA	No	BWW
0002OKI 088	88	pot piece pink/ green burned	Finished	9/19/1998	DP	22'x042 deg, Datum 1	OPS	NA	No	BWW
0002OKI089	89	pot piece green/white burned	Finished	9/19/1998	DP	22'x042 deg, Datum 1	OPS	NA	No	BWW
0002OKI090	90	glass curved rainbow effect	Finished	9/19/1998	DP	22'x042 deg, Datum 1	OPS	NA	No	BWW
0002OKI091	91	glass tri-shaped rainbow effect	Finished	9/19/1998	DP	22'x042 deg, Datum 1	OPS	NA	No	BWW
0002OKI092	92	glass greenish brown	Finished	9/19/1998	DP	22'x042 deg, Datum 1	OPS	NA	No	BWW
0002OKI093	93	glass blue rainbow effect	Finished	9/19/1998	DP	22'x042 deg, Datum 1	OPS	NA	No	BWW

SIDCO Artifact Inventory—0002OKI

Artifact Number	Entry Number	Description & Medium	State of Preservation	Recovery Date	Recovered By	Exact Provenience	Present Location	Samples	X-ray	Cataloguer
0002OKI094	94	glass rainbow effect	Finished	9/19/1998	DP	22'x042 deg, Datum 1	OPS	NA	No	BWW
0002OKI095	95	glass brown	Finished	9/19/1998	DP	22'x042 deg, Datum 1	OPS	NA	No	BWW
0002OKI096	96	wood canon quoin	Working	6/27/1999			sidco lab	Yes	No	BWW
0002OKI097	97	wood canon quoin	Working	6/26/1999	PO	16'x deg, Datum 3	sidco lab	Yes	No	BWW
0002OKI098	98	wood	Working	6/26/1999	PO	22'x deg, Datum 1	sidco lab	Yes	No	BWW
0002OKI099	99	slate gray 2 hole	Finished	6/26/1999	PO	10'x270 deg, Datum 4		NA	No	BWW
0002OKI100	100	rims gray/green	Finished	6/26/1999	RS	32'x160 deg, Datum 1	sidco lab	NA	No	BWW
0002OKI101	101	pot piece pink/blue	Finished	6/26/1999	RS	23'x143 deg, Datum 1	sidco lab	NA	No	BWW

0002OKI102	102	glass corner green	Finished	6/27/1999	RS	20'x31 deg, Datum 1	OPS	NA	No	BWW
0002OKI103	103	glass bottle bottom dk green	Finished	6/26/1999	RS	6'x170 deg, Datum 2	OPS	NA	No	BWW
0002OKI104	104	pot piece corner pink/ green	Finished	6/26/1999	RS	31'x045 deg, Datum 2	OPS	NA	No	BWW
0002OKI105	105	glass bottle neck green	Finished	6/26/1999	BT	2'x150 deg, Datum 3	OPS	NA	No	BWW
0002OKI108	108	pot piece pink/ green burned	Finished	6/26/1999	RS	24'x025 deg, Datum 2	OPS	NA	No	BWW
0002OKI109	109	glass curve	Finished	6/26/1999	RS	29'x019 deg, Datum 3	OPS	NA	No	BWW
0002OKI110	110	glass green thin	Finished	6/27/1999	RS	10'x280 deg, Datum 1	OPS	NA	No	BWW
0002OKI111	111	glass green	Finished	6/26/1999	RS	21'x050 deg, Datum 1	OPS	NA	No	BWW

SIDCO ARTIFACT INVENTORY—0002OKI

Artifact Number	Entry Number	Description & Medium	State of Preservation	Recovery Date	Recovered By	Exact Provenience	Present Location	Samples	X-ray	Cataloguer
0002OKI112	112	glass edge	Finished	6/27/1999	RS	20'x031 deg, Datum 1	OPS	NA	No	BWW
0002OKI113	113	iron shaft 1/8"	Finished				sidco lab			BWW
0002OKI114	114	china tri-shaped white/green	Finished	6/27/1999	RS	29'x019 deg, Datum 3	OPS	NA	No	BWW
0002OKI115	115	pot piece pink/blue	Finished	6/27/1999	RS	20'x025 deg, Datum 1	OPS	NA	No	BWW
0002OKI116	116	green pattern	Finished	6/26/1999	RS	20'x041 deg, Datum 1	OPS	NA	No	BWW
0002OKI117	117			6/26/1999	RS	20'x041 deg, Datum 1	OPS	NA	No	BWW
0002OKI118	118	pink/green w/rim	Finished	6/26/1999	RS	09'x200 deg, Datum 2	OPS	NA	No	BWW

00020KI119	119	glass green	Finished	6/27/1999	RS	44'x004 deg, Datum 3	OPS	NA	No	BWW
00020KI120	120	pottery handle stub	Finished	6/26/1999	RS	19'x041 deg, Datum 1	OPS	NA	No	BWW
00020KI122	122	white/blue/ yellow	Finished	6/26/1999	RS	24'x060 deg, Datum 1	OPS	NA	No	BWW
00020KI123	123	black/white stripe pink flower	Finished	6/26/1999	RS	44'x020 deg, Datum 2	sidco lab	NA	No	BWW
00020KI124	124	glass bottom blue/green burned	Finished	6/27/1999	RS	25'x030 deg, Datum 3	OPS	NA	No	BWW
00020KI125	125	brick rough orange	Finished	6/26/1999	DP	06'x060 deg, Datum 1	OPS	NA	No	BWW
00020KI126	126	wood cannon quoin	Finished	6/27/1999	PO	38'x042 deg, Datum 1	OPS	NA	No	BWW
00020KI127	127	brick orange straight edge	Finished	6/27/1999	DP	32'x180 deg, Datum 1	OPS	NA	No	BWW

Artifact Number	Entry Number	Description & Medium	State of Preservation	Recovery Date	Recovered By	Exact Provenience	Present Location	Samples	X-ray	Cataloguer
0002OKI150	150	china white/blue pattern	Finished	9/19/1998	DP	22' x 042 Deg, Datum 1	OPS	NA	No	BWW
0002OKI151	151	china white/green leaf pattern	Finished	9/18/1998	DP	22' x 042 Deg, Datum 1	OPS	NA	No	BWW
0002OKI152	152	china green burned	Finished	9/19/1998	DP	22' x 042 Deg, Datum 1	OPS	NA	No	BWW
0002OKI153	153	china dk gray/redbrown	Finished	9/19/1998	DP	22' x 042 Deg, Datum 1	OPS	NA	No	BWW
0002OKI154	154	china white/pink/red/black	Finished	9/19/1998	DP	22' x 042 Deg, Datum 1	OPS	NA	No	BWW
0002OKI155	155	china scalloped edge dk gray	Finished	9/19/1998	DP	22' x 042 Deg, Datum 1	OPS	NA	No	BWW
0002OKI156	156	china bottom pink/green	Finished	9/19/1998	DP	22' x 042 Deg, Datum 1	OPS	NA	No	BWW

SIDCO Artifact Inventory—0002OKI

0002OKI157	157	china tan green stripes	Finished	9/19/1998	DP	22' x 042 Deg., Datum 1	OPS	NA	No	BWW
0002OKI158	158	china curved dark	Finished	9/19/1998	DP	22' x 042 Deg., Datum 1	OPS	NA	No	BWW
0002OKI159	159	china tan/ green	Finished	9/19/1998	DP	22' x 042 Deg., Datum 1	OPS	NA	No	BWW
0002OKI160	160	china curved green flowers	Finished	9/19/1998	DP	22' x 042 Deg., Datum 1	OPS	NA	No	BWW
0002OKI161	161	china curved gray pattern	Finished	9/19/1998	DP	22' x 042 Deg., Datum 1	OPS	NA	No	BWW
0002OKI162	162	china curved tan/green	Finished	9/19/1998	DP	22' x 042 Deg., Datum 1	OPS	NA	No	Bww
0002OKI163	163	china scalloped edge gray pat	Finished	9/19/1998	DP	22' x 042 Deg., Datum 1	OPS	NA	No	BWW
0002OKI164	164	china thick green pat pale	Finished	9/19/1998	DP	22' x 042 Deg., Datum 1	OPS	NA	No	BWW

SIDCO Artifact Inventory—0002OKI

Artifact Number	Entry Number	Description & Medium	State of Preservation	Recovery Date	Recovered By	Exact Provenience	Present Location	Samples	X-ray	Cataloguer
0002OKI165	165	china/black/green/white	Finished	9/19/1998	DP	22' x 042 Deg, Datum 1	OPS	NA	No	BWW
0002OKI166	166	china burned red/blue	Finished	9/19/1998	DP	22' x 042 Deg, Datum 1	OPS	NA	No	BWW
0002OKI167	167	china white green edge	Finished	9/19/1998	DP	22' x 042 Deg, Datum 1	OPS	NA	No	BWW
0002OKI168	168	china burned green	Finished	9/19/1998	DP	22' x 042 Deg, Datum 1	OPS	NA	No	BWW
0002OKI169	169	china white	Finished	9/19/1998	DP	22' x 042 Deg, Datum 1	OPS	NA	No	BWW
0002OKI170	170	china red burned both sides	Finished	9/19/1998	DP	22' x 042 Deg, Datum 1	OPS	NA	No	BWW
0002OKI171	171	china red burned gray	Finished	9/19/1998	DP	22' x 042 Deg, Datum 1	OPS	NA	No	BWW

0002OKI172	172	china shiny green burned	Finished	9/19/1998	DP	22' x 042 Deg., Datum 1	OPS	NA	No	BWW
0002OKI173	173	china white feather pat burned	Finished	9/19/1998	DP	22' x 042 Deg., Datum 1	OPS	NA	No	BWW
0002OKI174	174	china rose-colored flower/feather	Finished	9/19/1998	DP	22' x 042 Deg., Datum 1	OPS	NA	No	BWW
0002OKI175	175	china burned green	Finished	9/19/1998	DP	22' x 042 Deg., Datum 1	OPS	NA	No	BWW
0002OKI176	176	china burned green	Finished	9/19/1998	DP	22' x 042 Deg., Datum 1	OPS	NA	No	BWW
0002OKI177	177	china burned green	Finished	9/19/1998	DP	22' x 042 Deg., Datum 1	OPS	NA	No	BWW
0002OKI178	178	china burned red	Finished	9/19/1998	DP	22' x 042 Deg., Datum 1	OPS	NA	No	BWW
0002OKI179	179	china burned red	Finished	9/19/1998	DP	22' x 042 Deg., Datum 1	OPS	NA	No	BWW

SIDCO Artifact Inventory—0002OKI

Artifact Number	Entry Number	Description & Medium	State of Preservation	Recovery Date	Recovered By	Exact Provenience	Present Location	Samples	X-ray	Cataloguer
0002OKI180	180	china burned red	Finished	9/19/1998	DP	22' x 042 Deg, Datum 1	OPS	NA	No	BWW
0002OKI181	181	china burned red-orange	Finished	9/19/1998	DP	22' x 042 Deg, Datum 1	OPS	NA	No	BWW
0002OKI182	182	china dk blue beige check pat	Finished	9/19/1998	DP	22' x 042 Deg, Datum 1	OPS	NA	No	BWW
0002OKI183	183	china white blue pat	Finished	9/19/1998	DP	22' x 042 Deg, Datum 1	OPS	NA	No	BWW
0002OKI184	184	china white heart/feather pat	Finished	9/19/1998	DP	22' x 042 Deg, Datum 1	OPS	NA	No	BWW
0002OKI225	225	china white heart/feather pat	Finished	9/19/1998	DP	22' x 042 Deg, Datum 1	OPS	NA	No	BWW
0002OKI226	226	china white blue pat	Finished	9/19/1998	DP	22' x 042 Deg, Datum 1	OPS	NA	No	BWW

0002OKI227	227	china burned blue on rim	Finished	9/19/1998	DP	22' x 042 Deg., Datum 1	OPS	NA	No	BWW
0002OKI228	228	china burned blue	Finished	9/19/1998	DP	22' x 042 Deg., Datum 1	OPS	NA	No	BWW
0002OKI229	229	china white rose clore pat	Finished	9/19/1998	DP	22' x 042 Deg., Datum 1	OPS	NA	No	BWW
0002OKI230	230	china red/ green white flower pat	Finished	9/19/1998	DP	22' x 042 Deg., Datum 1	OPS	NA	No	BWW
0002OKI231	231	china blue checked pat	Finished	9/19/1998	DP	22' x 042 Deg., Datum 1	OPS	NA	No	BWW
0002OKI232	232	china white heart/feather pat	Finished	9/19/1998	DP	22' x 042 Deg., Datum 1	OPS	NA	No	BWW
0002OKI233	233	china white burned	Finished	9/19/1998	DP	22' x 042 Deg., Datum 1	OPS	NA	No	BWW
0002OKI234	234	slate gray rust textured	Finished	9/19/1998	DP	22' x 042 Deg., Datum 1	OPS	NA	No	BWW

SIDCO Artifact Inventory—0002OKI

Artifact Number	Entry Number	Description & Medium	State of Preservation	Recovery Date	Recovered By	Exact Provenience	Present Location	Samples	X-ray	Cataloguer
0002OKI235	235	china white flower pat	Finished	9/19/1998	DP	22' x 042 deg, Datum 1	OPS	NA	No	BWW
0002OKI236	236	china burned blue	Finished	9/19/1998	DP	22' x 042 Deg, Datum 1	OPS	NA	No	BWW
0002OKI237	237	slate gray textured	Finished	9/19/1998	DP	22' x 042 Deg, Datum 1	OPS	NA	No	BWW
0002OKI238	238	china burned heart/feather blue	Finished	9/19/1998	DP	22' x 042 Deg, Datum 1	OPS	NA	No	BWW
0002OKI239	239	china burned white curved	Finished	9/19/1998	DP	22' x 042 Deg, Datum 1	OPS	NA	No	BWW
0002OKI240	240	china burned hearts/feathers	Finished	9/19/1998	DP	22' x 042 Deg, Datum 1	OPS	NA	No	BWW
0002OKI241	241	china flowered pat	Finished	9/19/1998	DP	22' x 042 Deg, Datum 1	OPS	NA	No	BWW

0002OKI242	242	china white blue hearts	Finished	9/19/1998	DP	22' x 042 Deg, Datum 1	OPS	NA	No	BWW
0002OKI243	243	china white blue feathers/ flowers	Finished	9/19/1998	DP	22' x 042 Deg, Datum 1	OPS	NA	No	BWW
0002OKI244	244	china burned white blue check	Finished	9/19/1998	DP	22' x 042 Deg, Datum 1	OPS	NA	No	BWW
0002OKI245	245	china burned hearts/feathers	Finished	9/19/1998	DP	22' x 042 Deg, Datum 1	OPS	NA	No	BWW
0002OKI246	246	china white hearts/feather pat	Finished	9/19/1998	DP	22' x 042 Deg, Datum 1	OPS	NA	No	BWW
0002OKI247	247	china burned red/blue	Finished	9/19/1998	DP	22' x 042 Deg, Datum 1	OPS	NA	No	BWW
0002OKI248	248	china white sm ridge	Finished	9/19/1998	DP	22' x 042 Deg, Datum 1	OPS	NA	No	BWW
0002OKI249	249	china burned white curved	Finished	9/19/1998	DP	22' x 042 Deg, Datum 1	OPS	NA	No	BWW

SIDCO Artifact Inventory—0002OKI

Artifact Number	Entry Number	Description & Medium	State of Preservation	Recovery Date	Recovered By	Exact Provenience	Present Location	Samples	X-ray	Cataloguer
0002OKI250	250	china burned blue/white pat	Finished	9/19/1998	DP	22' x 042 Deg, Datum 1	OPS	NA	No	BWW
0002OKI251	251	china burned white w/flowe pat	Finished	9/19/1998	DP	22' x 042 Deg, Datum 1	OPS	NA	No	BWW
0002OKI252	252	china burned white/blue cir pat	Finished	9/19/1998	DP	22' x 042 Deg, Datum 1	OPS	NA	No	BWW
0002OKI253	253	china burned white/blue feathers	Finished	9/19/1998	DP	22' x 042 Deg, Datum 1	OPS	NA	No	BWW
0002OKI254	254	china burned check pat	Finished	9/19/1998	DP	22' x 042 Deg, Datum 1	OPS	NA	No	BWW
0002OKI255	255	china burned blue/white	Finished	9/19/1998	DP	22' x 042 Deg, Datum 1	OPS	NA	No	BWW
0002OKI256	256	china burned red/blue	Finished	9/19/1998	DP	22' x 042 Deg, Datum 1	OPS	NA	No	BWW

0002OKI257	257	china burned white blue pat	Finished	9/19/1998	DP	22' x 042 Deg, Datum 1	OPS	NA	No	BWW
0002OKI258	258	china white blue hearts/ feathers	Finished	9/19/1998	DP	22' x 042 Deg, Datum 1	OPS	NA	No	BWW
0002OKI259	259	china burned white	Finished	9/19/1998	DP	22' x 042 Deg, Datum 1	OPS	NA	No	BWW
0002OKI260	260	china burned white	Finished	9/19/1998	DP	22' x 042 Deg, Datum1	OPS	NA	No	BWW
0002OKI261	261	china burned red	Finished	9/19/1998	DP	22' x 042 Deg, Datum 1	OPS	NA	No	BWW

NOTES

CHAPTER 1

1. Details courtesy E.W. O'Neal Jr., his historical materials collection and *Ocracoke Island Stories; Part of the History,* 3rd edition (N.p., May 2007), 21–22.
2. Samuel W. Newell, "A Maritime History of Ocracoke Inlet, 1584–1783," master's thesis, Department of History, East Carolina University, 1987.
3. Ibid.
4. The long wooden pieces fit together to form the outsides of the barrel.
5. David Stick, *The Outer Banks of North Carolina* (Chapel Hill: University of North Carolina Press, 1958), 13–17.
6. David Stick, *Graveyard of the Atlantic* (Chapel Hill: University of North Carolina Press, 1952), 4.
7. Ibid.
8. Ibid.
9. Ibid.
10. William P. Cumming, *Mapping the North Carolina Coast* (Raleigh, NC: Division of Archives and History, NCDCR, 1988), 36–38.
11. Instruments of Protest, Hyde/Carteret County District Court, North Carolina Colonial Records, 1723.

12. Ibid.

13. Newell, "Maritime History."

14. Ibid.

15. Ibid.

16. Ibid.

17. Courtesy of local author and historian Ellen Marie Cloud.

18. Newell, "Maritime History."

19. Ibid.

20. Ibid.

21. Wade G. Dudley, "No Mischief Shall Be Done: The Ocracoke Raid of July 1813," *Tributaries* 17 (October 2012): 31, North Carolina History Council Publication.

22. Ibid.

23. *Raleigh Register*, September 9, 1814.

24. William S. Powell, editor, *Encyclopedia of North Carolina* (Chapel Hill: University of North Carolina Press, 1919–2006), 546.

25. Newell, "Maritime History."

26. Article courtesy Ellen Marie Cloud, local historian and author.

27. Emanuel Raymond Lewis, *Seacoast Fortifications of the United States: An Introductory History* (Washington, D.C.: Smithsonian Institution Press, 1970).

28. Stick, *Outer Banks*, 79–80.

29. *Harper's New Monthly Magazine*, December 1863, 3.

30. Dudley, "No Mischief," 31–36.

31. Ibid.

32. *Harper's New Monthly Magazine*, December 1863, 14.

33. Dudley, "No Mischief," 31–36.

34. Ibid.

35. *Harper's New Monthly Magazine*, December 1863, 14.

CHAPTER 2

36. Robert Fowler O'Neal and Jessie Lee Dominic, oral interviews with the author.

37. Jay Barnes, *North Carolina's Hurricane History* (Chapel Hill: University of North Carolina Press, 1999).

38. John F. Sanders, "Hurricane of 1913 Submerged Oriental," *Sun Journal* (New Bern, NC), Wednesday, June 29, 1983.

39. Barnes, *North Carolina's Hurricane History*.

CHAPTER 3

40. Abstract logs of CSS *Ellis* and North Carolina naval steamer *Beaufort*.

41. William Henry von Eberstein Papers, Special Collections, 148.1–148.2, Joyner Library, East Carolina University, 148–245. Courtesy of Mr. Edward L. Harding, his great-great-grandson, Washington, North Carolina.

42. John F. Hoke to Ellwood Morris, Raleigh, North Carolina, April 29, 1861, Adjutant General's Letter Book.

43. Letter from Major Thomson to John Whitford, May 23, 1861. Courtesy of our friend Ellen Cloud, author and historian.

44. David Schenck Diary, June 28, 30, July 1, 1861.

45. Ellwood Morris to John F. Hoke, Beacon Island, Ocracoke Inlet, May 28, 1861. As recorded in "North Carolina Mobilizes: Nine Crucial Months, December, 1860–August, 1861," master's thesis by Richard W. Iobst, University of Chapel Hill, 1968.

46. *Official Records of the Union and Confederate Navies in the War of the Rebellion* (referred to as the ORN), vol. 6, 222.

47. Schenck Diary, June 28, 30, July 1, 1861.

48. Letter from James Bradford to Warren Winslow, New Bern, August 20, 1861, Henry T. Clark Papers.

49. Schenck Diary, June 28, 30, July 1, 1861.

50. Lee Dominick, interview about her life on Portsmouth Island, March 1998.

51. P.E. McDuffie, Civil War Fortifications, http://civilwarfortifications.com. Professional archival data for research only—do not build these structures yourself!

52. Schenck Diary, June 28, 30, July 1, 1861.

53. Official report of Lieutenant James Y. Maxwell, USN, September 18, 1861.

54. McDuffie, Civil War Fortifications.

55. D.H. Mahan, *An Elementary Course of Civil Engineering for the Use of Cadets at the United States Military Academy* (New York: John Wiley, 1849).

56. "Magazines," www.fieldfortifications.com.

57. Rod Gragg, *Confederate Goliath: The Battle of Fort Fisher* (Baton Rouge: Louisiana State University Press, 1991), 233–35.

58. Fred M. Mallison, *Civil War on the Outer Banks* (Jefferson, NC: McFarland & Company, Inc, 1989).

59. Letter to the Editor, *New Bern Daily Progress*, June 8, 1861.

60. Richard W. Iobst, "North Carolina Mobilizes: Nine Crucial Months, December 1860–August 1861," thesis, University of North Carolina–Chapel Hill, 1968, 644.

61. Von Eberstein Papers.

62. *The Confederate Field Manual* (Richmond, VA: Ritchie and Dunnavant, 1862), 4–5. There were only three sources for artillery for the Confederates: purchase from private or previously owned government mills, purchase from England and other countries or seizure from captured U.S. Army forts and facilities, including federal ships. Because of this, a great deal of mismatched guns were gathered for each new fort installation, based on what was available at the time. Then, of course, the carriages had to be built to suit the new use of the particular weapon.

63. Dean S. Thomas, *Cannons: An Introduction to Civil War Artillery* (Gettysburg, PA: Thomas Publications, 1996), 55.

64. Harold L. Peterson, *Round Shot and Rammers* (South Bend, IN: South Bend Replicas, Inc., n.d.), 76.

65. Ibid.

66. Thomas, *Cannons*.

67. *Confederate Field Manual*, 116.

68. *ORN*, Report from Captain Chauncey aboard USS *Susquehanna*, September 19, 1861

69. Edwin Olmstead, Wayne F. Stark and Spencer C. Tucker, *The Big Guns: Civil War Siege, Seacoast and Naval Cannon* (N.p.: n.d.), 41–43. Provided by Paul Branch, historian, Fort Macon State Park.

70. Ibid., 20.

71. Ibid., 6.

72. Warren Ripley, *Artillery and Ammunition of the Civil War* (Charleston, SC: Battery Press, 1984), 52.

73. Von Eberstein Papers, 148.1–148.2, 148–245.

74. Letter to the Editor, *New Bern Daily Progress*, June 8, 1861.

75. Von Eberstein Papers.

76. Ibid.

77. William Augustus Parvin Papers, 1861–1907, East Carolina University, East Carolina Manuscript Collection, 536.

78. Ibid.

79. Von Eberstein Papers.

80. *ORN*, vol. 6, 221, Official report of Lieutenant James Y. Maxwell, USN, September 18, 1861.

81. *Confederate Flags Fact Sheet*, Museum of the Confederacy, Richmond, Virginia, as seen in *Flags of the Confederacy* by Earl P. Williams Jr., (Gettysburg, PA: Thomas Publications, n.d.), 15

82. *ORA*, Series 2, vol. 2, 573, Affairs in North Carolina, Report from Brigadier General Richard C.Gatlin.

83. *ORN*, vol. 6, 78.

84. Ibid., 80, Letter from Daniel A. Campbell, August 12, 1861.

85. Abstract log of the North Carolina naval steamer *Beaufort*, Lieutenant R.C. Duvall, commanding.

86. Martha Matilda Fowle Journal, Brown Library, Washington North Carolina, 4–5

87. Series of three handwritten letters to and from Fort Ocracoke on or about August 12, 1861, regarding munitions and stores needed at the fort. Courtesy of Ellen Cloud, author and historian.

88. Letter from James A.J. Bradford to Warren Winslow, New Bern, August 23, 1861.

89. Schenck Diary, June 28, 30, July 1, 1861.

90. Parvin Papers, 6–10.

91. Von Eberstein Papers.

92. Ibid.

93. Ibid.

94. Ibid.

95. Thomas Sparrow, "The Fall of Hatteras," in *Histories of the Several Regiments and Battalions from North Carolina in the Great War 1861–1865*, vol. 5, 3rd ed., edited by Walter Clark (Goldsboro, NC, 1901) 35–36.

96. Abstract log of the CSS *Ellis*.

97. Sparrow, "Fall of Hatteras," 35–36.

98. Abstract log of the CSS *Ellis*.

99. Sparrow, "Fall of Hatteras," 35–36.

100. Major Thomas Sparrow diary, Tenth Regiment, North Carolina Troops, August 28–29, 1861.

101. *ORN*, ser. 1, vol. 6, 120.

102. Sparrow diary, August 29, 1861; "Fall of Hatteras," 51.

103. *ORN*, ser. 1, vol. 6, 122.

104. Ibid.

105. The entire confederate force was later sent home in a prisoner exchange where the Seventeenth became the Seventh North Carolina Volunteer Troops.

106. *ORN*, ser.1, vol. 6, 127.

107. *Scientific American*, October 1861, 162.

108. Ibid.

109. *ORA*, series 1, vol. 4, 636–37.

110. Ibid.

111. Von Eberstein Papers.

112. Ibid.

113. Ibid.

114. H.T. Clark Papers, Minutes of War Council, held at Fort Oregon, August 31, 1861, North Carolina Archives and History, Raleigh, North Carolina.

115. *ORN*, vol. 6, 161.

116. Ibid., 162.

117. *ORN*, vol. 6, 221, Official report of Lieutenant James Y. Maxwell, USN, September 18, 1861.

118. Ibid.

119. Ibid.

120. Official report of Commander S.C. Rowan, Flag Officer, USN Atlantic Squadron, USS *Pawnee*, September 18, 1861.

121. Letter from John Whitford, October 6, 1861, Governor Henry Clark Papers, G.P. 155, North Carolina Archives.

122. *Field Manual for the Use of the Officers on Ordnance Duty* (Richmond, VA: Ritchie and Dunnavant, 1862), 14–15.

123. *ORN*, Letter from Commander Rowan to Captain Chancey, Atlantic Blockading Squadron, U.S. Navy, September 16, 1861, and Letter from Commander Rowan to Captain Chauncey, September 18, 1861.

124. Report from Samuel Sawyer, Steamer *Albemarle Number 7*, to John Whitford, Commander C.S. Forces, New Bern, September 18, 1861.

125. *ORN*, vol. 6, 221, Official report of Lieutenant James Y. Maxwell, USN, September 18, 1861.

126. *ORN*, vol 6, 223.

127. *ORN*, Letter to Flag Officer Stringham, September 19, 1861.

128. *ORA*, Series 1, vol. 4, 617–19.

129. *ORN*, vol. 6, 221.

130. *ORN*, vol. 6, 225.

131. *New Bern Daily Progress*, October 2, 1861.

132. Information courtesy of historian and author Drew Pullen.

Chapter 4

133. Ervan G. Garrison and Richard J. Anuskiewicz, "Underwater Archaeology by Braille: Survey Methodology and Site Characterization Modeling in a Blackwater Environment: A Study of a Scuttled Confederate Ironclad, CSS *Georgia*," American Academy of Underwater Sciences, 1992.

134. Ibid.

CHAPTER 5

135. Von Eberstein Papers.

136. *ORN*, Letter to Captain Chauncey, Commanding USS *Susquehanna*, from S.C. Rowan, Commander, USS *Pawnee*.

137. *ORN*, Letter to S.H. Stringham, Commanding Atlantic Squadron, from S.C. Rowan, Commander, USS *Pawnee*.

138. *ORN*, vol. 6, 221. Official report of Lieutenant James Y. Maxwell, USN, September 18, 1861.

139. Ibid., attachment to, Letter from S.C. Rowan to Flag Officer S.H. Stringham, September 18, 1861.

140. Report of Camp Equipment, Arms, Hospital Stores, etc. of the Forces at Ocracoke Inlet made by T. Sparrow, Senior Commanding, June 12, 1861, to Walter Gwynn, Brigadier General Commanding.

141. *ORN*, vol. 6, 221, Official report of Lieutenant James Y. Maxwell, USN, September 18, 1861.

APPENDIX 1

142. Information provided by Edward L. Harding, great-great-grandson of Sergeant Major William Henry von Eberstein.

INDEX

ABOUT THE AUTHOR

Robert K. Smith has been a diver for more than thirty years and was an archaeological technician on the Blackbeard Shipwreck Project. In 1996, Robert founded SIDCO, a nonprofit archaeological dive team dedicated to the study of historic shipwrecks and submerged sites in North Carolina waters for the express purpose of education and display. He has since led ten shipwreck investigations throughout the state.

Visit us at
www.historypress.net
....

This title is also available as an e-book